No Cross-Country
for Old Men

A story of loss, resilience… and
running

Brian Gardner

No Cross-Country for Old Men

© Brian Gardner 2022

ISBN 9798839444416

Thank you:

To friends and family who read the drafts and encouraged me to persevere
To the Calne Wordfest Writers Group, for their expertise and inspiration
To Colin Youngson, for going above and beyond to support this project
To my wife, Jane, who put up with years of my highs and lows in sport, and then months of my writing about it

To the best of my recollection, everything in this book actually happened. The names of some places and people have been changed. I don't think they'll mind.

For Mum and Dad

Prologue

I'm shivering on the edge of the football pitch, head hanging in shame, kicking bits of slag. Someone told me that the pitch is made of slag: spoil spewed up from old mines, but I don't know about that. It's supposed to be an all-weather surface but I'm shuffling up and down a ditch carved out by the rain that hasn't stopped all day. It's cold. My clothes are soaking wet and I'm getting wetter and colder with every minute that I spend kicking bits of slag around, trying and failing to keep warm.

Now and again, I look up and see grey everywhere. The nearest building is the factory where most of our parents work. It's grey. Grey rain from grey clouds batters down. Squinting, I can make out the puddle-strewn road in front of the factory. It's grey too. Chinks of light from the factory windows pierce the grey gloom. Grey cars splash along, headlights illuminating waves of grey water sloshed onto grey pavement. Behind grey smoke belching from the factory's grey chimneys is the huge, grey shadow of a bing: a mountain of discarded slag. In the opposite direction, a grey path of grey slag crawls up a grey hill, past grey wasteland towards our school; also grey.

We've all trailed down the hill because our football trial has to take place today. Aye, it's a trial, right enough. I'm on the outside, looking in, paradoxically not on trial. Because I'm not playing. It feels like punishment without trial. Condemned to kick at slag on the sidelines. My school clothes and shoes are ruined. Mum's not going to be impressed. Our janitor won't be happy with me kicking his precious pitch to bits, but he's too busy refereeing and passing judgement on potential players to notice me, dressed in grey and immersed in grey. Incessant rain stinging my face. Cold and wet seeping through clothes and skin, all the way to the bone. Convulsively sniffing up snotters and the putrid, chemical smell from the factory. A bitter taste lingers in my bile. Rumbling of thunder, or is it factory noise, deep and foreboding, contrasting with high pitched, eager shouts from twenty-two happy boys, keeping warm by splashing around on the pitch and chasing a ball for ninety minutes. Ninety minutes of shivering for me, wishing I was anywhere but here.

But why am I here, on the outside, not part of the crowd? Why am I not playing with everyone else? Well, I'm no good at football. They call me the Muffin Man because I'm always muffin' it. The only thing boys ever do at playtime is play football on the playground. Except I don't: I always play quietly on the side with one or two friends (who, strangely, are not in school today). The janny would stand at the door from time to time and watch us play. He's picked two teams from what he's seen, and he hasn't seen me play. So I guess it's my own fault that I'm left out. Not only that but to choose two eleven-a-side teams for the Primary 7 trial, he's had to raid from our Primary 6 class for a few boys to make up the numbers. It wouldn't occur to him to play with smaller sides on a smaller pitch or, Heaven forbid, let girls play. Nor did anyone consider that maybe they should play for fewer than ninety minutes, especially in this downpour, or postpone until the weather improves. But none of the teachers is interested and Janny is doing his best. I get all that. I even understand why I have to be here in the cold and rain, doing nothing at all for ninety minutes: it wouldn't be the 'done thing' to leave me behind in the warm and dry with the girls. It's bad enough being rubbish at football, which means rubbish at sport, which means rubbish at everything, but to stay behind with the girls? Life wouldn't be worth living, ever again. So here I am, crying on the sidelines.

But no one notices me.

Eventually, Janny blows the final whistle. Eleven boys cheer. The other eleven don't. Neither do I, and we all trudge back up the hill.

That's football.

That's sport.

That's life.

It's 1967, I'm eleven years old and rubbish at everything.

Part One

The Start: Schooldays

Chapter One: Brigade

It wasn't always grey in Airdrie: far from it. Months after that dismal day on the edge of the football pitch, the sun came out and it was time for the Primary 7 athletics trials. 'Why don't you have a go?' someone suggested to me. 'You can run.'

How do they know I can run? I wondered. *Can* I run? *Could* I give the trials a go? *Should* I? I'd like to… but no, I'm rubbish at everything.

Too shy and low in self-esteem, I didn't take up the offer and the opportunity was lost.

It's not completely true that I was rubbish at everything: academically, I was quite bright. Not the brightest, but one of the brightest. I did make it to the top, or the front, of the class, briefly. Our teacher was transparent in her method of ranking pupils according to brightness: based on the results of regular tests, she would sit her top pupil in the front row, nearest to her desk. The second brightest would be on the next seat of the front row, and so onto the second row until eventually the least bright pupil was sitting in the back row, in the corner furthest away from the teacher. Test by test, I edged my way along the second, then the front row, until I was sitting at the most prestigious desk. Shortly afterwards, in a rare moment of enlightenment, our teacher reconfigured the ranking order so that the least bright pupil was at the front and the brightest at the back. The pupil at the front deservedly gained extra attention by sitting nearest to the teacher, while I was shunted to the back, on the edge again. In the coming weeks I slipped down the rankings and shuffled along the back row. Not that any of my classmates noticed: academic prowess didn't make you one of the cool kids. Being good at football was much more important.

And so a pattern was set: lacking in confidence, I couldn't see myself being much good at anything.

It was difficult to believe at the time, but there were other activities besides football. I had an active childhood. My sister, Susan, and I walked to and from school every day: about three quarters of a mile each way. We didn't have a family car, so we got used to walking everywhere. I would be playing outside after school and most of the day at weekends and school holidays, always with one or maybe two close friends. During long and sometimes hot summers we would go exploring along the canal path and into the woods to climb trees, challenging ourselves to see who could reach the highest branch. We would run up the bankings (railway embankments) and roll down. The bing, which from the sidelines had seemed so threatening on that grey afternoon, became our playground in the sun. You could slide down and pretend you were skiing. There was a pond with a huge pike that no one could catch; the Sea of Plastic where someone had dumped a load into a hollow in the slag. We used to launch ourselves into the middle, never thinking what might be lurking underneath the millions of pieces of dusty plastic. When the fields were commandeered for housing, we played creatively on the building site after hours, imagining that we were in an adventure series on TV. We knew every inch of

Cairnhill, stayed out as long as we liked and came home when we were hungry.

Mum and Dad provided a happy home for Susan and me. Mum devoted her life to looking after us all. She was always there when we needed her. When Dad came home from work, he always showed an interest in what we'd been doing. At weekends, he would arrange things for us to do together: shopping for tropical fish, playing with our many cousins or swimming at Airdrie Baths. The first time Dad asked me if I'd like to come along to watch football with him, I wasn't keen, for obvious reasons. But one day I joined him and enjoyed the match so much that I became a lifelong supporter of Airdrieonians F.C.

My primary schooldays were mostly happy ones. I don't remember much bullying: the incident on the football pitch sidelines was an exception. I just wasn't in with the In Crowd. Most of the time I didn't mind: I never felt comfortable in a crowd and preferred the company of a few friends with shared interests. However, even at that young age I was aware that something was missing in my life. I craved acceptance, and that motivated me to try to be good at something. It wasn't about health or fitness. Not only did I want to be good: I wanted to be the best and I wanted people to know about it. The trouble was, I had no idea what that something might be.

****

It's always daunting when you move up to the big school but I loved Airdrie Academy. It was more varied and interesting, learning different subjects in different parts of the school, rather than staying in the same room all day, and I was more active, too. Walking about a mile and a half each way between home and school, walking between classrooms, and for miles at weekends to see new friends. There was a large choice of after-school clubs. I'm not sure why I chose rugby: I'd never played before and didn't follow it on TV, even when Scotland were playing. Maybe I thought that this could be the thing I was good at, because all the kids who were good at games would be playing football.

I wasn't good at it, but I wasn't rubbish, either. It was fun learning something new at practices, although they backfired on us at our first match. Our coach was from the North of England; he loved his rugby and made training fun. We played small-sided games, where you rolled the ball back under your foot after being tackled, to keep the game flowing. The first time we played against another school, the referee kept penalising us for not releasing the ball. We didn't know that we'd been practising rugby league instead of union.

We were the scruffiest team ever: the team kit was a disgrace, frayed and ripped at the collars and cuffs. But we laughed it off and embraced the scruffiness as part of our collective identity. For the first time in my life, I was in a team, enjoying the camaraderie, especially on the team bus to away games on Saturday mornings. For some reason, I was picked at flanker: a forward, a strange choice for someone as small and skinny as I was. I didn't see much of the ball but I was quite good at tackling, diving at the opposition's legs. Maybe my reckless abandon at the

Sea of Plastic had prepared me for the rough stuff on the rugby pitch.

However, one particularly dark, windy, cold and wet training night midway through my second season, I felt too numb to tackle and was fed up with aimlessly chasing around. I'm ashamed to say that I dropped out, never to play rugby again. So that was the end of that. What was I going to be good at? I was doing okay academically, never troubling the top of the table but plodding along. There had to be something else, but what?

Salvation came in the unlikely form of Subbuteo.

Subbuteo is a table football game like no other. The players are smaller than a finger, and the skill is in your finger control. There are tactics in how you position your players and direct your flicks. When we played, there was violence on the pitch, and injuries were rife: unless you were lucky to have a spare table in your house, you had to spread the pitch out on your carpet, and you couldn't help kneeling on a player and breaking his legs.

The teams were painted in your favourite club colours. Unfortunately, Airdrie's shirt was too complicated for the Subbuteo artists, so we had to buy Walsall (white shirts, red shorts, red socks) and paint the red diamond on the shirts. There were leagues, cups and international tournaments, not that I scaled those dizzy heights: more like stumbling in the foothills, although I did win our street league. Well, I organised it and the opposition were all younger than me.

Nevertheless, I was better than most of my mates of the same age and I could pretend that I was no longer rubbish at football. Waking up some mornings, I had to pinch myself because I couldn't believe that I was actually good at 'sport' at last. It didn't stop me losing 0-8 once, though. I wasn't put off, but my interest waned eventually.

I was vaguely aware of the 1970 Commonwealth Games in Edinburgh, where Ian Stewart won the 5,000 metres for Scotland and Lachie Stewart (no relation) did the same in the 10,000 metres. It should have inspired me to take up running but it didn't. Football was my number one sport: not playing but, with great dedication and a season ticket, making a pilgrimage with Dad to the hallowed ground of Broomfield every second Saturday to support my beloved Airdrieonians. Our team's success in the Texaco Cup, losing narrowly in the final to Derby County, then the best team in England, did inspire me to do something: I joined the Boys' Brigade, because the Airdrie captain, Derek Whiteford, spoke warmly of his time in the Brigade.

Plodder, underachiever, outsider, introvert, and now another pattern began: late starter —it was unusual to join the Brigade in your mid-teens—and late developer.

For the next few years, I attended our group at the church hall behind South Bridge Street every Friday evening, and church and bible class every Sunday. With anchor as our emblem and 'Sure and Steadfast' as our motto, we strove to achieve 'obedience, reverence, discipline, self-respect and all that tends towards a true Christian manliness'. We learned drill and took part in parades; earned badges for being active and creative and serving the community; held jumble sales to raise funds for charity; and we went to Southport on a fortnight's camping holiday. At fifteen years old, it was the first time I'd been away from home. As a squad leader and assistant quartermaster, I enjoyed the responsibility of leadership. The Brigade was exactly what I needed, and filled a gap in my life. It gave me new purpose and made me feel part of a community. I even won our group's Best Boy award, presented by Derek Whiteford. Cynics declared it would have meant more if the Rangers' captain, not Airdrie's, presented the award, and that the main reason I won was that I was the only boy who never missed bible class. Which was ironic since, despite my dedication, I did not consider myself a Christian. Oh well, the award was mine, and finally I was the best at something.

And then the Brigade gave me an opportunity amongst many opportunities: cross-country running. This time I did not allow the chance to be lost. Although I was still shy, the Brigade had encouraged me to develop obedience, discipline, self-respect and a new confidence to say, 'Yes, I'll do it.'

The Airdrie and Coatbridge race, a qualifier for the Scottish Boys' Brigade Championship, was approaching, and half a dozen of us took time out of drill on Friday evenings to run. We were the cross-country team, but it was too dark to run over fields, so we ran around the streets of Airdrie, nothing like the terrain that we expected in the race. Being out in tee-shirts and shorts on a freezing cold night amongst Friday night drunks probably wasn't in the Brigade's manual of things to do to achieve a true Christian manliness, but there was safety in numbers, and if threatened we could run away.

A week before the race, I decided to run on the country to prepare myself properly. This would be my first solo run and I didn't want anyone to see me. I woke up early on Saturday morning and, with tee-shirt, shorts and gutties (plimsolls) tucked under my arm, walked to the fields at the foot of the old bing. Looking around furtively, I changed under a disused railway bridge, stashed my clothes next to a pile of abandoned beer cans, and, meerkat-like, looked again to make sure no one was around. The sun was rising into a clear, blue sky, the air was crisp and fresh, and the muddy fields stretched out ahead, long shadows from the bing enticing me to start my first ever cross-country training run. Final check that no one was looking, and I was off at a scamper, eager to finish before anyone else woke up. The scamper was too quick: after only a few hundred metres my chest was hurting, breathing irregular, legs aching, and I was tripping on tufts of grass and slipping in the mud, the low sun straining my eyes. I had to slow down, stop, bend over to take some deep breaths, walk for a while and start running again, this time more conservatively. About ten minutes later, I made it back to the bridge, changed into my everyday clothes and walked home. Nobody had seen me, and I was saved any embarrassment.

Or so I thought.

****

Another muddy field. Another Saturday morning. A few dozen boys in tee-shirts and shorts, shivering on the start line of the Airdrie and Coatbridge Boys' Brigade cross-country race. Huddled together against the wind, chatting amicably and giving each other manly and Christian encouragement. We're eying up the opposition, and for some reason my team-mates think I'm the favourite. I'm the fastest in our group, we think we're the best group, so I must be the best in Airdrie and Coatbridge. It's flawed logic but, despite years of low self-esteem, I believe it. There's a downhill section directly in front of us, followed by a path uphill to a gate into woodland. Beyond that is the unknown, although the starter has explained that there will be flags and marshals to guide us around the two mile course. It's not only the cold that makes me shiver: I'm nervous, weak at the knees, butterflies in my tummy. (Why butterflies?) I need the toilet but it's too late.

Bang! We're off, hurtling down the slope. I'm the fastest at hurtling because I'm in the lead. By the time we reach the bottom of the hill I'm way out in front, sure that I'm going to win.

And then we start climbing the hill. How have I not realised that it's much harder to run uphill than downhill? Airdrie, like Rome, was built on seven hills (and there the resemblance ends). This must be one of them, and it introduces me to a new kind of pain in my thighs and calves. Despite the good work of the Brigade to inspire discipline, we're somewhat ragged as we trudge up the hill. I must be more ragged than most but

I'm still leading as we reach the first flag at the gate. Stumbling over tree roots into the woods, I slide around the mud in my gutties. How did the Romans manage in their sandals? Just about staying upright, I spot the first marshal at the end of the woodland path. I'm still leading as I follow his directions to cross the next field. It's a relief to be coasting, not hurtling, downhill, and I'm still winning when the ground levels off, but now I'm fighting against a headwind, and I can hear noisy breathing close behind. (Is that what I sound like?) I try to speed up to hold off the chasing runner. Ascending the next hill, my thighs, calves, chest, back, arms— everything—is hurting, and my mud-caked gutties are dragging me down. Shoulders rolling and jaw clenched in pain, I have to slow down and give way. The chaser, in spite of his laboured breathing, pulls away from me. I lose sight of him after he rounds the next flag, and then someone else overtakes me.

Eventually we return to the first gate, and I can see the finish at the other side of the valley. I'm in fifth place and the first of our team. But one of my team-mates catches me up. He must be hurting too, but he manages to tell me to keep going.

'Where. Do we. Have tae. Go now?' I gasp, although I know where we have to go—down the hill and up the other side—I just can't wait for it to be all over. I can't keep up with him as we run downhill, the last reprieve before the agony of the final climb to the finish line. He holds his form, I don't but no one else overtakes me and I stagger over the line in sixth and stop, bent over again, hands on knees, heaving noisily to reclaim lost air.

****

Our dark Friday night wanderings on the dark streets of Airdrie and my furtive, early morning dash hadn't prepared me for the physical pain and the embarrassment of getting it so wrong. It was a lesson in pace judgement, another trial. I hadn't won but I'd qualified for the Scottish Boys' Brigade Championship to take place a few weeks later. All was not lost. An aim was in sight: my first national championship, in only my second race.

Having heard of Airdrie Harriers, I asked a pal if he'd come along with me one night to join the club. We arranged to meet at the Top Cross to walk along to the track in Rawyards Park. At the appointed time, I waited. And waited. And waited. My pal didn't turn up and I went home. On another night, I waited for a girlfriend at the same place and she didn't show, either. Maybe I should have arranged to meet at the Bottom Cross, which coincidentally is where I ended up making most of my phone calls to girlfriends. We had no phone at home, so I used to walk to the nearest phone box at the corner shop about a quarter of a mile away. More often than not it was vandalised, so I'd walk another quarter of a mile to the next one at the train station. When it was out of action, I'd walk on to the Bottom Cross in the town centre, another quarter of a mile, phone a girlfriend, who wouldn't be in, and I'd walk the three quarters of a mile back home again.

These wasted journeys built up my endurance, although that wasn't my intention: I really wanted to join Airdrie Harriers and I really wanted a girlfriend. I didn't know which girl, but I liked the idea of having a girlfriend. Maybe, again, it was a longing for acceptance. But it always ended in tears: I didn't know what to say or how to behave, and I was dumped, on average, after about three weeks. In so many ways I was a late developer.

It was time to put these disappointments aside and focus on the forthcoming Scottish Boys' Brigade Championship. Airdrie Harriers could wait, and who needs a girlfriend, anyway? They always dump you. After a few more Friday night and secret Saturday morning runs, I boarded the minibus at the Bottom Cross with the rest of the Airdrie and Coatbridge team, and we set off for Callander Park in Falkirk to challenge ourselves against the best in the land. Well, the best of those who were in the Boys' Brigade and liked running, or were asked to run.

This time I paced myself more sensibly, starting steadily and threading my way through the field. Noisy Breathing Guy, the Airdrie and Coatbridge Champion, adopted the same tactic and we had a race-long battle, settled only by a sprint down the home straight. He pipped me, I beat everyone else in our team and finished in the top fifty out of about two hundred.

Dad said that if I could hold my own amongst that lot, I had a promising future in athletics.

The next week, he took me to Rawyards to join Airdrie Harriers.

Chapter Two: Harrier

Meanwhile, I was plodding along almost diligently at Airdrie Academy. Reports included the classic comment: 'could do better'. I was in the fifth year and on my way to passing four Higher exams: two B's and two C's, nothing spectacular. I was hoping that Airdrie Harriers was my chance to shine, to be the best at something other than being ever-present at bible class.

The senior harriers encouraged me to start as a sprinter and move up to longer distances at a later date. Under their guidance I learned to run fast—well, faster than my cross-country pace—with short sprints on the track and slightly longer runs up the adjacent hill.

Gutties were discarded, and Mum and Dad bought me my first pair of training shoes, spikes and the maroon club vest. I was ready for my first competition on the track: Airdrie Highland Games, one of many gatherings that took place all over Scotland every summer. A couple of weeks before the Games, we were not allowed to train on the (cinder) track in spikes. During the final week, we were barred from running on it at all: the track and surrounds had to be in pristine condition. The Games attracted thousands of spectators and it was exciting, hearing all the bands warming up: the skirl of the pipes. Skirl is a unique word and sound: it starts with a drone (some say that's all it ever is), proceeds to a wail and develops into melodies that are cheerful and jaunty or haunting and melancholic. There's nothing like that sound to build up atmosphere and anticipation. To this day, the sound of bagpipes and the smell of cut grass and tarpaulin sends shivers up my spine. There was tossing the caber, running, dancing, wrestling and pipe bands. Susan was in the dancing, and I was in the 100 metres and 200 metres.

There's a photo of me lining up at the start. Everyone is built like a sprinter except me: I'm shorter and skinnier than any of them. It's so obvious that I'm made for distance running, not sprinting. I'm also the youngest, because I joined the Harriers just before my seventeenth birthday on 25 March, and on the first day of April, I moved up from the youth (under seventeen years) age group to junior men (under nineteen). However, there were hardly any junior races, so I was thrown in at the deep end with the senior men. It was no surprise that I finished last in both races.

Undaunted, I kept sprinting and even won a couple of minor prizes in handicapped races where, based on current form, you started at different points around the track. In longer races, the slowest runner could be halfway round the track before he started. How anyone heard the starting gun, with all that skirling and wailing going on, I'll never know.

My first endurance running training session was an education. Until that day my track running had been flat out all the time, and that's what I did on my first 300 metres run. I finished well clear of the group and felt great. It was only after a 100 metres jog round to the 300 metres mark that I realised that I couldn't maintain that speed for the second 300 metres, or the next six of them. That was my initiation into repetition running: you repeat the same distance several times with a short rest (usually a jog), long enough to bring your heart rate and breathing rate down but not a complete recovery. Your training pace is usually a wee bit faster than race pace, in this case 800 metres pace, and this is how you prepare for the demands of races. But I didn't understand that, or hadn't been listening. By the fourth or fifth 'rep' there wasn't much difference in speed between my 300 metre reps and my 100 metre jogs. I started each rep with a view of my clubmates' backs. They looked so relaxed and easy, running fast. As their backs disappeared into the distance, I wished that I could run that fast and look so relaxed.

The Highland Games skirled and wailed their way around Scotland throughout the summer, and I followed by bus to other Lanarkshire towns such as Coatbridge and Shotts, and by train and boat to idyllic locations further afield such as Dunoon (Cowal Peninsula), Rothesay (Isle of Bute) and Brodick (Isle of Arran). My favourite was Brodick. It was a fun day out that I would repeat year on year: train from Airdrie to Glasgow Queen Street, walk to Glasgow Central, train to Ardrossan, ferry to Brodick. Standing on deck during the hourlong sailing, while Goatfell and the other mountains on the north side of the island drew closer and closer. Arran is known as a Miniature Scotland, the Highland Line dividing the island into rolling farmland in the south and rugged mountains to the north. Anticipation mounted as each landmark came into clear view: the Holy Isle, Brodick beach, the ferry terminal. Then walking along the promenade, past the crazy golf and gift shop to Ormidale Park. Unlike the other games, where a 300 metres or 400 metres track was more or less accurate and flat, no one was quite sure how long Brodick's sloping and bumpy track was, but nobody minded: everyone was friendly and relaxed. We runners were more relaxed after our run and would enjoy a cold dip in the sea, followed by a couple of pints. Sometimes we would stay the night and make a weekend of it. It was the highlight of the summer, never to be forgotten. Back home in Airdrie on a clear day, you could easily make out the 'Sleeping Warrior': the shape of the 'Arran Alps', a different world, all those miles and memories away.

On more conventional tracks, I persevered with less memorable sprint races, never running faster than twelve seconds for 100 metres or twenty-five seconds for 200 metres. Well, I think those were my times: only the first three finishers were timed; all other times were estimated. I ran a few races at 800 metres, ending the season with a best time of about two minutes and twelve seconds (2:12). I might have done okay at 400 metres but there were no races. Nobody at school knew about my prowess or lack of it until I was an unspectacular sixth in the Lanarkshire Schools 800 metres and then first in the Airdrie Academy Sports Mile. However, the Mile was at the end of the programme and most people had gone home, so my quest for acceptance, and perhaps fame and adulation, dragged on.

Meanwhile, I discovered Athletics Weekly ('AW'): the bible of my new sport. It was a black and white A5 magazine, packed with features, fixtures, reports and results. I devoured it from cover to cover as soon as it arrived on our doormat. It was the start of a love affair that would continue unbroken for nearly fifty years (and counting). Never has an issue been missed. In 1973 I read about David Bedford's world record 10,000 metres at Crystal Palace, the progress of Frank Clement as Scotland's top 1500 metres runner, Brendan Foster's move up from 1500 metres to 5,000 metres and Alan Pascoe's from 110 metres to 400 metres Hurdles. The fixture list included the European Athletics Cup Final, to be held this year in Scotland and I asked Dad if we could go.

On a wild and windy day (is there any other kind?) at Meadowbank Stadium, Edinburgh, I was enthralled, watching the victories of people I had previously only read about: Chris Monk in the 200 metres, Andy Carter in the 800 metres, our own Frank Clement in the 1500 metres and Brendan Foster (Big Bren) in the 5,000 metres. Alan Pascoe said after his 400 metres Hurdles win that when he turned into the home straight it was like hitting a brick wall, the wind was so strong.

It was the first time I had been to international athletics, and I was inspired. My own performances in my first track season could never be described as inspirational, but I had shown dedication, made some progress, enjoyed the summer and discovered an everlasting passion.

****

'Sun 4 Nov. 1973

'A.M. 2 mi. on Scarhill track (raining, uneven ground, puddles) managed it in just over 11min

'P.M. about 3/4hr mobility work at Caldervale. Then run home, about 2.5-3mi., steady pace / managed all right, enjoyed it'

Nothing remarkable about that, except that it's the first entry in my first training diary, and, like reading 'AW', became a habit that I would keep up forever.

I had nine months of running behind me, and the cross-country season was already underway, but 4 November was the first time I put pen to paper and recorded details of my training. The Scarhill (or Scrawhill) track was a disused oval of black cinders and debatable distance, overgrown and hidden amongst slag foothills, fields and travellers' sites, close to our house in Cairnhill. I must have overestimated the distance or miscounted the laps, because no way was I quick enough to run two five and a half minute miles. I recorded a total mileage that week of thirty-five, but it was probably under thirty, given my tendency to exaggerate.

The entries follow with unfailing regularity: runs on the road and over the country; indoor games, flexibility and strength sessions; hill repetitions and the occasional track session or race. Until that winter I used to walk everywhere to get from A to B for a purpose, such as going to school, or to Broomfield or to meet a friend. Now it was a novelty to run the same routes in a much shorter time. I had read Alan Sillitoe's *The Loneliness of the Long Distance Runner*, and I enjoyed the solitude. You rarely saw another runner, and if you did it would be a clubmate or someone from another club. Road runs were not without their challenges. People would shout insults. 'Get them knees up, hup, two, three!' was the mildest of their ingenious proclamations. There were much worse, some so bad that it could put you off running altogether. Stubbornly, I ran on. And on. And on.

My cross-country runs took me beyond my childhood playground of woods, canal, bankings and bings, to more of Airdrie's seven hills and through foreign lands such as Calderbank and Chapelhall to riverbanks and lochs far from home. My training diary included complaints about colds and niggling aches and pains. There were names of people I trained with: Jim Carr (who became a race walker), his brother John (club captain), Andy Henderson (the quietly spoken son of the rector of Airdrie Academy), Neil Douglas (who was studying to be a P.E. teacher and led the sessions at Caldervale) and Neilson Taylor (club secretary, who also co-organised Brodick Highland Games). There is no mention of girls: there were few at the Harriers, which saved me the embarrassment of being dumped again.

It's claimed that self-recording leads to personal achievement, and it worked for me: I ran faster and longer as the winter progressed. Despite not feeling comfortable in large groups of people, I didn't let running or study stop me having a social life. One week's entry in November included a list of activities outside of training and school. For an introverted outsider, I was surprisingly sociable:

'Sunday: cinema (the Exorcist, which scared the willies out of me)

'Monday: homework

'Tuesday: Club Marcos, Airdrie's upmarket discotheque, much cooler than the Countdown

'Wednesday: Hampden Park, Glasgow, watching Scotland get hammered 0-5 by England

'Thursday: part-time evening job, distributing and collecting football coupons

'Friday: Uriah Heep concert, Green's Playhouse, Glasgow

'Saturday: Airdrieonians game'

I was slowly creeping out of my shell and enjoying life 'outwith' the In Crowd. In my sixth and final year at Airdrie Academy, it's just as well that my social life wasn't busy every week, because I was trying to improve my grade in Maths as well as taking two new Highers and C.S.Y.S. English. The Certificate of Sixth Year Studies wasn't a qualification: it was preparation for university. It bridged the gap in standard between Highers and the first year of even higher education. Our English teacher, Miss Sneddon, inspired in me a love of literature: reading Shakespeare, Burns and my favourite author Graham Greene, whose protagonists were often outsiders. My critical analysis and creative writing skills developed at the same time as I ran further and faster. *Mens sano in corpore sano.* The two people who helped me most to achieve an

26

active mind within an active body were Miss Sneddon and our new Physical Education teacher, Mr McLean.

Early in the school year, when I asked Miss Sneddon which grade I was achieving so far she told me, 'Currently, your *best* work is at D, but I fully expect it to improve to C, perhaps B.' Patiently, she guided me along my literary journey and eventually I did achieve a final grade of B. Meanwhile, Mr McLean took me under his wing on a similar but different journey.

****

It's the end of a school day in December. It should be dark but there's lightness in the sky and on the ground. It's been snowing all afternoon; proper snow, big, fluffy flakes close together in an unbroken sky of white. It's thick and deep underfoot, and none of the students seems to be in a rush to go home: how often do they get a chance like this, to play in the snow with so many of their friends at the same time? They're pelting each other with snowballs, which Mr McLean and I dodge as we run out of the school gates. 'Ouch!' A thump on the back of the neck then a cold dollop of snow sliding under my collar and down my back. We laugh it off, escape the bombardment as the crowd thins, and turn into the Golfhill housing scheme.

I've been helping Mr McLean with the boys' cross-country team, and he's been helping me with my running: pacing me on these runs and giving me tips based on his experience as a former cross-country runner and steeplechaser with Shettleston Harriers. Never overbearing, never interfering with the Airdrie Harriers' way of doing things, he's a positive role model and a comforting presence during my first winter of regular training. It's fun running in the snow, which hasn't had time to turn into icy ruts or filthy slush. The soft surface cushions your footfall and although we're running on pavements, it's more like cross-country running: good preparation for races.

However, as we climb the hill towards Glenmavis, something doesn't feel right. It might be the increased resistance of the snow, but it feels worse than that. It's not only aching legs but also a general weariness, which becomes overwhelming as Mr McLean's back becomes less and less distinct in the whiteness up ahead. What started as anticipation and thrill has become an ordeal.

He stops and waits for me. 'Are you okay?'

'Not really. I'm. Really. Tired today.'

'Okay, let's take it easy. You're not coming down with something, are you?'

'No. Don't think. So. Just. Tired.'

'What sort of training have you been doing lately?'

'The usual. Road. Country. I've run. Five days. In a row.'

'Is it not time you took a break, then?'

'Guess. So.'

We run on, more slowly than before. My breathing settles into a more comfortable rhythm. I'm still tired but I'm listening intently to Mr McLean's words.

'It sounds like you're doing some tough training, but you can't run hard all the time. You need some easy running between the hard sessions. You're a good runner. In the short time I've known you, I've seen a lot of improvement. You're dedicated, you've got basic speed and you're talented.'

I can't answer. It's not because I'm tired: I can't think of what to say. No one's ever spoken to me like this before

'Look, you could get a medal at the Scottish Schools Championships, and I'm not talking about silver or bronze.'

I still can't speak. For the first time in my life, someone is telling me that I can be the best at sport. I'm not alone: someone else believes in me. We can do this. I can do this.

We turn a corner onto the Carlisle Road. The snow has stopped falling, the wind is behind us and it's nearly all downhill back to the Academy. Suddenly, I feel like I could run all the way down to Carlisle. I'm engrossed, as Mr McLean suggests a few tweaks to my training: weekly, rather than occasional track sessions; longer reps; recovery runs between hard sessions; a longer run of between an hour and an hour and a half on Sundays. All sensible stuff, bringing more structure to my programme.

As we run back though the school gates, weariness left behind somewhere on the Carlisle Road, I feel inspired again.

But this is different.

This is real.

It's 1973, I'm seventeen years old and I'm going to be Scottish Schools Champion.

Chapter Three: Steeplechase

The 1974 Commonwealth Games were held in Christchurch, New Zealand, during our winter. It was the first major athletics event that I followed religiously. I studied the preview in 'AW', watched as many TV sessions as possible, often giving up sleep, and devoured the results.

I was enthralled by Tanzania's Filbert Bayi's world record in the 1500 metres as he led from gun to tape, holding off the home nation's John Walker, who also broke the old world record. Those two left in their wake: Ben Jipcho of Kenya, Rod Dixon of New Zealand, Graham Crouch of Australia, Mike Boit of Kenya and our own Big Bren. England's Ian Thompson, after a surprise, rags to riches win in the English trial, won the marathon. Alan Pascoe hit another wall of sorts when, in his excitement after winning the 400 metres Hurdles, he started to run his lap of honour the wrong way around the track, discovered painfully why hurdles are set up in a particular way, smashed two of them and gave up, smiling and waving sheepishly to the crowd. John Davies of Wales fell over in the steeplechase but picked himself up to finish second to Jipcho. It was a lesson in perseverance and triumph over adversity that I would never forget.

Meanwhile, back in the UK winter, there were limited opportunities to race. I ran the Lanarkshire and Western District Cross-Country Championships, but six miles against grown men was quite a leap from two miles amongst boys in the Brigade races, and I had neither the experience nor the maturity to be competitive at that distance. I did, however, notch up my first win, in the only local inter-schools race in my age group. Mr McLean said that the gently undulating course on a good surface suited my 'free-flowing' stride. I was flattered that someone had noticed and took the time to point it out to me. I was good at being prepared and sometimes guilty of overthinking things, but free and flowing? I could take that.

More significant than that first win was the day that the Academy's 1st X1 football squad joined me on a training run and I outran them all. It proved that I wasn't only good at running because footballers didn't do it: I was better at running than the best footballers. Seven years after my humiliating rejection on the side of that football pitch of shame, not one of the twenty-two boys who played that day had made it into the Academy's first team squad. Was this retribution? Not really: it was only a training run.

I finished forty-seventh in the Scottish Cross-Country Union Junior Men's Championship in Drumpellier Park, Coatbridge. It was a much better performance, against club runners, than my similar run against Boys' Brigaders the previous year. However, that race and a tenth place in the Lanarkshire Schools race at Cleland Estate proved beyond doubt that I had no chance of being Scottish Schools Cross-Country Champion. Nevertheless, Mr McLean and I were quietly confident of an improved performance as the day of the Big Race approached.

This is how my final diary entry of the 1973/74 cross-country season described the race:

'Scottish Schools c.c. champs. (17-19yrs) 4mi. Clydebank

'Terrain: heavy, steep hills

'Weather: cold, windy

'Comments: the race was two laps of a hilly course. I got off to a good start and was in the first half-dozen or so at the burn (200 metres). I stumbled and had to make up the lost ground at the bog and the hill which followed. The hill was a 'killer'. I took it fairly easy the first time and by the time we were at the bottom of it on the other side, I was in about twentieth position. From then on I made up places going up the hills but lost them going down them. At the ditch, the second time round, I fell but made up two or three places on the hill. With 300 metres or 400 metres to go, I sprinted and made up another two or three places, but as we entered the bog with about 150-200 metres left, I lost a place, then sprinted away from the guy behind me. My final position was sixteenth. (about 140 starters.) I'm quite pleased with this race. It more than makes up for my disappointment at the Lanarkshire. The start made all the difference. This race ends the c.c. season on an optimistic note. I've improved more than I could ever have hoped for back in November. Before then, I could hardly keep going for as little as 3mi. in a training run. I hope that I can carry this rate of improvement onto the track now.'

****

'Sixteenth is good,' said Mr McLean. 'Look, those sixteen have four races to choose from at the Scottish Schools Track: 800 metres, 1500 metres, 5000m and... how do you feel about the steeplechase?'

It was no surprise that he suggested that I try his old event. He wrote me a sensible training schedule: track sessions with reps of varied distances, grouped in sets to maintain the pace; recovery days of easy running; long run at weekends. I ran a few local races: 800 metres in 2:05 and 1500 metres somewhere around 4:25. My training pace was much quicker than that, so I was frustrated at running more slowly in competition, although much faster than my debut season. We also incorporated hurdles practice and I took to it quite well. However, there were no steeplechase barriers at Rawyards and of course no water jump.

'There's nothing to the water jump,' Mr McLean assured me. 'One foot on the barrier, one in the water, back into your stride, you'll be okay.'

Not only were there no steeplechase facilities nearby but there were also no junior races before the day of the Scottish Schools Championships. So, encouraged by Mr McLean, I entered the senior 3,000 metres Steeplechase at the Western District Championships.

****

I'm on my own. I don't know anybody here. I recognise a few athletes and I'm on nodding terms with some of them but I don't really know any of them. Neither Dad nor Mr McLean could make it today, so

34

I've come to Grangemouth on two buses. Grangemouth isn't even in the West but there aren't many 'tartan' tracks in Scotland, so here we are in the East for the Western District Championships. Grangemouth is best known for its oil refineries, but I'm not feeling anything like refined. Everybody looks like they know what they're doing, with all the right gear, preparing for their events. I don't know what I'm doing here, full stop. I haven't ever run a junior championship on the track yet, but I'll be lining up for a senior championship soon and it's the steeplechase and I've never done one before. And it's 3,000 metres and that's one and a half times longer than the distance I'm due to run at the Schools. I've never been over a steeplechase barrier before, never tried the water jump, never run a flat 3,000 metres on the track, never run on tartan before. Who ever thought that this was a good idea? What if I can't get over the barriers? What if I trip at the water jump and everyone laughs at me falling flat on my face? What if I finish last? What if I don't finish? For the fourth or fifth time in the past hour I go to the toilet. And there's still two hours to go until the start.

The barriers aren't set up on the track yet but I practise hurdling one of them a few times on the grass on the infield. I get over okay, and then try a few with one foot on top because I'll probably be too tired to hurdle all the way. Feeling a wee bit more confident, I venture over to the water jump. Is the water not supposed to be deeper than this? I take a run at the barrier and hesitate at the top. The water seems a long way down, although this barrier is no higher than the others. 'There's nothing to the water jump: one foot on the barrier, one in the water, back into your stride, you'll be okay.' I drop off the top and clear the water, not hard to do because the pit is only half full. The track slopes upwards out of the low water and my foot hits the dry surface at an awkward angle. My ankle clicks. Oh no! My first ever go at the water jump and I'm injured! But it doesn't hurt, and I try a few more times, with slightly more success.

Walking back to my lonely seat in the stands, I spot someone I know in a group of red-jacketed officials. It's Mr McLean! He's made it, after all. Great! He'll know what to say. I'll be okay now. Approaching the group, I open my mouth to greet him but my words stick in my throat: it's not him. There's a passing resemblance in build and hair colour but it's not Mr McLean. Of course it's not: he told me he couldn't come and why would he be wearing an official's jacket, anyway? He's not an official. So, I'm on my own: deal with it.

There's an hour to go until the start. I've collected my number, so that means I've registered, right? Or is it 'declared'? No, that's when you report at the start, fifteen minutes before the start time. Or is it ten? Half an hour drags by. I check the timetable for the tenth time. Events are behind schedule, so I don't need to warm up yet, do I? But what if they catch up and get back on schedule again? I'll still be warming up or not warmed up at all. I decide to jog within sight of the start line, just in case. I wear my club vest with the race number pinned on, under my tee-shirt, and carry my spikes, in case I forget them. I visit the toilet again. My ankle hurts a bit.

After an interminable time, jogging up and down, punctuated by anxious glances towards the start and another visit to the toilet, the starter's marshal calls us over to check in. I don't recognise any of the other competitors but they're all taller and older than me. They'll find it easy to clear the barriers and they've got years of running in their legs, so I'll have no chance of keeping up. I'm going to be last.

I stride down the straight a few times to complete my warm-up, like everyone else, but their strides are longer and faster than mine. An image of me sitting comfortably at home watching TV with Mum, Dad and Susan distracts me. I wish I was there, with no worries, rather than suffering this. And we haven't even got to the start line yet.

Now we're at the start and I'm hating these last few minutes, waiting for the call to our marks. Please can I go home now?

'On your marks...'

Crash! My nerves settle slightly as we start running; at least I'm doing something other than waiting. The first 100 metres or so feel surprisingly easy. This race is going to be twice as far as my more familiar 1500 metres, so it seems slower. Then I'm surprised by the first barrier. I don't know why I'm surprised: this is a steeplechase, and I know it's coming. But I'm at the back of a group of runners and I don't see it in time to adjust my stride, which I have to chop as I jump up onto the barrier and drop over the other side. I manage to hurdle the next one; I have a clear view of it because I'm already several metres behind anyone else. The race has hardly started but the pace no longer feels easy. The first water jump looms ahead. I'm terrified, but I leap up onto the top of the barrier and stumble over the other side. My ankle clicks again as I land on the track but it doesn't seem too painful, so I carry on, drifting further and further behind and not enjoying myself at all. One lap later, I trip and fall at the water jump; the ghouls who always gather there laugh and shout unhelpful comments; I remember John Davies and his determination at the Commonwealth Games, and pick myself up, but at the next barrier I don't even try to clear it: I stop and walk off the track. My ankle hurts, I'm hobbling, it's too painful, I'm humiliated, and I don't want to do this anymore.

****

My sister and I are paddling in the sea at St. Andrews. The doctor has diagnosed strained ligaments and advised me not to run for two weeks. That's going to take me up to the week before the Scottish Schools. Mum and Dad suggested that sea water would help my recovery, so here we are at their favourite spot on the coast. It's taken a couple of hours to drive here, over the Forth Road Bridge into the Kingdom of Fife, stopping midmorning at the Powmill milk bar, then parking next to the famous golf courses overlooking the West Sands.

We're laughing like a pair of toddlers at the seaside for the first time in their lives. The sea laps gently against thousands of pebbles, each one individual in its shape, size and colour. Next to this small beach is a pool, carved out of rocks framing still and clear water. It's about the shape and size of a typical indoor pool and looks inviting, but not that inviting. I've been swimming at Airdrie Baths during the week but I'm not going to swim in this pool, no matter how still and clear: it's too cold in Scotland's early summer. The ruins of the castle and white, fluffy clouds in an azure sky are reflected perfectly in the pool. The sandy colour of the castle walls complements the various shades of grey, brown, yellow and white of the rocks and pebbles, and contrasts with the blues of sky and sea, all of these watched over by drifting clouds, like tourists strolling along the promenade above the shore.

We skim stones: mini splashes—one, two, three, four—ripples emanating from pinpoint sources. Concentric circles widening, glinting in the sunlight, until they fade away, absorbed into the sea.

We look up and wave to Mum and Dad, who are walking arm in arm towards the cathedral and harbour.

****

'That was poor,' says Mr McLean as I rejoin him after finishing third in the 1500 metres at the Lanarkshire Schools Championships. It wasn't his most motivating speech, but he's the one who made me believe in myself, he's encouraged me every step of the way, he's got me here, and I should have won.

I agree: it was poor, and I'm disconsolate. I took half of the doctor's advice, returning to easy running after one week, not two. That was a week ago. After a few days, the ankle felt much better, so I completed a track session. Big mistake: on the way home, both calves tightened up, the next day it was painful to walk, I returned to the pool and hoped for the best. And now, on a grass track in Hamilton, every step has hurt, and I've struggled to a mediocre third place in a race that was mine to win.

Mr McLean softens his approach and reassures me. 'It would have been worse if it was a tartan track instead of grass: grass is easier on the legs. You'll be fine after a week of easy running and swimming. You've done the work; a couple of weeks off won't make any difference to your fitness; the rest will do you good. And just think: a year ago you were sixth in this race and would have loved to get a medal. Now you've got one and you're gutted. You're aiming higher. Keep that in mind this coming week.'

Only one week to go before the biggest race of my life.

****

I'm back in Fife, sitting on a grass bank outside the track at Pitreavie, with Gerry Bollen from Coatbridge, who has just won the 200 metres Low Hurdles. Gerry and I have practised hurdling together at Rawyards, and now one of us is a Scottish Schools Champion. My race, ten times as long, is approaching, and a strange calm settles upon me.

My calves feel fine, not tight or painful any more, the ankle injury forgotten. I've followed instructions to the letter and done nothing all week other than easy running and swimming on alternate days. No one could describe the past few weeks as perfect preparation, but they have been part of over a year of building up to this, my final chance to shine as a schoolboy. Friday night dashes in the dark, secret runs under railway bridges, the embarrassment of my first cross-country race, learning my trade on the track, memories made at Highland Games, those runs after school with Mr McLean, the promising performance at the Scottish Schools cross-country, a new training schedule, improvement in my first few track races, injury and recovery, and now the inspiration of Gerry: if he can do it, I can do it. Further back into the depths of time: Best Boy at the Boys' Brigade, winning and losing at Subbuteo, diving into rugby tackles and then dropping out, all that endurance unknowingly developed while walking and playing outside, my shyness when declining the chance to try for primary school athletics, that miserable afternoon on the edge of the football pitch when I believed that I was rubbish at everything and always would be. It all comes down to this one race. I'm on the start line of my first and only Scottish Schools Championship on the track, the final lesson of my final day of school.

I'm in second place and it's too slow. I hurdle the first barrier smoothly and take the lead. The first water jump passes without incident; this time my foot lands in the water and I'm back into my stride: nothing to it. By the next barrier I'm back in second but the new leader is slowing down: too slow, so I regain the lead and pick up the pace, which chops and changes as I slow it down again. But there are no negative thoughts this time: it's a tactical decision to slow the pace. I don't have to run fast at this stage: I've got basic speed; I can beat them in a sprint finish.

It's still slow, I'm tired and no longer hurdling: putting my foot on each barrier now. The opposition is breathing down my neck, but I'm not worried: I know they won't be breathing down my neck when I'm sprinting down the home straight. Where has this new-found confidence come from? Best not to wonder about that: concentrate on the task in hand. No one is laughing as I clear the water jump again and round the bend towards the final barrier of the penultimate lap. I'm over it, and seconds later, the bell rings, a cacophony that usually causes a surge in adrenalin and an increase in pace as you start to squeeze out your last drop of energy around that final circuit.

But I'm not going to run faster yet. Patience, patience. Wait, wait. For the sprint finish. It's still slow. My shadow is still behind me, as he has been for most of the race. He must have the same idea: wait for the sprint. Or maybe he can't run any faster. I'm tired but not too tired. Maybe he's really tired. Hold that thought. Be confident. I can do this.

The final water jump is in clear sight, as clear as my will to win. This is it: I'm on top of the barrier, leaping into the water, slightly stumbling on landing but I'm okay. I'm out of the pit and sprinting round the bend. I'm flying! The wind is in my ears, and I can't hear any breathing behind me. Entering the home straight, I risk a glance over my shoulder, and there's nobody there! *And I'm* not tired! *But it's not over yet:*

there's 100 metres to run and one more barrier to clear. Don't trip! Don't mess up now!

I'm over cleanly—I've actually hurdled it—and I'm still sprinting, sprinting to the finish line. In every previous track race, I've always had a view of another runner's back at this point. But this time, no one's there: it's just empty space up ahead. Breaking the tape, I raise my arms spontaneously and immediately, and self-consciously, lower them. I slow to a stop and turn to shake hands with the other runners but they're a long way behind. It's only a few seconds but I savour that time like it's years of triumph against a lack of confidence, low self-esteem and poor attainment.

No more feeling low on the sidelines.

This is high.

This is running.

This is winning.

It's 1974, I'm eighteen years old and I'm not *rubbish at everything.*

I am Scottish Schools Champion.

Part Two

The Early Laps: Coming Of Age

Chapter Four: Retribution?

So, I was a Scottish Schools Champion but was it retribution?

It was a triumph over adversity but it wasn't a great run. My time of 6:45 for 2,000 metres Steeplechase was the fastest in Scotland in 1974 but only three of us had toed the line at Pitreavie and no one else ran the event all year. Boys of the same age in England were running much faster. Not something that you would normally shout about but I wanted all my athletics friends to know about my injury, my slow but tactical run and my sprint finish. I was making excuses for winning.

I also told everyone else, who would listen, that I was the champion. When Susan made a new friend I asked, 'Did you tell her about your brother, the famous athlete?'

What a wanker.

Due to go on holiday with some mates later in the summer to Dawlish Warren in Devon, I entered a competition in Torquay. I wrote to the organisers and asked if there was anyone I could train with down there for a fortnight. I told the whole story about the championship and what sort of training I'd like to do. To their credit, they replied with recommendations.

Two days after Pitreavie, I started work at the Scottish Widows Fund and Life Assurance Society in Glasgow. In spite of my B in CSYS English and my love of literature, I did not have the confidence to apply for university and had decided to enter the world of work instead. On my first day, I told them all about the race.

Everyone and his auntie were fated to hear my story. After years of perceived failure, I couldn't cope with success.

That evening I ran up to the track to complete a set of 150m reps. Roy Baillie of Bellshill YMCA Harriers, one of the top 800 metres runners in Scotland, was training alongside his coach, whom I didn't recognise. I was tired at the end of my first day at work, so soon after such an emotional race, and was struggling to train on my own. The three of us exchanged a few words, and of course I inflicted them with the story of my Great Victory. The coach listened patiently and commented that it sounded like a tough race, sympathised that it was going to be difficult commuting by train to work instead of walking to school, suggested that it would be a good idea to take it easy for a few days, and finally, that I should think about running my 150 metres reps with the breeze behind me instead of into a headwind.

The coach was Tommy Boyle.

Not quite everyone was subjected to the story of my race: no one at school knew, because I'd already left. The 1st X1 footballers didn't know. The rugby team didn't know. None of the girls knew, ending any chance I might have had of impressing any of them and persuading them to go out with me. And none of those twenty-two boys from my former primary school knew.

But Mr McLean knew: I had phoned him up to tell him the good news and to thank him profusely for all of his support. He arranged for me to be invited to the Academy's annual awards evening, when I would be presented with my school colours: yellow and blue braid to sew into the collars and cuffs of your school blazer. I'd watched the top sportsmen at school parading around in their blazers and braid, a clear statement that they were Good at Games. Now I was going to receive mine. That I was never going to wear the school blazer again didn't matter: the braid was a symbol of success. And I had an opportunity to show off in front of my peers at last. I accepted the invitation with pride.

On the evening of the awards, I walked proudly into the assembly hall and along the front row of seats named and reserved for award winners, looking for the one with my name.

There wasn't one. The speeches were about to begin and there was nowhere for me to sit. I spoke to one of the teachers, who quickly shoved an extra seat on the end of a row for me. I was on the edge again.

The rector mentioned me in a list of sporting achievements, and I thought: oh well, I don't have a seat but I haven't been forgotten; I'll be on the stage, and everyone will see me collecting my award.

One by one the award winners walked up as their names were announced. There were academic awards, competition prizes, recognition of volunteers and finally, the sports awards. Amidst much applause, the winners climbed the steps and received their award and handshake from the rector. It was nearly the end of the evening and I hadn't been called up yet. Maybe the rector was going to save the best until last: no one else had won a Scottish Schools Championship that year.

But no: the evening ended and everyone went home. I had been forgotten. There was no award for me. No braid. No applause. No recognition. I was left out again.

****

Back on the track I ran a personal best (pb) of 4:19 in the heats of the junior men's 1500 metres at the Scottish Amateur Athletics Association Championships but it wasn't fast enough to qualify for the final.

'You didn't even make the final?' remarked my boss at work the next day. 'That's not very good. I thought you were the Scottish Champion.'

'I'm not *the* Scottish Champion,' I confessed. 'I'm *a* Scottish Schools Champion. There's dozens of us.'

I had now realised that I'd better stop boasting about my win at the Scottish Schools. Far from being the final retribution, it was only the start of a fledgling career in athletics. I had a lot to learn.

On the first day of our holiday in Devon, I went for a run and then made a half pint of cider last all night in the bar. I was trying to be the epitome of a healthy athlete, and I had that race in Torquay coming up. However, by the end of the second day I was having such a good time that I stopped running, withdrew from the race and did what most lads do on holiday: drank multiple pints in the bar, ate junk food, messed around by the pool and on the beach, and went out with girls.

****

The break was exactly what I needed. Refreshed, I returned to work, training and the Highland Games circuit. Running 800 metres and 1500 metres handicapped races, I won prizes and even finished first a couple of times, thanks to generous 'marks'. I ran some pretty good times but not for the full distance, of course. I thought I was running quicker than my equivalent 'scratch' times but it was impossible to tell.

Brodick was my favourite again. I was a close second in the (approximately) 800 metres scratch to Danny Knowles of Edinburgh A.C., who had run 1:57 for 800 metres and 3:52 for 1500 metres that season. Then I beat him on the first leg (300 metres) of the medley relay. 'I beat Danny Knowles!' I shouted, not realising that he was within earshot.

'Never mind,' he replied, smiling. 'It was a good laugh, anyway.'

He was right: it was a fun way to end a season that had been on the whole successful and enjoyable. Travelling home with my mates on the ferry, looking back at Arran across a shimmering sea, I reflected on how good a decision it had been to take up running. Athletics, for me, had started as a desire to be the best at something, to prove myself and to show others that they shouldn't leave me on the sidelines. It now seemed highly unlikely that I would ever be the best but I was improving. Besides, it was a healthy activity, I had made new friends and had become part of a community.

I set myself the modest targets for the following summer of breaking two minutes for 800 metres and winning the 1500 metres Handicap at Airdrie Highland Games.

But first, winter was coming.

****

Winter was dark. Every morning I walked to Airdrie Station in the dark, sat in a stuffy train carriage with nothing but darkness outside the grimy windows, walked in the dark from Queen Street Station to the office, sat at a desk in a smoky office all day, repeated the dark journey in reverse after work, and then when I got home, ran in the dark. The only time I saw daylight during the week was walking in George Square at lunchtime if it wasn't raining.

I enjoyed running on my old training routes at weekends but my cross-country races against the seniors were less than successful and not much fun. Then an opportunity came along to attend a sprinters' training day in Bellahouston Park, Glasgow. It had been a long time since I had done any sprinting, and the day clashed with a cross-country race, but this was a chance to learn something new. I chose sprinting over cross-country. One of the elite athletes demonstrating was Chris Monk, winner of the 200 metres in the European

Cup in 1973, when Dad and I had watched international athletics for the first time.

And one of the coaches was Tommy Boyle, who kindly gave me a lift home. The training day had been educational, it felt good to be running faster again, and it was a refreshing change from my dull winter's routine. Realising that I needed a change that would last more than one day, I plucked up the courage to ask Tommy to coach me.

Tommy invited to me to join his squad at Bellshill.

And opened my eyes to a new way of running.

Training with a coach at Bellshill caused no conflict at Airdrie: by then Airdrie, Bellshill, Monklands, Lesmahagow and Motherwell had amalgamated to form Clyde Valley A.A.C.. The intention was to create a Super Team in the north of Lanarkshire. It brought together international runners of the calibre of Jim Brown, Ron McDonald, Ian Gilmour and John Graham, backed up by solid team men such as Roy Baillie, Ian Moncur, Joe Small and Eddie Devlin. The newly amalgamated club also benefited from coaching expertise. I was excited about the prospect of training and racing at a higher level.

There was no track in Bellshill but Tommy made the most of the local environment: circuits and fitness tests in the YMCA hall, hill reps under streetlights, and fartleks (speed play) and steady runs on the roads. As the 1975 summer season approached, most of our sessions took place on a black, rubber-like track at Carluke, where I learned how to train specifically for 800 metres races. Complementing more traditional sessions, there were changes of pace within reps, for example 4x400 metres x15–20mins (four repetitions of 400 metres, with a full recovery of 15–20 minutes); the first 200 metres in 29–30sec and the second 200 metres flat out, for times of 55.3, 55.5, 56.0 and 54.3. Another was a series of 300 metres reps of blast/coast/blast: you would run flat out for 100 metres, 'take the foot off the pedal' but still run fast for the middle 100 metres, and then sprint to the finish, with full rest between each run. I trained with the much faster Roy Baillie, sometimes joining him for the last 300 metres of his 400 metre reps, and we would pace each other. How about this one? 200 metres (28 sec), two minutes jog recovery, 200 metres (28), two and a half minutes, 300 metres (43), three and a half minutes, 300 metres (42), five minutes, 600 metres (87.5), thirteen minutes, 600 metres (88).

This type of training was a revelation to me, and my times came tumbling down in early season: I opened with a pb of 4:13 for 1500 metres and my 800 metres was hovering just outside two minutes.

Then, a year after my distressing experience in the 3,000 metres Steeplechase in Grangemouth, the Western District Championships came around again.

****

I'm on my own in the shower, after the 800 metres final, and I'm crying. I've shaken hands, left the track, completed my cool down jog and walked to the shower room, all as normal. Suddenly, without warning, I'm overcome with emotion. It starts with the chin wobbling, then shoulders shaking, and now— great, gulping sobs. Uncontrollable tears. Thank goodness I'm alone and the tears are washed down the drain with sweat and shampoo. No one sees me struggling to pull myself together. I manage to hide my feelings on the way out of the Westerlands stadium, and all the way home from Glasgow to Airdrie. That evening, I phone Tommy for a de-briefing.

****

Really; what was I crying about? Bubbling like a big baby. I had broken two minutes for 800 metres for the first time and qualified for my first senior championship final. And I was still a junior. I had finished eighth and last in the final in a slower time of 2:01.8, and that had felt like failure. After the elation of setting a landmark time and the excitement and anticipation of reaching the final amongst the elite, the crash back down to earth had been overwhelming.

But it wasn't that bad. I had run the best 800 metres of my life in the heat, and only an hour later I had been competitive and only failed to avoid last place by the narrowest of margins. It was miles better than my equivalent performance at the same championship only twelve months ago. And I was having a good season. A season that got better and better.

Within a week of achieving the first of my modest targets, I achieved the second: at Airdrie Highland Games I won the 1500 metres Handicap after running the 1,000 metres (scratch) invitation race the same afternoon. (Yes, I was invited to an elite race.) By the end of the season my 800 metres had come down to 1:58.0, although that was in the heat of the Scottish Junior Championship and, like last year, I didn't make the final. However, I won the 1500 metres at the (less prestigious) Scottish YMCA Championships and improved my pb to 4:08.0. So, my 800 metres and 1500 metres pbs were now, respectively, seven and eleven seconds quicker than last season. As a regular in Clyde Valley's relay team, I ran more 400 metres relay legs than 1500 metres races. In a fitting climax to the season, we were third in the senior 4x400 metres at the Scottish Relay Championships. Our time was 3:24.54 and my split was just under fifty-two seconds. That was my first national senior medal.

****

The 1976 track season, my first as a senior, started promisingly with an 800 metres pb of 1:57.4 for second place in the Lanarkshire Championships. However, I didn't improve, and the season petered out, although it ended with another national senior medal: silver in the 4x400 metres.

The novelty of travelling into Glasgow on the blue train for work had long since worn off. I was tired all the time. I never missed a track session but I was skipping some of the recovery runs in between. Work as a new business insurance clerk was boring and brought me no job satisfaction. The next change in my life was long overdue.

Never having stopped reading literature since leaving school, I added philosophy, psychology and sociology to my reading list. I had kept in touch with

Miss Sneddon, who encouraged me to apply for a place at university. Wishing to stay fairly close to home, family, club and coach, I applied to read English Literature at Stirling or Edinburgh. And was rejected by both. Maybe I would have had more success if I had cast the net wider but it was too late. However, there was still time to apply for colleges of higher education, so I applied to Jordanhill in Glasgow to train as a teacher of Physical Education. After all, I was enthusiastic about sport and literature in equal measures. But that application met with rejection too. What could I do next? Another year with Scottish Widows was not an option. Convinced that full time study was for me, I found out that there were a few places remaining at other colleges up and down the UK. Showing a rare sense of adventure, I took a risk and applied to all remaining colleges with vacancies. My first interview was at Chester, and it was successful. A twenty-year-old late starter, I was going to leave home and start a new life in England.

I said goodbye to friends in Airdrie, at work and at the club. Nearly all of my clubmates were at the opening of the new tartan track at Langloan in Coatbridge, where at the end of the season, a host of international runners had been invited to mark the occasion of the grand opening. Most of the large crowd had never seen athletics before and were unsure how to react. One young lad, clutching his autograph book, scampered across the track in front of Nick Rose, one of the best distance runners of all time and now in full stride, mid-race. Unflustered, Nick skipped aside and without breaking stride ran on to win. I don't know if he signed the lad's book after the race, but, approachable in more ways than one, he probably did.

At the final club session in Bellshill before my departure at the end of September, I thanked Tommy from the bottom of my heart. What he did mattered. How could I ever repay him for what he had done for me? He said it was no bother but one of the club coaches had called in sick; would I look after the youngsters that evening? I guess I had asked for that.

They played me up so much that, exhausted, I was glad to get home that night. It wasn't the best introduction to PE teaching before I had even started. The most disruptive of the group was a wee nyaff called Tommy McKean.

That wee nyaff would grow up to be World Champion indoors and European Champion outdoors at 800 metres.

Tommy McKean's glorious future as an athlete was ahead of him. Tommy Boyle's growing reputation as a coach would be forged in years to come. Meanwhile, a different sort of future awaited me but what would it be? What would I be doing in three or four years' time?

The car laden with books and running gear, Mum, Dad and I set off down the A74 towards England and into the unknown.

Chapter Five: Bannister

'None of you run like athletes. I repeat: none of you run like athletes.'

These are the wise words of 'Jack', athletics specialist, PE Department, Chester College of Higher Education. It's the first athletics lesson of the First Year PE course and we're running in circles around the sports hall. I'm standing behind Jack, hands on hips, aghast. Okay, I'm not a superstar but I have run some good times, won some decent races and I do run like an athlete. I am an athlete.

'Carry on. Elbows and knees. Elbows and knees. Always at right angles.'

No they're not. Anyone who's looked at a photograph or video of a runner can't fail to notice that the elbows and knees are not always at right angles: they extend to an almost straight position at a certain point of the running action.

'After this warm-up we'll learn how to high jump. We'll start with the Straddle and move on to the Western Roll. We will not be doing the Fosbury Flop: who wants to land on your neck?'

Such enlightened views.

I should have seen it coming: when I attended for interview last year, the first thing the Head of PE said to me was, *'You're not very big, are you? Not a rugby player, then?'*

Rugby comes first at Chester College, football second, athletics nowhere.

During the winter, I scored two goals in the final basketball session, but too late to avoid a D+. Gymnastics was even worse: I missed three weeks of practicals—and running—after colliding with the 'horse' and crumpling in a heap, causing a huge haematoma in my thigh. I was better at swimming: after years of messing about at Airdrie Baths, I was taught how to swim front crawl properly. I could finally do the breathing thing, and that helped to raise my average grade. I was looking forward to athletics to show what I could do. Would Jack notice? Not in a month of Sundays. Our respective views of athletics are miles apart.

Next comes cricket, a sport I never experienced at school in Scotland, or anywhere else. We're practising bowling. I must be taking to this new sport quite well because the teacher invites me and another student out to the front to demonstrate.

But no, he picks on me to demonstrate how not to bowl, and contrasts my pathetic efforts with those of the other, much more proficient student. Outstanding teaching skills. How to de-motivate, deflate and humiliate in one easy lesson. What's the lesson for me? Don't play cricket? Don't try to be a PE teacher?

Once again, I was the Muffin Man.

****

My first year at teacher training college was trying. At the beginning of term, my first run had been with the football and rugby squads. It was a two mile circuit and in a scene reminiscent of the day the Airdrie Academy 1st XI joined me for a run, I led them home at a steady pace.

'Right, guys,' said the rugby club captain. 'Five minutes rest, and we go again.'

Groans all round, but not from me. 'Okay, I'll just put my track suit away in my room, and I'll be ready.'

He was joking. I was serious. It set us apart from then on. On the basis of that run, the PE students thought I was a good runner but serious and a bit odd. An outsider again.

The PE students strutted around arrogantly like they owned the place. They thought they were the kings of the college. I was a PE student too, but I wasn't part of that particular In Crowd. Nor did I want to be: just like at school, I made a few close friends and enjoyed relatively quiet times with them. I even had a girlfriend at last, and our relationship would last for longer than three weeks: Gemma and I would be together for years.

Despite being on the sidelines again I loved college life. The routine of going to lectures, training in daylight and meeting friends for coffee or in the student bar was a world apart from life as an office clerk and commuter. The halls of residence were too noisy—PE students thought nothing of coming back drunk in the middle of the night and playing cricket in the corridors—but, on the upside, your friends were never far away. No more long walks along a trail of vandalised phone boxes for a few words with friends. Life seemed so much faster without those long gaps between seeing people.

The cross-country team was a collection of misfits but we were friendly and had regular, well organised 'matches' on Wednesday afternoons. I won a few races, all at distances shorter than the six milers that had put me off in my early days back in Scotland. In summer, the college track appeared and to say the least, it was unusual. The grass circuit was more like a circle than an oval: huge bends and short straights. On hot and sunny days you couldn't train on it because students were sunbathing across the lanes. During the occasional athletics matches, no running could take place during the Shot Put, because they putted across the bend.

None of the other college runners trained much, so I joined Chester & Ellesmere Port A.C. and trained with Paul, nicknamed Dylan because of his hair style, like the rabbit from the Magic Roundabout. There was also Martin Weston, a farmer from across the border in Wales, who walked mile upon mile all day long at his work and claimed to get by on low running mileage, and he pushed me along at least once per week. Most of my training was based on helpful letters from Tommy and memories of old sessions. Almost inevitably, my training times were slower, and I graduated to longer sessions suitable for 1500 metres and above. As Tommy pointed out, on grass I wouldn't be able to run as fast, but it would be easier on the legs.

My 800 metres races were also slower but I was developing into a better racer on the college scene and in local races, winning more often than not, feeling and looking relaxed. After searching for better competition, my 1500 metres time came down to 4:03 in an open meeting at Kirkby, Liverpool. This meant nothing to the PE students or staff: the forthcoming Inter Year Sports was seen as the pinnacle of athletic achievement at Chester College. The year captains picked their teams, and non-athletes volunteered to run, jump or throw, intent on earning bragging rights. The PE staff acted as officials and a large crowd of students gathered to cheer on their favourites. I won an entirely unremarkable 800 metres/3,000 metres double and was to enjoy a couple of weeks of minor, undeserved adulation. Even Jack said, 'Well done.' I was tempted momentarily to reply, 'Not bad for someone who doesn't run like an athlete,' but I resisted. I wasn't confrontational. Unfortunately, not everyone could resist petulance: a rumour developed out of the 4x400 metres relay, where I started the final leg just behind Ross, College's top sprinter. I had dashed into the lead but lost during the second 200 metres as Ross easily pulled away. Like Chinese whispers the story was exaggerated to the extent that Ross had taken the baton 100 metres behind me and finished 100 metres in front.

Meanwhile, although struggling with the sports science course, my understanding improved through hard work and perseverance, which brought my grades up but didn't impress my classmates. There was an anti-intellectual element within the PE fraternity.

It was a completely different culture amongst students of my 'second' subject, English Literature. I loved the discussions about twentieth century novels,

Gothic classics, romantic poetry and Shakespeare. Gemma and I joined the Literary Society's trips to Bronte country, theatres in Liverpool and a production of *The Hitchhikers' Guide to the Galaxy* at Theatre Clwyd.

Gemma's work on her placements at primary schools also intrigued me. When the time came to choose options for the forthcoming second year, when you were to drop your second subject, I decided to drop PE and continue studying Literature.

I had enrolled for college, intent on teaching PE at secondary school. Now I could study the subject that was closest to my heart. And I was going to learn something new and unexpected: a quirk of the timetable meant that I would be training as a primary school teacher.

****

On the day of my twenty-second birthday, Dad and I are standing in the rain at Bellahouston Park, Glasgow, watching the men's race of the World Cross-Country Championships. Greta Waitz has run away with the women's event, and now, as the rain falls more and more heavily, I find a new hero. It's John Treacy of Ireland, who wins through sheer guts and determination. And he's only twenty. Scotland's first finisher, in seventh, is Nat Muir, a local lad from Salsburgh, near Airdrie, another twenty year-old. Also running for Scotland are Scottish Champion, Allister Hutton, and Frank Clement, who loses count of the laps. As he passes us he shouts to a friend, 'Is this the last lap?' He's an Olympian; how can he not know how many laps he's run? His friend confirms that this is indeed the last lap, so he knows how far he has to run.

But what about me? How far do I have to run? What am I aiming for? What's my World Cross?

****

It was the end of my second cross-country season at college. I had usually finished in the top twelve of cross-country league races—nothing to write home about—but I enjoyed a consistent winter of training and increased my mileage to at least sixty per week, sometimes into the eighties. It was a solid base for the 1978 track season.

I had also embraced new wave and punk, although, typically, I was late to the party. At first I reacted negatively: 'That's not music, it's just a racket, they can't play their instruments...' However, like many others of my generation in the late seventies, I was bored by the pretentiousness of Uriah Heep, Yes, Genesis and other stalwarts of heavy metal and progressive rock. Punk was a breath of fresh air. Buzzcocks, the Sex Pistols, the Clash and thousands of less famous bands showed the world that you could pick up a guitar, learn a few chords and join a movement that meant more than the music. Sticking two fingers up at the authorities, punk gave young, rebellious people a new voice. It brought outsiders together and gave them a new confidence to challenge what was taken for granted. Things had to change. Nobody was sure what that change would look like but that didn't stop them trying. Punk stood for a lifetime of trying. Punk was on the edge.

In my case, it was a mild rebellion against the PE Department and its arrogant students. Long ago it had been the football players at primary school. Gemma and I followed the bands, and I kept on running, challenging the taken for granted in my own way. Unlike the punks, I thought I knew how to change things. My way was to run, run, run. I was going to be a better runner, better at sport than any footballer or rugby player I knew. I didn't know how good I could be but I was going to find out.

****

'Where have you been? You've missed the 1500 metres!' shouts Jack across a crowd of students.

'What d'ye mean? I'm in the 3,000 metres.'

'The 3,000 metres was cancelled, and we had to pull someone off the tennis courts after four sets to run the 1500 metres. He came last and was lapped.

'Well, I didn't know any of that.'

'Where have you been? Somebody said you'd gone out on a road run.'

'I was out warming up, like a good boy.'

'Well, you'll have to run the 800 metres instead. Have you done one before?'

Clearly, Jack has forgotten my Glorious Victory at last year's Inter Year Sports.

It's Chester College vs. Alsager College, and the afternoon isn't going well. We've barely scraped a *team together. It was always going to be a tough match against one of the best college teams in the country. We've been outclassed in the opening events, and now the 1500 metres/tennis debacle has made us look ridiculous.*

'I read this one in the Beano,' I overhear an Alsager athlete mutter.

So, it's 800 metres, not 3,000 metres. It's the first race of the season. After a winter of relatively high mileage, I haven't cut into speed work yet. Never mind, I have more experience at 800 metres; it'll have to do.

Then I find out that Dave Mission is running for Alsager.

Dave is the reigning British Colleges 1500 metres Champion: he won last year when I was fourth. His times are much better than mine. He's going to beat me easily in front of our home crowd. Everything is black and white with them. Last year they thought I was brilliant because I won the Inter Year Sports at a canter. Now they're going to think I'm rubbish. I'll probably have to put up with comments like, 'Why do you bother doing all that training? It doesn't do any good: you lost.'

I've heard a rumour about Dave's training, related to a recent article in 'AW', but no... forget that. I need to get warmed up again.

The shot putters clear the bend and sometime later so do we. Entering the back straight for the first time, Dave has already built up a lead of a few metres. One lap later and he's further ahead. I knew this would happen; he's beating me easily. Entering the final bend, oh well, I'd better try to muster up a sprint finish, make it look good. I pick up the pace, and something unexpected happens: it looks as though Dave is struggling... I'm gaining on him... It's a big gap... Surely I can't make up that distance... But I'm getting closer and closer... Ten metres, five metres... The long bend leads into the home straight, and I'm right behind him... But it's a short straight, he could hold me off... He moves out wide, forcing me to run even wider... The crowd yells encouragement: 'Come on, Chester!' I draw level with him, go past, sprint towards the finish... I've won. I've beaten the British Colleges Champion.

In the space of two minutes and four seconds I've metamorphosed from zero to hero. Dave, gracious in defeat, nevertheless can't understand why he has run so slowly: after all, in training he completed a set of eight reps of 800 metres, all of which were quicker than 2:04.

There's something I need to ask him about his training...

****

The article in 'AW', written by regular contributor, Cliff Temple, was about a study of statues of ancient Greek athletes. The study demonstrated that in 93% of a hundred and twenty statues, the left leg was more developed than the right. The obvious conclusion was that ancient Greek athletes ran around the track in a clockwise direction. Round the bends, the left leg would have a longer stride, therefore had to be more developed. Modern athletes circle the track anticlockwise; we have been getting it wrong; things will have to change. The article went on to point out that equipment at the finish line and the best seats in the stand were in the wrong place: there would be financial implications. It was so well-written that it was convincing until the penultimate paragraph, which indicated that the steeplechasers would be the most affected: they would have to clear twelve feet of water and *then* scale the three-foot barrier.

Then you noticed the date at the top of the page: 1 April.

It was a superb hoax, and apparently Dave had taken it seriously and was doing all his track running, including that 8x800 metres session, in a clockwise direction. Until that afternoon on our oddly shaped track.

Dave had been fooled but he had the last laugh: he defended his 1500 metres title at the British Colleges Championships later that summer, while I was left on the sidelines, crying again. I had been spiked during the first lap of the final. A chasing runner's spike had scraped down the back of my calf and lodged briefly in the heel of my shoe, pulling it away from my foot. What do you do when that happens? Do you carry on with the shoe half on, half off? Do you kick off one shoe and run on? If you can't kick it off, do you stop to pull it off? Or do you stop to pull it back on? Every one of those options would slow you down.

I ran on awkwardly for 100 metres or so, hoping that the shoe would work its way off my foot. It didn't, so I stopped and pulled it back on, while the entire field of 1500 metres finalists ran further and further away from me. I could catch only one of them and finished second last.

In spite of that disappointment, it was a good season. I ran twenty-five track races, won nine of them and finished second four times. My 800 metres times were hovering around two minutes again but I set a new 3,000 metres pb of 8:33. And at 1500 metres, my own Bannister-esque moment arrived on 6 May at the Stretford Track League in Manchester.

'I've got to tell you this,' I announced as Dylan answered the phone. 'Three…'

'Well done!' Dylan interrupted. He knew that sub-four was my target and how much this meant to me.

On 6 May 1954 Roger Bannister had become the first ever to run the mile in under four minutes. The announcer read out his winning time: 'Three…' and the rest was drowned out by ecstatic cheering. Bannister's ground-breaking time was 3:59.4. Exactly twenty-four years later I had run faster at 3:58.8.

Except that my run was shorter by 109 metres.

Chapter Six: Breakthrough

The first race of the cross-country season is one of anticipation. A long, cold, dark winter is ahead, but in early October, signs of late summer remain. It's still quite warm; you don't need your extra layers or woolly hat and gloves yet. Most trees are still in full leaf, groundsmen are still cutting vast expenses of green grass, and it's firm underfoot.

Next month will be cooler. There might be a strong wind bringing together myriads of scattered leaves to dance. An earthy smell will become more and more pungent with each age group race, as the course cuts up under the feet of hundreds of runners rushing to finish before the gathering dusk. Mud, more mud, and leaves, all around. Shades of brown, orange, yellow, red and more brown.

Later in the season it will be bitterly cold. Howling winds, maybe snow or frozen, rutted ground. The promise of a post-race hot drink as strong a motivation as not wanting to let the team down or of striving towards individual targets: for some, win the league or championship, representative honours; for others, beat a close rival or simply finish higher than last time. There will also be bright, crisp and invigorating days, exciting and enticing days after weeks of gloomy evenings.

All of that is ahead of today's runners. Brightly coloured club tents, each distinctive, draw in its athletes to share stories and encouragement, strip off their track suits, pull on spikes for the first time. When they arrive today, runners are greeted by a bewildering array of flags and tape. But after crowding around the only map of the course they rehearse in their minds where the course will take them, perhaps planning when to make their big effort. Now it's that smell of cut grass and tarpaulin, a chorus of nervous laughs, a kaleidoscope of multi-coloured vests, the thunder of many feet as runners set off on the first of their winter adventures.

****

It's a scene repeated at various venues up and down the country, including Liverpool's Clarke Gardens where I finished ninth in the first round of the Liverpool & District League (L&D). The following week I was third in the Cheshire League at Stockport, then returned to the L&D, this time Warrington and an unprecedented second. I was much improved and buzzing. And it was only November.

Next, a month of teaching practice. Pressure to perform, tiredness, arriving back at college to an evening of marking and preparation. Squeezing in dark runs on the roads, looking forward to running on the country at weekends. Not surprisingly, there was a slight drop in my performances: fifth in the L&D in Birkenhead and seventh in the Cheshire League, over the Welsh border in Connah's Quay. I enjoyed the teaching but was glad when the practice came to an end and it was time to go home to Airdrie for Christmas.

There was nothing inventive about my training that winter. It was miles, miles and more miles. The only diversion was a weekly hill session, or Alsatians, as Gemma called them.

It was an accent thing: I said that hill sessions weren't my favourite. She said that she didn't like them either: they bite. Well, they do bite but not in the way Gemma meant: she heard 'Hull sations'. And from that day, hill repetitions were always known as Alsatians.

Apart from the Alsatians, it was steady running, lots of it, with longer, slower runs twice per week, mostly solo. Shorter runs tended to be on local footpaths, streets or the city walls: an almost unbroken two miles around the ramparts surrounding the Medieval city. The walls overlooked the Roodee racecourse, where you could run on good grass inside the circuit. A path from the Roodee led to a golf course made for runners, as long as no one was hitting hard, dangerous balls with a stick. Alongside the racecourse was the River Dee, which took you all the way to Wales. I had imagined running freely along an idyllic, tree-lined riverbank but I was disappointed: the river had been redirected in a straight line through a featureless, man-made landscape. Ironically, the man-made canal was much more natural and picturesque than the river, winding its way out of the city and between rolling hills. Amongst my favourite runs was one along the canal bank and back to college via a path through the zoo. One minute you were hurdling fishermen's poles—'Hey, I'm tryin' tae run here!'— and the next you were dodging giraffes and zebras. Not really, they were safely behind a high fence.

Back home in Airdrie the countryside was different but no less interesting. Some of my former playground of fields was now housing. But a run down into the Monkland Glen was a journey into history and heritage. Paths meandered through thousands of trees and along the banks of the North Calder Water. Look up, and the remnants of a huge bridge towered over you. It used to traverse the valley but now only one of the uprights remained, pointing to nowhere. Look down, over railings, and there were deep weirs, which seemed out of place: they must have been something to do with power for the old mines. I didn't know much about that: it was my training ground, and I was there to enjoy a run. There's a scene in *Apocalypse Now*, the Vietnam movie, where the soldiers are drifting along an idyllic river in the jungle, and they suddenly come across a crashed helicopter, balanced precariously in the trees. Here in the Monkland Glen, it was an abandoned car, rusted by years of neglect, trapped in low hanging branches and clinging for dear life on the edge of the North Calder Water. Out of the trees and along the towpath of the canal, you could see a long, pale green pipeline on stilts, standing high above an abandoned cricket ground. The club had to give up long ago because its club house had been continually vandalised. No wonder cricket was new to me when I came to college.

My weekly mileage had crept up to sixty, seventy, eighty and now, over Christmas and New Year in Airdrie, it dropped to fifty: it snowed for three weeks. Deep drifts made running in the woods a lottery. Pavements were frozen with dangerous ruts. Suburban roads were sheets of ice. Fields were so deep with the still falling snow that you developed muscles you didn't know you had: lifting your knees much higher than usual and for once justifying the catcalls of 'get them knees up!' The best of the bunch of bad surfaces was out on quiet country roads where the snow tended to be more compacted, cushioning your footfall. A ten mile run felt like fifteen but on a day of blue skies and bright sunshine it was glorious. A runner's high.

When distance runners are going well in training they talk about feeling strong. It's not the 'strong' that you gain from weights training. Strictly, it's not strength: it's endurance. But you feel strong, and with that feeling comes confidence. A confidence that I took with me, along with the snow, back to college in January.

By the third week of the month the snow had finally cleared, and I returned to Warrington to finish second in an interclub race. I wrote in my training diary that I had felt strong but too fresh, and annoyed that I couldn't find another gear to pick up the pace and challenge the winner.

One week later the pace of the season was to pick up. And so did my form. Those runners who have experienced a breakthrough always remember when and where it was achieved. Mine was on the final weekend of January 1979, in Runcorn.

****

It's the West Lancashire Championship but it could be anywhere: in this fog it's difficult enough to see the next flag, never mind any Lancashire landmarks. We've run about a mile and I'm in fourth place. I can see Mike Turner and Dave Lindsay just ahead and I think I can make out Frank Davies in front, rounding the next flag... Halfway, Mike and Dave have caught Frank, I've dropped back but I'm feeling good; there's a long way to go, plenty of time to catch them... Something's wrong with Dave; ankle trouble? I pass him and start to close in on Mike... It's the last mile and it feels like I'm floating through the fog, past Mike and into second place... I'm in the silver medal position at a senior championship... The fog is drifting, and I can see Frank, but he's too far ahead... Half a mile to go; hold on, hold on... But I don't need to hold on, because I'm flying! Keep pushing, keep pushing... A marshal looms out of the fog, directing lapped runners on to the final circuit, finishers into the finishing straight... 'Hey!' he shouts, 'You're not finishing!' 'Aye am ur!' *I shout in defiance.... He doesn't understand my accent, doesn't believe me—I'm an unknown—but nothing is going to stop me sprinting towards the finishing funnel... 100 metres to go, seventy-five, fifty, last few strides... I'm over the line and I'm second, my first ever senior medal, and I* don't feel tired: *this is pure elation. I've never beaten Mike or Dave before; I've always admired them from afar... Fog envelops the entire field but there could be a shaft of sunlight shining on me alone.*

Never mind fog.

Never mind cold.

Never mind mud.

This is where I want to be.

Right here.

Right now.

****

My name was in 'AW'!

I had a line to myself: the first three names on the race result stood out because they were listed individually; all the other names 'ran into each other'. The West Lancs. didn't merit a race report, but it didn't matter: I was in 'AW'. Then the Chester paper proclaimed: LOCAL RUNNER SECOND IN CHAMPIONSHIP RACE and described my rise up through the ranks.

Nobody in the PE department at college noticed, but the British Students Championships were to take place one week later; a good performance would guarantee selection for the British Colleges in an end of season representative match, which would bring prestige to our college and the PE department. More to the point, it would be a pinnacle of achievement for me in my final year as a student. And it could be a springboard for the next stage in my development.

There was a lot at stake as I boarded the train at Chester station for Glasgow and then home. The championships were at Stirling University, scene of one of my rejections. There was going to be more than one point to prove in the foothills beneath one of Scotland's most historic strongholds.

****

It was a disaster.

My training diary demonstrates a depth of disappointment bordering on depression:

'British Students Sports Federation cc champs

'(incorporating British Colleges Sports Association cc champs)

'Stirling University; 7mi; 72nd (350); 39:37

'(colleges race – 13th)

'A very, very frustrating race for me. I felt a stitch coming on right from the start of the race, yet after the first of three 2.5mi laps, I was in the first twenty-five and about the seventh college runner. Halfway round the second lap the stitch was so painful that I felt like I was crawling round the sides of these big, ploughed up hills. Also, a few college runners had passed me. I felt really bad, so I dropped out and walked off the course for a few minutes. However, I found that to get back to the start I had to rejoin the race, so I did, and discovered that the stitch had gone. When I got round to the start again I must have been about 120th, and Dad shouted to me that I was seventeenth college runner. It's not in my nature to give up and I felt like I still had a chance of getting into the first nine college runners (for selection for British Colleges team) so I 'flew' round the last lap and passed about fifty runners, I think. But it looks like I won't be selected. I *know* I could have finished in about the first twenty today if I hadn't got that stitch. I *know* I'm good enough to be in the British Colleges team. What can I do now?'

Disappointed, depressed, but also defiant.

What I could do was talk to the British Colleges team manager, Harry Morris from Alsager. I explained that today was an uncharacteristically poor run: I had run much better several times during the season. Would he consider selecting me? Harry listened sympathetically but pointed out that he had to have faith in those who had run well at the trial. It was a strong colleges team. But would I write to him with a list of my races from earlier in the season? He would consider my request.

Technically I had cheated: I had dropped out for only the second time in my life, and had joined back in. I'm not sure if I cut a corner and therefore gained an unfair advantage, but the fact remained: I stepped off the course and rejoined it somewhere else. I gave up, and then changed my mind. I wasn't going to give up a second time: I was going to fight for selection.

So I sent Harry a list of my races, from the ninth place at Clarke Gardens to second in the West Lancs., and hoped for the best.

One week after the students' race I was back in Scotland, lining up for the Scottish Senior Championships in Livingston.

****

It's freezing, the ground is rock hard and the wind is howling. This is cross-country in Scotland. We've run the first of seven and a half miles and I'm in the leading fifteen runners. Fifteen! The highest I ever finished in the juniors was twenty-seventh, and here I am in the first fifteen seniors. I'd better slow down: I don't want to blow up. It was a disaster last week: I don't want that to happen again. Take it steady: there's more than six miles to go.

Mid race; I'm in the top twenty and feeling great. Allister Hutton and I are having a seesaw battle. The same Allister Hutton who won this race last year. The same Allister Hutton I was supporting in the World Cross under a year ago. And here I am, going toe to toe with him. But what's he doing, down in twentieth? He's wearing trainers (not spikes) and tracksuit bottoms: an announcement that he's not giving this race his most serious attention. Maybe he's carrying an injury but needs to show face to get in Scotland's World Cross team again.

We're about three quarters of the way and I'm still in the top twenty. I recognise the faces and club vests of some of the runners closest to me. I'm sure that I've never been this close to any of them before. I'm not losing any ground: I'm not going to blow up. Let's push on.

At the start of the last lap, without breaking stride, I turn to Dad on the sidelines and shout: 'Is this the last lap?'

I know it's the last lap. I'm thinking back to last March at the World Cross: Frank Clement shouting the same question. It's my tribute to Frank, I want to be like Frank, but today Frank Clement is behind me. *Way behind me: I'm going to beat Frank Clement, Olympian. I've also dropped Allister. What's going on?*

'Aye, it's the last lap! You're in seventeenth! This is brilliant!'

Dad's enthusiastic support drives me on, into sixteenth... I can catch the next runner... fifteenth... into the finishing straight... one more effort... fourteenth! I've finished fourteenth in the Scottish Senior Championship. I thought the West Lancs. was a breakthrough, but this isn't breaking through: this is smashing *through.*

****

Later, I examined the results in detail. Nat Muir won from Lawrie Spence and Clyde Valley's own Jim Brown. Of the thirteen in front of me, two were Irish: I was twelfth Scot. Scotland would take nine runners to the World Cross and name three non-travelling reserves. But I never thought that I had a chance of selection. I was realistic: the selectors would choose runners with proven pedigree. (They picked Allister, for instance.) I was the new kid on the block. My time would come. Maybe next year? I dared to dream.

There were more races to run, and I hoped that my finale would be representing British Colleges against the British Universities, Combined Services and English Cross-Country Union. If the Scottish selectors could choose Allister, a form runner who had an off day in the selection race, Harry could pick me for exactly the same reason. I wrote again, describing what had taken place in Livingston, twenty-seven miles from Stirling, but a world away in terms of performance. This had been the best race of my life.

A few weeks later I wrote again:

'4 March 1979

'Dear Harry,

'I hope you are well. I am writing to tell you about my latest three races: fifth in the Cheshire League, sixth in the Liverpool & District Championship and 190th (263 places higher than last year) at the English Senior Championship.

'Thank you for considering my request for selection for the colleges team.

'Yours sincerely…'

They were solid performances but not as exhilarating as my breakthrough at Livingston. I still hadn't been selected for the colleges, and despite this season's improvement, I was yet to win a senior cross-country race. Both were to change on 10 March at Madeley: I won an interclub race at a canter and returned to college to read a letter from Harry:

'8 March 1979

'Thank you for your letter of 4 March. Your performances make interesting reading. However, I am surprised that you did not mention your fourteenth place at the Scottish National. It was you, wasn't it?

'I am delighted to confirm your selection as first reserve for the BCSA to face the BUSF, ECCU and CSAA at Camberley, Surrey on Saturday 31 March. Travel details are enclosed. Please stand by: if past experience is anything to go by, I fully expect to confirm your place in the team by early next week.

'Congratulations!

'Yours sincerely,

'Harry'

Ten months after my Roger Bannister moment, this was my *Tess of the D'Urbervilles* incident. In Thomas Hardy's novel, Tess writes a letter to her lover, Angel, confessing her 'indiscretions' with Alec Stoke D'Urberville. She pushes the letter under his door. When he greets her affectionately the following morning, she assumes that he has forgiven her. Later, however, she discovers the letter hidden under the doormat: Angel has not seen it. This changes the course of the story and contributes to Tess's tragic demise.

As far as I'm aware there was no doormat to blame for my letter about the 'Scottish' not reaching Harry. However, unlike the tragic Tess, I was rescued, by my old friend and rival, Dave Mission, and 'AW'. Dave, at Alsager College with Harry, showed him the results printed in the magazine.

My place in the colleges team of nine runners was confirmed within a few days. It was my responsibility to find the money to pay for the train fare to the meeting place in London. It was assumed that your college would meet your expenses, so I applied to the treasurer of Chester College Sports Association, who promptly rejected my application. Once again I should have seen this coming: back in the summer I had declined to turn out for College in an athletics match. I apologised but explained that I had bigger races to prepare for. Was it petulance on my part? Was I being elitist? Could I not just have run and treated it as a training session? Regardless, I had an immediate problem: I couldn't afford the train fare, so I went above the treasurer's head, to the dean of students.

Meanwhile, I received a message to call back Jim Brown of Clyde Valley A.A.C. This was not an easy thing to arrange, and it must have been important for Jim, an international athlete and a big name at our club, to go to all this trouble. Jim had phoned the college office. The receptionist put a handwritten note in 'Piggies' (pigeon holes arranged alphabetically by surname). Sometime afterwards I checked 'Piggies', read the note and then queued at a public phone box to return Jim's call. He wanted me to run in the Edinburgh to Glasgow road relay.

The 'E to G' was not an official national championship but it was the most prestigious road race in Scotland. Some say that Clyde Valley A.A.C. was formed for the sole reason of winning the 'E to G'.

I had never been good enough for selection.

Until now.

It was the same day as BCSA v BUSF v ECCU v CSAA.

I thanked Jim for his confidence in me but, as this was my last year as a student, I wanted to prioritise the representative match, provided that I could afford to get there. Jim said that Clyde Valley would pay for me to travel to the 'E to G'. I said thanks again but sorry, I really wanted to run in this match. There would be other years to run the 'E to G'. (I never did, though.)

When the dean heard the story so far, he acted on my behalf. I could hear both sides of the conversation when he phoned the treasurer.

'I don't think we should cover his expenses: it would be like sponsoring him,' claimed the treasurer, conveniently forgetting that the rugby club had received thousands of pounds to travel to away matches all season and to entertain the opposition—which involved copious amounts of alcohol—at home matches.

'I think that young athletes should be sponsored,' replied the dean. 'We should support emerging talent. Besides, he's also been chosen to run for Scotland on the same day but he would prefer to represent College. Scotland has offered him expenses. We need to do the same here.'

That's not quite what I had told the dean, but it did the trick: he overruled the treasurer, and I became even more unpopular. I got my expenses and was on my way to London for my first representative honours since running for Airdrie & Coatbridge Boys Brigade six years previously.

The race itself was an anticlimax. I needn't have worried about not being selected: the colleges team was so depleted that I probably would have been in it without the exchange of letters. Outclassed, we finished last of the four representative teams. I ran reasonably well: although only twenty-fifth out of thirty-three runners, I was second home for the colleges. It wasn't a bad run, and I enjoyed the challenge of mixing it in a small, select field of some of the best runners in the country: Julian Goater, Graham Tuck, Steve Jones, Barry Knight, Ray Crabb, Bob Treadwell, Glen Grant, Kevin Forster, John Wild, Scotland's Alastair Douglas and Fraser Clyne; the list goes on. The whole day— travelling from Chester to London on the train, meeting my teammates, completing the journey in the team minibus, pulling on the representative vest, meeting the opposition, travelling home with a sense of achievement—was valuable experience.

I had been in demand, made a difficult choice, and made an enemy. My inner punk prevailed. Surely there would be further adversity ahead, but I was ready for it. The approaching track season was going to be my best yet. I was going to be British Colleges Champion at last. I was going to smash all my pbs. Then, next cross-country season, I was going to force my way into the Scotland team. I was going to run in the World Cross.

Never before had I been so confident between seasons.

Chapter Seven: Fall

Pride comes before a Fall.

I had shared my ambitions only with Gemma and my training partners. Unlike my foolish boasting after the Scottish Schools, I wasn't boring everyone with delusions of grandeur. But it was Pride, and I couldn't see the Fall coming until it was too late.

At first I was sure-footed.

****

I'm sitting next to Jim Brown on the runners' bus from Motherwell to Law, heading for the start line of the Tom Scott Ten Mile road race. Jim doesn't seem to hold it against me that I didn't turn out for Clyde Valley in the 'E to G'. He's telling me about the time he ran two fives in thirty-nine and forty-two. Only distance runners understand this code: 2, 5, 39, 42 means that he ran two 5,000 metres races in 13:39 and 13:42. I try not to dream about running so quickly or to bother Jim with questions. Not today: we both need to focus on this point-to-point race, which is another unofficial Scottish Championship.

This is my first ten miler. The route is generally downhill, with a sting in the tail during the final mile, which seems a long way from the start line as we line up, shivering in the horizontal sleet.

After three miles someone shouts out a time of fourteen minutes, and I think, Wow! If I can run that for the first three of ten miles, I should be able to run close to the same time for 5,000 metres on the track.

Jim wins in 48:04 and I finish eighth in 50:45. That's 5:04 per mile: have I really run that fast? I overhear a conversation in the tea bar after the race: 'Ye know, they say that this course is downhill and it's short, but every time they measure it, it comes out as a good, solid nine and three quarters.'

****

So maybe it wasn't as fast as 5:04 miling but three weeks later, in a close run race on a lapped course in Wrexham, I ran my second 'ten' in 51:25, finishing second. One month later I was at Stretford, lunging for the line in an 800 metres race where I was second again, with the same time as the winner: 1:57.8. It was my second fastest ever, only four tenths of a second outside of my pb, and that was after a slow first lap of sixty seconds. Those two competitive performances, at opposite ends of my spectrum and only a month apart, demonstrated a range that I hadn't known I possessed. In between, I set a new pb of 8:28.4 for 3,000 metres. I had every reason to expect that my slow pb of 15:50 for 5,000 metres was going to be obliterated at the imminent British Colleges Championship, where I was confident of winning at last.

That was Pride.

I was about to have a glimpse of the future. It was to be my first stumble on the way to the Fall.

****

I'm leaning on my knees at the end of the British Colleges 5,000 metres, chest heaving, gulping air noisily, concentrating on not falling over. I've just finished third but narrowly avoided being lapped by Dave James. His Welsh teammate, Ioan Ellis, passed me with two laps to go. That final 800 metres was agony; all that kept me going was the thought: Don't let anyone else pass me. I stayed on Dave's shoulder for the first four laps but had to let him go. From that point on I was slowing down all the way. It's the worst possible way to run a race. It's no consolation that 15:31 is a pb: I was on course for around 14:20 (which Dave ran) but I've been outclassed. My pride caused me to get it completely wrong.

Dave and Ioan approach me later, offering 'support'. 'We've been talking about it,' Dave says. 'We were wondering if you knew my times.'

A bit cocky but who am I to judge?

'I knew,' I reply. 'I thought I could keep up with you, but I was wrong: you were too fast. Well run.'

It's a sportsmanship that I don't feel. All I feel is failure.

There was worse to follow.

****

It didn't happen immediately. The following week I improved my time by eleven seconds. It was the Western District Championships again and the opening laps were so slow that a fast time was never on the cards but I ran competitively to finish fourth. The next one would surely be faster, although fourteen minutes looked to be out of reach.

The next one never came. Term finished earlier than usual because of our final exams, and the season was over before you could shout 'track'.

But not before the grudge match of the summer.

In the era of Coe vs. Ovett, a far greater duel was about to take place. Never mind the Olympics, never mind British Colleges: the Inter Year Sports was coming around again. And this time there was a challenger to knock me off my high horse, and the PE students were taking bets.

Colin McLachlan came to college with a reputation as a decent runner, particularly at 5,000 metres. We had done the odd run together, but he hadn't really kept up his interest in athletics. He had decided not to enter the British Colleges but he was about to make his mark, running for First Year in the Inter Year Sports.

'You're gonna get beaten, for once,' the treasurer goaded me. 'He's run faster than you twice at 5,000 metres.'

The treasurer had ever taken interest in times at obscure events such as 5,000 metres before, so there was only one way he could know: Colin had told him, which meant that everyone who was running, jumping or throwing for First Year and Third Year knew. Second Year didn't get a look in. This was Third Year vs. First Year. Title Holder vs. Challenger. Old Hand vs. Young Pretender.

It was only a couple of students running on an oddly shaped grass track, probably my least important race of the season but in the best tradition of petulance, honour was at stake.

Colin followed a rugby player in the 3,000 metres, shouting to his 'fans', 'I love this pace!' before running away to an easy win. Which was disrespectful to his fellow competitors. I had a similar, easy win in the 800 metres, minus the shouting.

And then came the final race of the day: the 1500 metres.

****

Colin is leading with three laps to go. 'First one for me!' he announces to the crowd. Just in case I hadn't heard, he turns to me and declares: 'I won the first lap.' So it's like that, is it? But I don't rise to the bait. When we reach the actual end of the first lap he moves out wide, inviting me to take the lead, which I do, but I don't raise the pace. He tucks in behind me and at the bell he's still there, but I'm not worried. 100 metres later he moves alongside me noisily, tries to take back the lead. I don't let him past and hear an exasperated sigh as he has to ease back when I move away. I win with 4:06 by about 40m, which is almost the length of this ridiculously short home straight on a ridiculously shaped track at the end of a ridiculously hyped up non-contest.

****

That was my only 1500 metres of the season. A season that had just ended on the grass at Chester

College before it really got going. A season that had promised so much but delivered so little.

Gemma had completed her honours year and would soon be taking up her first teaching post. I decided after all that this wasn't my final year: I was coming back for honours, too. We had a relaxing week's holiday in Ilfracombe, forgot all about being students, about teaching, and surprisingly for me, about running.

In a rare moment of adventure seeking, I accepted the offer of a summer job at a south-west education centre for students from overseas. It was relevant to teacher training and not terribly adventurous, but it was more daring than my job in a summer playscheme in Airdrie the previous year, which in turn had been more exciting than my first summer job. Unbelievably, I had returned to the Scottish Widows, even though I had known that I wouldn't enjoy it, so anxious was I to ensure that I had employment. But now here I was, cutting my ties and spending the summer far from home, family and friends and away from competitive running. It would be my last chance to travel and experience a different lifestyle for a whole summer before my final year as a student and then re-entering the world of work. I was confident that I would keep my fitness ticking over, that the break from routine would do me good, that I would return to college in September, refreshed and better prepared for the twin challenges of advanced study and the pathway to international athletics.

My confidence was misplaced.

There are times when you look back and think, What if? What if Dad hadn't taken me along to Airdrie Harriers? What if I had been accepted at Stirling or Edinburgh University and had never come to England? What if I hadn't decided to return to college to study for honours? What if I had been preparing for my first teaching post instead, and not spending the summer travelling into the unknown?

I'll never know.

This is what happened next...

I hitched from Airdrie to the south-west, which was risky in more ways than one. Anyone or no one could have picked me up. I couldn't say for sure when or if I would arrive at the education centre to start work. Not only was it risky but it was cheeky. Here I was, starting a new job, and didn't think it was odd that I couldn't commit to a start date. I even stopped off on the way at a mate's house in Lancashire for a few nights. And I ran along the way. I ran on the Lancashire hills and then when I eventually reported for work, on the rolling countryside of the south-west.

It was no surprise to either me or my new employer that we didn't see eye to eye. Usually reliable and conscientious, that summer I rebelled and for once put socialising before work. Only ten days after arriving late for the job, I left to see a friend in London: the birthplace of new wave. A perfect place to release my inner punk. After a couple of gigs, I hitched up to Nottinghamshire to touch base with Gemma, who was preparing meticulously for the first step of her new career: so different from my new-found, if temporary, freedom. After a run along the River Trent and an emotional farewell, I was back on the road, rucksack on my back and thumb stuck out, flagging down a lift to Scotland, and, briefly, home.

Jobs were easy to come by that summer. The Airdrie & Coatbridge Advertiser carried an advert for a full-time job in a pub down the old railway path in Coatbridge. The New Me had the nerve to walk into the pub unannounced one lunchtime and ask for a job. The landlord took one look at me and said, 'It's a bit rough here, y'know. We've had to dae a bit of fighting to get established. I'll have tae let ye know.' One run later, I received a call and an offer of a job. 'Let's see how ye get oan.'

Against all odds, this student from the soft south was accepted by the punters. I was enjoying myself but still applying for jobs. Two offers arrived at the same time: assistant manager of a hotel at the foot of Tinto Hill in the south of Lanarkshire, and kitchen hand in a holiday park on the Isle of Wight. I chose the Isle of Wight. When I politely declined the offer from the hotel manager, he assumed that I'd accepted the rival offer because of better salary and conditions. I explained that it wasn't that: it was because I'd never been to the Isle of Wight before. The hotel manager, and the pub landlord in Coatbridge, accepted my decision in good grace, and I was off again.

Pausing to visit friends and of course to run, it took several days to reach the Isle of Wight. There was a tradition in the kitchen that whoever arrived last washed the pots. Two of us arrived on the same day. As

I had arrived at an earlier time, the kitchen staff assumed that I would exercise my right not to wash pots. But I didn't: I offered to share the chores. The other newcomer was called Matt, and we have been great friends ever since. People thought that we were alike: skinny, shaggy-haired, and with the same taste in music. We called ourselves the new wave pot washers, and still do.

It was a physical job with long hours: three shifts per day at mealtimes, six days per week. We relaxed by night, dancing and drinking in the bar or having barbecues on the beach. We swam and slept at odd times during the day. And I was running every day. It was a great place to run, along clifftop paths and up and over the downs, with sea views all around. One day I was so carried away that I was late for my shift. 'We thought you'd run off the island,' the boss said good naturedly.

I borrowed a bike on my days off and explored parts of the island too far away to run. And I played (badly) for the staff football team in weekly matches against the campers. The team captain also played for one of the island's semi-professional clubs. He had trouble coming to terms with how bad I was, although I didn't tell anyone that I was once known as the Muffin Man. He failed to hide his relief when I asked to be excused from football. It was late August and my first race for three months was coming up: a road race at a village sports day.

Word had got around the camp that I was a runner, and Walter, the elderly manager of the complex, took me under his wing, gave me time off work and drove me to the race. A large crowd cheered the runners on as we ran laps around the village green. I won by a big margin from villagers, holidaymakers and a few local club runners. I was more worried about my benefactor than the opposition: when I finished, Walter came running over, arms spread out to hug me. I was concerned for his health because I'd been warned that he had a weak heart. Luckily, Walter survived, my conscience was clear, and we arrived back at camp with the trophy.

He was treating me like a long-lost son. I had won a prestigious trophy for the complex. He engaged a professional photographer to take my picture, which he had framed and displayed behind the bar with the trophy and a newspaper report. I was the talk of the camp.

But something was wrong.

I had felt a clicking in my left knee throughout the race, which didn't hurt, so I ran the next day. I felt sore, which wasn't unusual the day after a race, so I ran again the day after that. This time a pain inside the knee was so acute after I stopped running that it was painful to walk. On the third day after the race the pain seemed to have eased. I kept on running and wrote in my training diary that it was 'just a nagging injury'.

The lack of common sense amongst runners is at times staggering. This was no exception. On the day after that diary entry I ran seventeen miles, painfully limping the last few. The fierce, stabbing, throbbing pain kept me awake at night. Stupidly, I kept running through the pain.

'Leg hurt more as day went on… afterwards it was really painful… knee hurt towards end but wasn't bad afterwards… wasn't too bad later… leg really hurt afterwards… not too bad…'

The idiotic diary entries kept on coming after equally idiotic runs. I was clutching at straws, paying more attention to the 'not too bad' statements than the startlingly obvious signs of serious injury.

Walter kindly took me along to a local GP. 'All right, all right, less of the boasting,' interrupted the doctor while I was trying to explain how much running meant to me, that I was nearly at international level. He said it was only a strained muscle, and that the reason it wasn't healing was that I wasn't using it properly.

I didn't tell him about the seventeen mile runs.

He gave me an elastic support bandage and recommended straight-leg lifts and deep-knee squats. I later learned that the bandage wouldn't have done any harm, that straight-leg lifts were good practice for strengthening the muscles around the joint, and that deep-knee squatting was probably the worst exercise possible.

Except more running.

Which is exactly what I did.

How could I have been so stupid? I even increased my mileage and ran faster, only slowing down when it became too painful, which it did with monotonous regularity. Then came the Fall.

Running down a steep hill, the knee gave way, I stumbled, toppled and fell, rolled painfully downhill and skidded to a stop in a ditch. It wasn't the fall that caused the pain: it was the pain that caused the fall. And it was running that caused the pain. I didn't understand what it was about my running that had brought on the injury. All I could think about was that I'd already had a break from competition. I couldn't afford to rest. I needed to get fit for the cross-country season. It was my destiny to represent Scotland in the World Cross. I had to keep running. I just had to. After all, I had recovered from injury before.

But this was different. It was a fall, but it wasn't a fall from a steeplechase barrier or gymnastics horse. They were both impact injuries caused by a trauma. This was a fall and trauma of a different sort. I didn't realise at the time, but it was a wear and tear injury, which usually takes much longer to heal.

Finally, an outbreak of common sense caused me to stop running. I hitched back home to Airdrie and only a few days later travelled back to college for my honours year. At the end of the last cross-country season I had so much to look forward to. So much promise. Now I was about to start my final year at college. A new cross-country season was on the horizon. But I couldn't run. I was injured and I didn't know what the treatment was. I didn't know when treatment would start. I didn't even know what the injury was. I didn't know how I was going to cope.

Chapter Eight: Despair

When you're injured, well-meaning people ask, 'How long will you be out for?' or, 'When will you be back?'

Olympic athletes and professional footballers always know the answer: 'I should be back in training after six weeks but I'll have to give the Olympics a miss this time.' Or: 'I'll be back in the gym next week and should be able to rejoin team practice by March, in time for the business-end of the season.'

Club athletes never know the answer. We have no idea when we'll be back. We're not sure how long the recovery will be. We don't know what the treatment will entail. The GP doesn't know, either. The waiting list for physiotherapy on the NHS is too long. We're wondering if we can afford to go private. We haven't even had a diagnosis yet.

I didn't understand what I was dealing with. I only knew that it hurt and wasn't getting any better. It had been a month since the injury first appeared, and I was none the wiser and no further forward. I couldn't cope with the uncertainty. Time was ticking away. The cross-country season was about to begin. Weekly sessions with a student physiotherapist were making no difference. I didn't know where to turn.

Then Dylan told me about a new coach at CEPAC: John Banks. John had previously held a national coaching position and now, in his retirement, had moved to Chester and wanted to help at the local club. Could John be my saviour? He had a look at my knee and said, 'I'm no medical expert, but I know a man who is. We'll get you fixed up to see Doctor James Bartholomew in Manchester. Nobody knows more about joints than Old Jim.'

I translated: 'We'll get you fixed up to see…' as: 'I'll drive you to Manchester,' and: 'Nobody knows more about joints…' as: 'He's the top man in the country.'

Neither proved to be the case.

****

I'm on my own, limping in and out of puddles along a back street in Manchester. The reason is not knee pain, as if that wasn't bad enough: I sprained my ankle pogoing at a punk gig last night. And now, after a journey by train and two buses, I'm trying to find Dr Bartholomew's surgery.

The ankle bandage has worked its way loose and is trailing into the puddles. After reapplying the bandage and making several wrong turns, I arrive at a nondescript building. I'm early for my appointment, despite the delays.

Nobody is expecting me. I'm not in the book. Putting on my most helpless and disappointed face, I explain that I've come a long way in the rain because Dr Bartholomew has been highly recommended to me. The receptionist apologises for the miscommunication and offers to speak to the doctor if I would care to wait until the end of his surgery.

It's a long wait: hours of rainwater dripping onto the carpet of the waiting room. Plenty of time to observe the other patients: an elderly lady, a young parent with a child, an overweight man taking up two seats. None of them looks like they're here for a sports injury clinic or an appointment with the top man in the country. It looks like any GP waiting room, anywhere in the country.

It's dark when I'm invited in to meet Dr Bartholomew. He listens sympathetically, examines my knee and concludes that it's a 'nipped cartilage', and the only recommendation he can make is to 'have it out'. He promises to write to the college doctor with his conclusions. I thank him for his time, and he says something odd in reply: 'I'm interested in joint injuries.'

Of course he's interested in joint injuries: he's the top man in the country. I'm confused, but more concerned about dodging puddles and worried about what's going to happen next. Cartilage: one of the most dreaded injuries at college. I've heard about one of our footballers who saved up his holiday job pay to have his cartilage removed in a private clinic. He was in hospital for three weeks, in a cast and on crutches for another six, and when he started training again, the muscles on the injured leg had deteriorated so rapidly that he had to rehabilitate for a further six weeks. That would be three or four months off, but I haven't even had the operation yet: I could be out for a year or more. But at least I've got a diagnosis at last, three months after my running ground to a halt. It looks like I'll be out for a while longer. A long while. But at the end of it, I'll be fixed, and I can start running again. I can still make it as an international athlete.

****

It's three weeks later, and the college doctor is telling me, 'I don't believe that you should be in a rush to have your cartilage out: it's a drastic measure and your knee would never be the same again. I'm surprised that Dr Bartholomew didn't discuss this with you, even if he is the top man in the country. I strongly recommend a second opinion.'

The college doctor writes to an orthopaedic surgeon in Liverpool to request an examination. It's nearly Christmas and my waiting time has suddenly grown even longer.

****

Partly to stop people asking me about recovery times, I started to tell them that I'd given up running. It wasn't true: I hadn't given up hope. But it was taking so long. When would I hear about the appointment in Liverpool? What was I going to do with myself while I was waiting?

I cycled and swam but my heart wasn't in it. It wasn't the same as running. I fought against excuses to get out of cycling and swimming. The excuses usually won. My 'AW' magazines went straight into the drawer, unread. I didn't want to read about athletics, didn't want to hear about athletics, not even from my old clubmates. I deliberately lost contact with my running friends.

However, I still had coffee with friends at college most days, and I stayed in touch with others from afar. Matt, my fellow new wave potwasher, came to visit, and we enjoyed a few pints and a couple of gigs. But after he had gone, I began to crawl back into my shell. I started to decline invitations to coffee after lectures. More and more, I was becoming withdrawn, losing contact with student life. I even isolated myself my flatmates: quite an achievement as we were sharing a kitchen and bathroom.

Gemma and I saw each other at weekends. She was always tired after a week at school but spoke enthusiastically about her new career. I could offer nothing in return. I didn't complain much about being injured and not running but she could tell how I was feeling, and was sympathetic. It must have been trying for her. I wasn't much company but here she was, spending most of her precious weekends with me.

My heart wasn't in my studies, either. This should have been the time to work harder, concentrate on taking my understanding to the next level. However, rather than rising to the challenge, my attitude was: That'll be good enough, or: This'll do. It wasn't inspiring me. I was bored.

The truth is: I was depressed.

It was a crisis. Life had been fairly easy so far. My home life and childhood had been happy. Not exactly carefree, but nothing I couldn't handle. I got by with schoolwork and studies. I had become a decent athlete, overcoming challenges—ridicule, lack of confidence, two (only two) impact injuries—but none of them was a crisis. This was the first, and I didn't know how to deal with it.

I wasn't coping.

A year earlier, when I had returned to college after three weeks of snow, the sun rose to a new dawn of anticipation, inspiration and exhilaration. What a difference a year makes. The most exciting thing that happened as the nineteen-eighties began was that I received a letter inviting me to the long-awaited orthopaedic examination.

The examination itself was inconclusive but the surgeon booked me in for an exploratory operation in April. He would decide on the day if further intervention was required and, with my prior permission, would perform there and then any corrective surgery deemed necessary.

The next in a long line of long waits began. I spent most of my time in my room, emerging on weekdays for bland meals, uninteresting lectures and occasional, boring cycle rides or swims. The highlight of the week was spending time with Gemma at the weekend. But was it a highlight for Gemma?

'I know you're upset that you can't run,' she said, exhausted after a long week in the classroom, and exasperated with minimal response from me. 'But I don't want you to be thinking about running all the time. I want to be the most important thing in your life.'

It was uncharacteristic of her, selfless and caring as she had always been.

The writing was on the wall.

****

April came.

It was the week before the operation.

Final examinations to follow.

And Gemma ended our relationship.

Suddenly I was alone.

Alone and depressed.

It was my own fault. No one else ran me into the ground. No one else lost interest in my studies. No one else locked me in my room. No one else sent me into a deep depression.

The day of the exploratory operation was here.

****

'He didn't have to have anything done.'

Those are the first words I hear as I start to wake up from the anaesthetic. I'm aware of nurses lifting me from the hospital trolley onto the bed. I didn't have to have anything done? How can that be? My knee's been painful for nine months. How can I not have to have anything done? I've been passed around the houses, I've come here on my own by train and bus, I've brought three weeks of work with me, anticipating a long stay, clinging onto the hope of corrective surgery and recovery, a return to running, and they didn't do anything? Should I be allowed to hear that before I'm properly awake? Am I even supposed to be awake yet? After nine months of frustration, worry and depression, am I really no further forward, again? Has it all been a waste of time?

I ask if I can see the surgeon but he's finished for the day. I'll have to wait until the morning. But what does it mean: I didn't have to have anything done? Would the nurse be able to find out for me, please?

'*The surgeon found a roughening underneath the kneecap,*' *I'm informed later.* '*Which is normal. His opinion is that no further intervention is required.*'

'*But how can that be? I've been in pain for nine months. All my hopes have been in this hospital. There must be something he can do.*'

'*I'm really sorry: he says he can't do anything for you.*'

'*I'm sorry, too. I need to get out of here now. I want to go home.*'

'*But you need to rest. And there's a risk of infection. You should wait until the morning. Please wait until the morning. Things will look different then.*'

But I'm adamant. I don't want to spend another minute in that ward, where my hopes have been crushed. The nurse confers with her superior.

'*We really don't want you to go.*' *She's really trying to help, to care.* '*You're not in the right state of mind to make decisions straight after surgery. Please wait until the morning. We strongly recommend that you stay.*'

When I fail to change my mind, she comes back with a disclaimer for me to sign.

'Who's going to collect you?' she asks.

'I haven't got anyone.' Mum and Dad would have collected me in three weeks' time and taken me back to Airdrie. But not now: it's too soon. I'm trying really hard not to cry. The nurse looks concerned, says that the least that she can do is order a taxi.

And so, one late night in Liverpool, I'm folding myself into a taxi as the driver loads my bag of books into the boot.

He looks worried too, when he drops me at the station and waves me off as I struggle over to the ticket office.

An hour later I'm sitting in the train, left leg up on the opposite seat, when the ticket collector comes along and roughly lifts it off.

'Hoi! I've just had an operation on that knee!'

He apologises and edges his way down the aisle. He looks concerned too.

The first person I see when I arrive at Chester Station is one of our English Literature lecturers, Mr Edgecombe. I must be a pathetic sight; everyone is feeling sorry for me tonight. He kindly offers me a lift: where can he take me? There's only one person who can help me.

'Please can you help me?' is all I can say as, silhouetted against the hallway light, Gemma answers *the door. She's just broken up with me but she won't want me to deal with this on my own. Mr Edgecombe waits patiently as Gemma packs a few things, and then he takes us to my flat.*

Gemma does everything you could ask of anyone. She makes me as comfortable as possible, stays all night, and goes off to school early the next morning. I can't help feeling that I'm making the most of the situation, taking advantage of her kind nature to win her back.

I never see her again.

****

I really need to grow up and face this like a man. I'm being pathetic. There's a final essay to write. If I can get that done, I can go home to Airdrie, recover, prepare for the exams and come back to take them. Then I can get away from here for good and move on.

****

I'm feeding a donkey on the beach in Southport, scene of my first holiday without the family, nearly ten years ago with the Boys' Brigade. This time I'm here with Mum and Dad, and I appreciate their support. It's the second time we've been here in the last couple of months.

I finished that final essay overnight, and Dad collected me the following day. Walking along the seafront, only days after the operation, my knee gradually regained flexibility, while I regained my appetite and some weight. I had lost a stone, through worry and not eating.

The next few weeks dragged by as I waited for the exam results. I knew I hadn't done myself justice, partly because of the operation and the break up with Gemma, but mostly because of a whole year of neglect, not only of my studies, but also of my health: social, physical, emotional. The final ignominy was when the college doctor downgraded me medically from A1 fitness. That will be on my record when I apply for teaching positions. Not that I've applied for any: I have no confidence. I've been looking for temporary, summer jobs, but unlike last year, they're few and far between. I haven't contacted any old friends from school, and I haven't tried to touch base with college friends. So, when the invitation to the degree ceremony arrived on our doormat, there was no relief or pride: all I was feeling was the dread of having to face people again.

So, here we are once more in Southport, after the ceremony at Liverpool Cathedral. I was awarded a 2ii. With a better attitude and more effort, it could have been a 2i or maybe even a First. But it wasn't a Third, which would be a waste of a year. Which is exactly how I feel about my final year at college. I was underwhelmed by the presentation: we walked in turn, up onto the stage, and shook hands with a local dignitary. We wore gowns but there were no scrolls and none of those special hats. At least this time, unlike the presentation at Airdrie Academy years ago, my name was on a seat, and I was called to the stage. 'At least'… I'm making do again. I'm not excelling.

I did speak to a few ex-classmates, and it was nice to see them again but I couldn't wait to get away. My Leaving of Liverpool has been without exchanges of phone numbers or addresses. I'm not intending to keep in touch.

The donkey's lips muzzle against my palm. Sea breeze gently rustles the straw in the manger. Sand under my feet, taste of salt on my tongue, the sun's heat on my face, and on either side of me: Mum and Dad.

There are times when only your family will rally round.

****

Take One:

You need to pull yourself together. Be a man!

It's not easy. I'm injured, my girlfriend dumped me, I don't have a job. I don't know where to start.

And...?

Is that not enough to deal with?

So, you've got a sore knee; you haven't had your leg blown off in the war. Get over it! You're not the only bloke in the world to get dumped. Get another girlfriend. Get a job! You don't know where to start? What are you gonna do about that, then? Stop feeling sorry for yourself and get on with it.

Take Two:

Let's break it down, shall we? What's the worst thing that's bothering you?

*Well, all of it... Not being able to run, I suppose.
Not having any control over it, relying on doctors to fix
me.*

What's the next worst?

My girlfriend breaking up with me.

And the next?

*Not having a job. Not having the confidence to
start the career I've trained for.*

*So, the job is the least of your problems. What
is it that makes it less of a problem than the others?*

*Well, I'm doing something about it: I'm
applying for jobs.*

How's that going?

I haven't got one.

Yet.

Yet.

But you're trying?

Yes.

*Good. How confident are you that you will get
a job?*

*It's taking a long time, much longer than last
year. But if I keep trying, something should come up.
There's another problem, though.*

About jobs?

111

Yes: it's only holiday jobs I'm applying for. I don't have the confidence to apply for teaching posts.

Yet.

I suppose.

What's behind your lack of confidence? Let's break that down if we can.

Well, everything affects it. I didn't apply myself in my final year. I couldn't cope—can't cope—with not being able to run. I cut myself off from my friends. I was full of hope that my knee would be fixed when I went into hospital for the operation but they didn't think it was bad enough to fix. My girlfriend ended our long-standing relationship. And then the exams came along.

Okay, you've told me about what running has done for you: physically, mentally and socially. You've also explained that since you left home to go to college, you've been self-coached. You've planned your training and competitions and have enjoyed a great deal of success. You've met challenges and overcome adversity on the way. That's down to your determination, confidence and planning. How can you utilise these strengths to meet your present challenges, and overcome adversity as you've done before?

Phew! Well, I'm not planning to have a girlfriend, so we can put that problem to one side.

And how do you feel about that?

I'm still deeply hurt but I can't do much about it. I need to focus on something else.

And what comes first?

Getting a job. I'm not ready to apply for teaching. Yet. But if I get a holiday job that's residential, it'll be a fresh start somewhere else. I can build up the confidence to apply for vacancies in teaching.

And the injury?

It hurts. Physically, mentally, emotionally: it hurts. It's been a whole year, and nothing has changed. I can't seem to get anyone to take me seriously. There must be someone who can fix it.

When is your next appointment?

October, at the Monklands General. I'm seeing a specialist. I've written a long letter, in case he doesn't have time on the day or I forget anything.

How confident are you that this appointment will bring a resolution?

Not confident, but there's hope. There's always hope.

Anything else?

Well, there's nothing stopping me from contacting old school friends.

You sound so much more positive and confident than earlier. You're making use of your experience and your planning skills, taking one step at a time. When are you going to start?

Well, I'll have to wait for the hospital appointment, and I'm still applying for holiday jobs. But I'll phone one or two old friends tomorrow. They probably don't know I'm home. I owe it to them as much as to myself.

****

If only that conversation was real.

But it's 1980. People don't understand mental health, especially men's mental health.

But I'm beginning to deal with things on my own.

I have a plan.

I'm twenty-four years old and I'm about to turn a corner.

Part Three

The Middle Laps: Changing Perspectives

Chapter Nine: Resilient

During those last days of the summer of 1980, the corner that I needed to turn was a long way off. The Moscow Olympics had come and gone. Sebastian Coe and Steve Ovett had won each other's races. Scotland's Allan Wells won gold in the 100 metres and said that he actually liked coming back from injury: he loved the challenge of overcoming adversity.

Without a diagnosis, my comeback hadn't even started.

But things were beginning to change.

I did contact old friends and started to come out of my shell again: swimming at Airdrie Baths, playing bowls with Dad, going to the pub and cinema, and travelling into Glasgow for the odd gig.

And I got a job in a hotel in Inveraray on the banks of Loch Fyne, Argyll.

It wasn't all smooth sailing; there were bumps, lows and setbacks along the way. All of us found it difficult to work with Eilish, the manager's wife, but I seemed to manage it better than most: it was the least of my problems.

The staff, including the manager Hamish, were easy-going. Then there was James, the manager's brother, due to go on holiday to France soon; Robbie, a student who liked new wave; and Peggy MacDonald, a local who knew everything about everything local.

Inveraray Castle is the ceremonial home of the Campbells, unforgiven by the MacDonalds for the Glencoe Massacre of 1692, when the Campbells abused the hospitality of their hosts, the MacDonalds, by slaughtering many of them in their sleep. 'It disnae matter whit their name is,' declared Peggy, during one of her fag breaks. 'Ye can *aye* tell if they're a Campbell.'

The male staff accommodation was poor: camp beds in an unheated, unfurnished attic, sharing with a water tank that dripped all the time and made an extra racket when someone flushed the toilet. It wasn't the best way to treat staff. I'm not sure it was even legal. Sleep was difficult to come by.

I enjoyed the work, which helped me regain lost social skills. I gained a reputation for being available to listen and have a chat with the regulars at the bar. Time off was infrequent but, when we were able to finish early, Robbie or James and I would have a few pints in the other hotel in the village. During the day you could visit the castle, walk along the banks of Loch Fyne and take a break at one of the many tea rooms. One day, admiring the tranquillity of the smaller Dubh Loch, I was looking back on my life in running, thinking what an ideal place this would be for a run. Maybe I would come back one day and do it. For the first time in a long time, I was looking forward as well as back.

Sometimes I would walk the family dog, a sleepy red setter called Shaun, and take the manager's six-year-old daughter Fiona to school. I was as comfortable chatting with Fiona as I was with customers at the bar.

'Whose day off is it today?' she asked me one day, just like a boss's daughter.

'Nobody's. Nobody gets Sunday off.'

'Not even Shaun?'

'Och, he never has a day *on*. He never does any work.'

'Yes, he does: he chases cats.'

'Chases cats? Remember yon wild cat that wis in your room? Well, it ran rings around Shaun and he didn't even notice: he slept through the whole thing.'

'Well, it must have been his day off.'

I was beginning to think that I'd like to have more conversations like that one. Maybe I should think about taking a look at the job vacancies in the Times Ed.

And then I was brought back down to earth with a crash.

****

'You needn't have come all the way down from Inveraray today: we could have told you what you need to know when you finished working there for the season.'

Not a good start to my long-awaited consultation with the specialist at Monklands General.

It's a follow-up appointment. Previously the consultant had asked me to summarise my long letter because he didn't have time to read it. He had arranged a blood test, and the nurse had laughed at me when I felt faint. She even invited her friends along so that they could join in the fun at my expense. And now, another month later, he's telling me that there's nothing wrong.

'As far as I can see, you're perfectly fit. People get upset when they can't play badminton or something. But it's not serious and nothing needs to be done. I'm afraid you've wasted your time.'

And wasted his time. Could he make it any more obvious? Months after a specialist in Liverpool tells me that there's nothing he can do because there's nothing wrong, *another specialist, in Airdrie, is telling me exactly the same thing.*

How can there be nothing wrong? The knee hurts. It hurts when I walk, especially downstairs, and it hurts when I sit down with knees bent. It's a sharp pain inside the joint. Both joints: the right knee hurts now too. The pain has increased and my ankle still hurts, a year after spraining it. I'm not imagining this.

But what's worse than the physical pain is how this all makes me feel inside. All of a sudden, it hits me that the only thing that kept me going was hope, however slender, that I would be 'cured'. And now I'm back to Square One. The last year and a quarter— seeing the GP on the Isle of Wight, rehabilitation exercises, physiotherapy sessions, the 'top man' in Manchester, college doctor, exploratory operation in Liverpool, months and months of waiting and being passed from pillar to post, and now this doctor in Airdrie dismissing me—have all been for nothing.

Do these so-called medical experts not realise the damage their attitude causes to their patients? Do they not understand anything about mental wellbeing? Do they even care?

There's no hope any more. I can't go on like this. No career in athletics or teaching, dumped by everyone: Gemma, friends, doctors. In pain and miserable all the time. Dead-end job in a hotel. What do I have to live for?

Dead-end, nothing to live for... It would be easy: just walk out into the loch at night. No one would see me in the dark. I'm a strong swimmer, but it's cold, really cold. All I would have to do is swim until I'm too cold to carry on. Then just stop swimming, let the water engulf me. Sink...

No! I can't do that. It's selfish, cowardly. What have Mum, Dad and Susan done to deserve that?

There must be another way.

What about the plan?

But the plan stands or falls on hopes of a cure. If there is a cure, I haven't found any. All hope has been shattered.

What about the idea of searching for teaching vacancies?

But I haven't done anything about that, have I?

What about the friends you caught up with?

But where are they? I'm stuck in an attic in a dead-end hotel.

What about the friends you've made at the hotel?

But that's short-lived: the hotel will be shut at the end of the season.

What about your other interests: reading, music, watching football?

But what about them? They're only other interests. I can't do what I really want to do.

What about your positivity since moving to Inveraray?

But I'm not feeling positive now, am I?

What about your family?

But... Family. Hope isn't the only thing that's kept me going. Mum and Dad are always there for me. They pick me up when I'm down, they don't judge, they never dismiss me, they always listen. Their love is unconditional.

And now, at my lowest point, Mum says something that rekindles hope.

She's heard about a homeopath: a sort of chemist who prescribes drugs and helps people like me when the doctors have given up. Suddenly, there is a glimmer of hope again.

People like me.

I'm not the only one.

A light at the end of the tunnel.

Mum, a woman of faith, has provided hope, has seen the light.

I arrange to see the homeopath in Glasgow on my next day off. I don't even need to wait for an appointment: I can just turn up at his clinic and wait in turn. No long delay. Maybe things are looking up, after all.

Before hitching back to Inveraray, I bump into Ronnie McDonald, one of our top athletes at Clyde Valley. He tells me about a Doctor Walker, who runs a sports clinic in Berkshire, and has helped him get back to international standard after injury. Ronnie recommends that I write to ask for an appointment. It's worth a try.

So, now there are two lights, two hopes to cling to: homeopathy in Glasgow and a letter to Berkshire. I write the letter promptly, fully expecting to wait quite some time for a reply. Meanwhile, there's only a week to wait until my next hope.

****

Have you ever seen your boss writhing on the floor, screaming like a pig, helpless at 3am? That's exactly what I'm witnessing right now. It's the wedding anniversary of Hamish and Eilish, and the hotel staff are having a lock-in. Hamish has started with the wine and champagne then moved on to whisky: something we have rather a lot of in our bar. He's sampled every one of the twenty-odd malts behind the bar, and Robbie, James and I have joined in. Eilish normally keeps a tight rein on us, but she's letting her hair down. It's a free-for-all.

It's all a bit too much for Hamish, poor soul. I don't know what Eilish has been drinking but she's bossing us about, as usual, calling for help to drag her husband to the caravan in the back garden before any of the guests wake up. We'll drag him back this afternoon but meanwhile, we leave him in the arms of Eilish and stumble up to the attic.

****

A shaft of light encourages me to make an effort to open my eyes as the attic door creaks open and Eilish's face appears, alarmingly close to mine. It's 9am, and I'm the only one she can raise from the dead (the only one sober, as it happens). Will I go on duty at ten?

She actually asked me, didn't boss me into doing it, I ponder while tucking into a fried breakfast with Fiona; Shaun at our feet, giving us his best 'a dog is for life, not just for Christmas' look. It's been a strange morning.

'Where's Daddy?' asks Fiona.

'It must be his day off.'

****

Daddy is next seen at 1pm, being coaxed across the lawn, shuffling up the stairs to a cold shower. Binge

124

drinking is not to be recommended, particularly for athletes, at any time, but somehow this seems right. Bonding exercises such as these raise the spirits during dark times. We're all in it together.

****

I've been on a course of homeopathic drugs for a fortnight. The homeopath listened to me carefully and concluded that I have arthritis, although not an acute case, which is why the condition didn't show up on the blood test results. He told me that the drugs should start 'dissolving' the arthritis within a few weeks and could clear it completely after two months (by Christmas). First of all, after two weeks, the drugs should aggravate the condition. Around now, in fact. I keep taking the pills and powder, which I remember looked exactly the same as all the other pills and powder lined up on the shelf behind the homeopath's desk. But the only changes in my condition are that I'm going to the toilet more often and my breath smells of onions, garlic and honey: well-known cures for arthritis, apparently. But it's hope.

There's also hope that I'll receive a response from Doctor Walker before too long.

****

Another set-back: I've just received a letter from Scottish Education. I wrote to them to start the process of applying for teaching jobs, and they've told me that I can't: my teaching training was in primary and middle schools, whereas my main subject was at secondary level. I've fallen between two stools, they say. It's yet another dismissal. It makes no sense but that's their decision and I have to deal with it.

Rejected by my own country, I have two choices if I want to teach: complete a fifth year of training in Scotland or apply for jobs in England.

****

The letter from Scottish Education might have sent me back into a deep depression, but it didn't. Things were changing since I relocated to Inveraray. I was good at my job in the hotel and good at listening to people. I was sociable, making friends again, feeling part of a team. I was able to shrug off the discomforts of the staff accommodation and make the best of the location.

It was beautiful: the loch, the forests, the mountains, the sky, all looked different, every day, every hour, almost every minute. Hamish joked to guests that 'If you can't see the hills, it's raining. If you can see the hills, it's going to rain.' But to observe the ever shifting scene— every degree of colour with every movement of cloud, every breath of wind, every shaft of sunlight—was magical. To stand on the shore— feeling the sea breeze, tasting the salt, listening to the seabirds calling—was perfect for contemplation.

The medical dismissal at Monklands Hospital had been a huge set-back but Mum and Ronnie had helped me find ways to overcome my intense disappointment. Perhaps the homeopathic treatment would have no effect but if nothing else it was distraction therapy. I was still waiting for a reply from

Doctor Walker but there was genuine hope: if he had helped Ronnie get back into running, he could help me, too.

So, I couldn't teach in my own country. I had no intention of training for yet another year. So, what to do: teach in England or do something else? I decided to try for teaching in England. After all, I had studied there for four years, and I was used to travel and relocation. More significantly, I really wanted to teach. After months of depression, despondency and despair, I was following the plan, the next stage of which was to take the first step on my career path.

Other changes were afoot: the hotel was about to close for the winter and I was going on holiday. Some of my friends and relations across the border had made open invitations for me to visit, so I wrote letters to take them up on their kind offers. At the same time as applying for teaching jobs, I was planning a long trip, hitching all the way: to stay with Martin in Wrexham, Matt in London, Dylan at Durham University, back to London, Aunt Phemie on the Essex coast, and back home to Airdrie. I was going to be away for about ten days.

On my return, things would be different.

****

On a cold, damp and dark evening in the middle of December, I'm standing on a deserted road, waiting for a lift. Normally so well prepared, I'm annoyed that I let myself be dropped off here. It's a bad spot for hitching: poor visibility and no obvious place for the infrequent drivers to pull off the road. It's probably because it took me so long to flag down my previous lift that I accepted anything to get me another fifty miles up the road. But I've been here for over an hour. I tried walking for a while, but no one could see me, and with a heavy rucksack on my back, my knees hurt. So I've been standing here by a road sign, holding up my own sign—'Airdrie, please'—in hope. But…

I am not forlorn.

I am resilient.

****

Alone on that dark road, injured and jobless, I was nevertheless making progress. Homeopathy was not the promised miracle cure but in the absence of any other intervention, I was still taking the pills and powder. There had been no reply from Doctor Walker. But consultants are busy people. It had been two months but I was hopeful of a reply any day. Meanwhile, I had been on my holiday, hitching hundreds of miles up and down the country.

Martin was settled into married life on the farm with his wife and young child. I watched him race well in the North Wales Cross-Country League, a race that I might have run if I had still been fit. In more ways than one it was painful for me to watch. The shouts of encouragement that echoed across the valley as the runners appeared out of the trees, could have been for me. Those sounds and sights, the earthy, woody scent and the feel of mulch, twigs and fallen leaves under my feet, together with ever-present knee pain, all conspired to remind me of what I was missing. I may have turned a corner and was feeling more optimistic but I was no closer to a return to running.

Matt was in a flat-share in Earl's Court and introduced me to the night life in that particular corner of London: pints, kebabs, more pints and the widest choice of gigs I had ever known. You could see a different band every night if you had the stamina, and the money. The Revillos were due to play at the famous Marquee later that week. Matt and I had already seen them in Liverpool when he stayed with me in Chester. Now I was about to follow them to my next destination, Durham, and then back down to London.

Dylan, shorn of his Magic Roundabout haircut, proudly claimed that he was one of only a few working-class students at Durham University. Most of his fellow students, he said, were Oxbridge rejects and former public schoolchildren. That said more about Dylan's pride in his roots and his Scouse accent, even though he was from Cheshire. You would have paid premium rates in a hotel for the view that Dylan enjoyed from his window: a spectacular, sweeping vista across city spires and surrounding countryside. The Revillos were equally spectacular, and the next morning I set off to London again in pursuit.

After more kebabs, more pints and more Revillos, I travelled eastwards from London towards Dovercourt in Essex and childhood memories of holidays with Aunt Phemie. And then it was home to an invitation to attend an interview in Weston-Super-Mare, about four hundred miles from Airdrie. I decided to take a risk and hitch: I could claim for a return journey by train and therefore make some income from travel.

****

The only good thing about this quiet road is that you can see car lights approaching from miles away. The specks of moisture in the air twinkle against the headlights as a car draws nearer. It slows down to a stop as it passes my sign. At last, after two hours of waiting. I'm lifting tired and stiff limbs, stumbling towards the car, looking forward to the warmth, but wait, what's going on? The car's pulling away, round the next bend, lights dimming and then disappearing into the hills. Did he do that to torment me: build up my hopes and then leave me with nothing but disappointment?

Sounds familiar.

Oh well, at least it's not snowing.

****

I didn't get the job in Weston but I interviewed well, apart from when I foolishly mentioned my injury, prompting one of the panel to ask me if it would affect my ability to teach. On the whole I had been confident, and one of the lessons I learned that day was to forget about being injured and concentrate on the task in hand.

When I returned to the guest house after the interview, there was a message to phone Dad: I had received a second invitation, this time to a school in Bedford on the other side of the country. It was in only a couple of days' time: not worth going home to Airdrie first. So I began another long hitching journey, from west to east.

The Bedford interview was also unsuccessful but I was a close second. Given that there were a hundred applicants per vacancy, it was an achievement to be invited in the first place. Second was as close to success as possible and on this occasion, there was also a chance of a temporary job for one term teaching SMS Mathematics. I had been brought up on that in Scotland, so I left that interview with increased confidence.

No sooner was I home than I was invited to the next one: all the way to Canterbury, Kent. It was my longest hitch yet but I managed to arrive at my digs in time to frequent an alehouse and chat with the locals. For someone who had never felt part of the crowd and who had been through many disappointments in the past year or more, I was surprisingly confident, friendly and sociable. Nevertheless, after another all-day interview, there was no job for me in Canterbury. Maybe there would be news from Bedford when I eventually arrived home.

****

It's been snowing steadily for the past half an hour. Another car skids by without stopping. Am I going to be here all night, or longer? I'm wet through and numb with cold. My knees and ankle no longer hurt because I can't feel them. That's another good thing, I suppose.

A lift will come eventually. It always does. I've hitched thousands of miles and never failed to reach my destination. Sometimes you're breezing along and complete the whole journey in three or four lifts, with little or no delay between them. Occasionally, you go the whole way in one lift, although that's a rarity. On other occasions, like this one, you can be waiting for hours. But you always get there. Think positively. This was always going to be a tough one: overnight from Canterbury to Airdrie after a whole day's interview. Okay, it's turning out to be longer than expected but you'll get there. And when you do there are three official-looking letters at home: Dad told me when I phoned. I asked him not to open them: I just want to get home. Will one of them be a job offer from Bedford. Will one be a reply from Doctor Walker? What's the third one? Anticipation keeps me awake as I try not to freeze, waiting for a lift. Waiting, and waiting...

****

When I accepted lifts from strangers, I knew I was taking a risk. Anything could happen. You hear stories. However, I trusted people, gave them the benefit of the doubt, and never fell asleep on them: I always showed interest and made conversation. It was another way to develop my social skills and growing confidence. However, while hitching through Kent, a twenty-two-year-old military officer told me how good he was at leading men and how well he had done at such an early age. Two years older than him and jobless, I was on my way home from an unsuccessful interview. His life story wasn't exactly what I wanted to hear, but he was helping me out, so I listened and made encouraging comments.

****

When is this lift coming? When, not if: it will come. But when?

Can it get any colder?

But I've been through worse, much worse.

I am emerging from the other side.

I am tenacious.

I will get a lift home.

The snow stops falling.

The headlights of the next car illuminate my 'Airdrie, please' sign.

The driver pulls up alongside me. 'This is your lucky day,' he says. 'I'm going to Airdrie. Hop in!'

Now, I wonder what those letters are about...

****

Before collapsing into bed, I opened the three letters.

The first one was an apology from Bedford: they were unable to offer me the temporary job but wished me well in future applications and, if one came up in their school, they would be delighted to hear from me again.

The second was a reply from Doctor Walker. He apologised for his delayed response but would be delighted to help me if he could. All he needed from me was a letter of referral from my GP. There was an available slot at his clinic in Slough in a week's time. Would I be available to attend, and could I bring my GP's letter with me to save time?

The third was an invitation to an interview at a school in Milton Keynes.

On the same day as my appointment with Doctor Walker in Slough.

It was Milton Keynes in the morning and Slough in the afternoon. I looked at the map and phoned around to find out about bus and train times from Milton Keynes to Slough. I wasn't going to hitch from one to the other and risk missing the afternoon appointment. It could be done. *I can do this.* I could make both appointments on the same day. Could I possibly come back with a job offer *and* a cure for my injury?

Finally, I went to bed. Despite the long, cold journey through the night and without sleep, it took me a long time to drop off: my mind was spinning. Eventually, sleep overcame me.

Twelve hours later, I woke up and immediately started on another set of plans.

The next journey could be life-changing.

Chapter Ten: Fixed

Another waiting room.

A scene repeated many times.

Summer, autumn, winter, spring, summer, autumn, waiting.

And now in the depths of another winter, waiting again.

I'm here in good time. I had the cheek to ask to be the first to be interviewed this morning at Milton Keynes. I have another important appointment this afternoon, I explained. This is highly irregular: you have to attend all day. It's the rule: you have to wait until the end. All the other candidates are going to wait.

They still are. It's only 4pm, the results won't be known yet.

But I'm in a different waiting room: Doctor Walker's clinic where, after seasons of waiting, my last hopes remain.

He's quick, he listens, he prods, he makes me yelp, he diagnoses, he cares.

It's a roughening on the underside of the kneecaps. That's exactly what they said in Liverpool and the Monklands but wouldn't do anything about it. But Doctor Walker gives it a name: Chondromalacia Patellae, and he can do something about it. It's a simple operation—bilateral, lateral retinacular release—

which will allow the kneecaps to move more freely and therefore eliminate the pain.

And means that I'll be able to start running again.

Running.

But there's a problem: he probably won't fit me in until the end of the summer term, 1981.

Two years after the injury first surfaced.

But I'm not prepared to be under the surface any longer. From the depths below, I can see daylight.

I'm coming up for air.

I don't have a job, I explain. I can go in at short notice. I could do it tomorrow.

Doctor Walker listens. He checks his records. It's close to Christmas, and there's a cancellation. Could I come back in two days' time?

I have to hold myself back: I feel like hugging this kind man. This man with his can-do attitude. This man with the skill, the knowledge, the understanding to give me what I've been searching for all these weeks, months, seasons.

This man is going to save me.

I'm going to be whole again.

I call Matt from a phone box in the hospital lobby: can I stay for another couple of nights, please?

I'm so stunned that I catch the wrong train and travel several miles in the opposite direction.

****

'Hi, Dad. I'm not coming home.'

'Oh?'

'Yeah, I'm going into hospital for an operation.'

'Oh.'

****

It's the day after the appointment and I'm killing time, sightseeing. St. Paul's Cathedral, Marble Arch to board the open top bus tour of the city, Madame Tussaud's.

Today: tourist.

Tomorrow: patient.

The next day: athlete.

****

It's evening and we're in search of bands again. Another famous venue: the Hundred Club in Oxford Street. Matt has been the perfect host, once again dropping everything to entertain me. I feel guilty that I wasn't as hospitable when he visited me at college last year: I was miserable. But now I'm full of anticipation and excitement. After long days on my feet and with my legs tucked up on buses and trains, my knees are painful again but I know that those days are numbered. There will be more pain after the operation but it will ease. And I'll get my life back on track at last.

****

It's three days after leaving Airdrie, I'm in hospital, preparing for tomorrow's operation. I have a pre-op assessment and meet the anaesthetist and physiotherapist. Noticing that my arches have dropped, Doctor Walker has also arranged an appointment today with a podiatrist, Mr Ball.

'No wonder you've got sore knees,' Mr Ball remarks, observing me walk. 'You're coming down in one solid lump. In fact I should think your right knee is worse now.'

Mr Ball takes casts of my feet for orthotic insoles, explaining that these will help my ankle as well as knees. He also recommends a wobble board to strengthen my ankle muscles and regain my balance. He concurs with Doctor Walker that I should walk, swim and cycle before jogging, then running. I'm humbled and grateful that, at last, people of the medical profession are taking me seriously. They understand not only what the problem is and how to fix it but also how important it is for me to get back to running. It's part of me. It makes me who I am.

The ward is partitioned, so that you can enjoy some privacy without feeling isolated. It's so much more appealing than Liverpool, where the ward was open-plan and crammed with beds: it was like a production line. Here you're made to feel welcome like guests: old, young, male, female, some injured because of an accident at work and some athletes. How amazing to be in hospital and talking about athletics!

While a line of disabled children pass through the ward on their way to their Christmas party, Jimmy, an assistant cook who happens to be from Airdrie, pops in to say hello. He loves it here, enjoys the work, has a great social life, but misses Airdrie. (Who wouldn't?) He hears in my accent a voice from home and invites me out for a pint. It's a friendly gesture but of course I have to decline. Can you imagine if I sneaked out to the pub on the night before the most important day of my life? There would be no career-saving operation for me in the morning.

****

Now I've had a bath, shaved my own knees, had the first jab in my thigh. Ouch! Feeling dozy, in a happy stupor. I'm being wheeled me to the operating theatre. I'll be asleep soon and when I wake up I'll be fixed. The next needle stabs into my arm but I hardly feel it. I mumble something but nobody understands me.

'Oh, you're the one from Airdrie: we should bring Jimmy along to translate.'

'Aye,' I slur, 'I've met h-...'

The next thing I'm aware of is a throbbing pain in my knees, then the familiar sounds of the ward. I can smell shepherd's pie: it must be lunchtime...

It's dark when I wake up again, I drink some water, throw it up in a bowl, and fall back to sleep...

I ask the two guys, both athletes, in the beds either side of mine, how they're feeling, but I don't hear their replies because I'm asleep again...

I keep picking up a book, read two or three lines, and drop off to sleep...

This isn't like Liverpool, when I woke up while being lifted back into bed: I've been knocked out for the count...

When I wake up again, it's morning. That first cup of tea is nectar. I keep breakfast down and now I'm encouraged to start walking. Without crutches. It's painful, but these are my first steps towards recovery. Before you run you have to walk. And what a walk: I must have looked like a mish-mash of Frankenstein's Monster and the Mummy. But unlike the Monklands, these nurses don't laugh at their patients. They nurture me until I can make it to the toilet without having to hang on to their arms.

****

It's been only a few days but I'm accustomed to the routine here. Awake at 5:50am with a cup of tea and thermometer, breakfast at 7:30am, drink and thermometer mid-morning, lunch at noon, another drink and thermometer midafternoon, dinner at 6pm, a final drink and thermometer in the evening and then early to bed. The rest of the day you spend lounging around, chatting to nurses and fellow patients, in between having physiotherapy and learning to move again. It's a happy time, as exciting as it is comforting. I feel safe in this routine; I'm going to miss it.

140

Mum and Dad have come all the way down from Airdrie to collect me. It was just over a week ago that I left home, knowing that the journey would end in Slough, via Milton Keynes but wondering where it would really take me. Mum and Dad notice that I'm different: I may appear physically broken but, mentally and emotionally, I'm fixed. This must be what Allan Wells meant when he said that he enjoyed coming back from injury. My comeback started when I took my first steps after the operation. I'm stronger, happier and more optimistic than ever.

I can work with that.

I'm ready for the next stage of my journey.

****

New Year's Day, 1981: the dawn of a new age.

The stitches are out: a long blue strip on each knee, weaving in and out of the skin. All the GP had to do was gently tug them out. I have two thin, matching scars about an inch long. 'A very neat job', my GP remarks, nodding. 'Doctor Walker must be a remarkable man.'

I can bend the knees to ninety degrees now, although it still feels tender around the scars. I'm walking more comfortably about the house but I haven't ventured out yet: it's hardly stopped snowing since we arrived home. I'm scared that I'll fall before I've even started walking.

The snow thaws on the third day of the year, and I manage three quarters of a mile at a snail's pace.

We're at Strathclyde Park, looking along the loch towards Tinto, resplendent in the distance. It's good to get away from the confines of the house for a while, although I hope we get back before dark. It should be a great view across to Arran and the Sleeping Warrior. That's me: I'm a sleeping warrior.

I had genuinely forgotten about the job in Milton Keynes until I read the letter. I didn't get it but it doesn't matter now. Nor do all the other rejections: schools, Scottish Education, uncaring consultants, Gemma: none of it matters.

Because I'm an athlete again.

****

It's the middle of January. The orthotic insoles haven't arrived yet. I've been swimming and cycling gently. I can walk further and I'm getting better on the wobble board. But the knees still hurt and after exercise they swell up, puffy and red. Should I be making better progress by now?

We're in Cumbernauld Park on the last day of January. Dad finished thirty-seventh out of seven hundred in a fun run this morning. How great that he has taken up running to keep up the family tradition. I feel good about giving something back, supporting Dad after all the times he has done the same for me. After lunch in the sports centre, we return to the park to watch the main events of the day: the international and invitation cross-country races. Alison Wright from New Zealand wins the women's race. Steve Jones from Wales is first in the men's, holding off our own Jim

Brown, who is followed by England's Dennis Coates. Unlike a few months ago in Wrexham, I don't find it so awkward to watch this one: this time next year I could be lining up with these guys. My old running mates wish me well, although, by the end of the afternoon I'm tired of telling the same story over and again.

****

It's now the middle of February and my progress has stalled. I'm walking quite well but I have to be careful with cycling, especially uphill, and swimming, particularly breast stroke: my knees are still painful and swollen. Worryingly, they feel the same as they did before the operation. The orthotics still haven't arrived. I write to Doctor Walker requesting a follow-up appointment. I also apply for a full-time, permanent post in a primary school in Newbury, Berkshire, due to start after Easter.

****

Two weeks later I'm on the road again, hitching to the interview in Newbury and the, on the following day, to Slough for my follow-up with Doctor Walker. It's uncanny that two potentially influential events are taking place on consecutive days in the same county. Or perhaps I should give myself more credit: I'm growing more and more resourceful.

I'm making things happen.

****

It's March and my heart is thumping in my chest. It's a pang of terror: I got the job. I'll be a full

143

time teacher in about six weeks' time. I need to prepare. I need to find somewhere to live. My comfortable life is over. What have I let myself in for? I'd better get organised. But first of all, I'm packing for a residential stay at Farnham Park Rehabilitation Centre, near Slough. Because Doctor Walker told me that I should be running by now, and a period of rehabilitation would set me on my way to full fitness. At first it was déjà vu: there were no vacancies until the school summer holidays. But then there was a cancellation, and I'll soon be on my way, hitching once more. It's perfect timing: rehabilitated, housed, prepared, all in six weeks. It can be done. I can do this.

And now for my first run: as recommended by Doctor Walker, I'm going to run for one minute today (with the orthotics), two minutes tomorrow and so on. In a month's time I'll be running thirty minutes every day and I can count in miles rather than minutes. I could be running about thirty miles per week by the time I start school.

That's not rehabilitation: that's training.

****

It's my third week at Farnham Park and I'm making good progress. I love the routine and feel as secure here as I did in hospital. We sleep in a dormitory, much like a ward. Our meals are provided for us in a canteen, more like college than hospital. We're cared for, but we're here to work.

They—the PE teachers, fitness instructors, professional footballers, athletes, swimmers and other sportspeople—call me 'Holiday Man'. Typically for a late starter, my stay began three months after my operation, whereas everyone else started a week or so after theirs. I was put straight into the pre-work group: preparing for a return to training and competition. As my recovery is several weeks ahead of the others, I'm one of the fittest, if not the fittest. They think I'm not finding it as painful as they are, so I must be here for a holiday. It's good natured banter, part of the team culture of working together towards a common goal: to get back into our sport or profession. 'Holiday Man' is an improvement on 'Muffin Man', for sure.

Throughout pre-work, during rest periods and after hours, we get to know each other. The hardest workers are those who persevere as if their lives depend on it. Others are here only because somebody, perhaps an employer, told them to. The jokers make themselves known. There are weekly awards: pre-worker of the week, lifesaver of the week, lover of the week; the list goes on. One evening per week, we're allowed to go to the pub. It sounds like a holiday camp but we train hard and support each other with our aims and objectives.

Alongside us are people recovering from industrial accidents, car crashes, violent attacks, life changing injuries. Not concerned with sport, just trying to get back to some sort of normality. There are disabled people who are managing their condition. Some will do much more than that: learn a new love of life. For some, that's a new sport. We'll see some of them in the Paralympics.

Recovering from shattering injuries, changed forever and making the most of their altered selves: these are the people with the most at stake. They are the most inspiring amongst us. They make us feel humble.

Most people go home at weekends but those of us who live too far away, enjoy the peace and quiet of having the place to ourselves for a couple of days. It's an old manor house in spacious grounds and surrounded by fields and woods connected by footpaths and country lanes. I'm now running—running, not jogging—thirty minutes per day. Together with pre-work my general fitness is probably better than ever.

I'm also using my time at weekends to find accommodation in Newbury. And today, I've spotted a notice in 'AW' with the phone number of the general secretary of Newbury Athletics Club. I'm going to phone him now and arrange to join the club as soon as I can get there.

****

In September 1981 I was about to start my second term at school. The first term was tough. My knees swelled after long days in the classroom and after preparing at home in the evenings and weekends. I was always catching colds and the after-effects didn't go away easily. It might have been the Thames Valley atmosphere but more likely close proximity to children every day. However, I never had a day off sick and could genuinely say that I never once regretted my decision to enter the teaching profession. I loved teaching—literacy, numeracy, creativity—and revelled in PE lessons and after-school sports, finally being fit enough to give it my all. I was actually sad when term ended and the summer holidays began, although after a fortnight's break, I was back in the classroom every morning, preparing for the autumn term and exploring the countryside on my bike in the afternoons, wandering along winding, tree-lined lanes amongst rolling hills.

I had no idea that Newbury was such a beautiful place. The first time I went for a run and discovered a public footpath just around the corner, I was captivated. One footpath sign led to another and a whole range of running adventure opened out before me. I was out for longer than I intended and came back with sore knees but it was worth it. I was living across the road from the site of the opening chapter of *Watership Down* by Richard Adams. This was where Hazel, Fiver and the other rabbits began their journey of discovery. And with that first run I began mine. I could see the whole world from there.

My first run at the club was along the towpath of the Kennet and Avon Canal with new clubmates who have since become good friends. Alongside trees abundant with early summer leaves, it was the idyllic run of my dreams. A couple of weeks later I attempted my first track session for two years: it was an unambitious set of ten repetitions of 200 metres with seventy-five seconds rest. I was aiming for a modest thirty-five seconds per rep and hit the bull's-eye every time. After an absence of two years my legs remembered the pace.

Training was constantly interrupted by swelling in the knees, minor sprains to the still-weak ankle, colds and sheer exhaustion during that first term as a teacher. Nevertheless, I was making progress, running faster and longer. By the middle of June I was on the start line of the 1500 metres: my first track race for two years. Four minutes and fifteen seconds later I crossed the finish line and passed the first competitive landmark of my comeback.

And now I was about to enter the next stage, with season's bests of 2:01.0 for 800 metres and 4:06.0 for 1500 metres: fewer than four and eight seconds slower than my personal bests.

My first cross-country season for two years and my first full year of teaching were about to begin.

After an eighteen month-long battle between conflicting forces: frustration, hope; despair, determination; depression, resourcefulness; suicidal thoughts, tenacity; dejection, resilience.

Negativity was winning the battle a year and a half ago.

Until, step by step, the balance shifted.

Positivity prevailed.

The athlete in me won.

Chapter Eleven: Return

I'm pacing back and forth in our shared kitchen. I'm nervous, and I need the loo. I should eat some breakfast. I have to, because I'm racing this afternoon and I need the fuel: I can't run on empty. But my stomach is twisting itself into knots, and for what? It's a race but it's not worth starving or making myself ill.

My housemate Steve strolls in, yawning. 'Cup o' tea?' he asks.

Steve, always calm and quiet, is even quieter in the morning. He plays hockey but doesn't take it too seriously; sensible chap. His presence should be comforting.

'Tea? Em, I'd love one, but I'm too nervous.'

'What are you nervous about, then?'

****

In January 1984 I was having a decent cross-country season. I'd had a solid fortnight of training back in Airdrie: cross-country reps in the Cairnhill Woods, steady runs in the Monklands Glen, longer runs out into the North Lanarkshire countryside, and pushing it along with my Clyde Valley clubmates on club road runs. My mileage was increasing: touching on ninety miles per week. I wouldn't keep that up, now that I was back at school, but the training was in the bank.

I was ready.

****

What am I nervous about?

Steve doesn't fully understand but he humours me. Geoff, our other resident and my clubmate, would know, but he's away this weekend. How do I explain to Steve what makes this race so different? Why is it causing this ridiculous turmoil? This is my hobby; it's supposed to be fun. I've just had a hard week at school, I should be relaxing instead of pacing up and down here like a prisoner on Death Row. It's not my execution; it's only running. I love running.

I love running, but I don't love this anxiety. Have I not had enough of mental health problems in the past? Running is good for your mental health, isn't it? Those relaxing runs in the countryside just across the road suddenly seem tempting. I could call up the club, tell them I'm not feeling well (which is true) and that I can't make it this afternoon. Then I could pull on my running gear, lace up my trainers and step out of the front door. Within minutes I could be running across the fields towards Newtown Common, coasting along the gravel paths, breathing in the tranquillity of the heathland, twigs and pine cones crunching under my feet, birds chirping cheerfully overhead, far away from this torture. I could climb up Beacon Hill, exalting in the effort and then breeze down the other side and choose any one of several routes to bring me home, looking forward to a well-earned, delayed breakfast. And then laze around like a normal person for the rest of the day.

150

But I won't do any of that: I can't let the team down. I can't let myself down. I don't give up easily.

But it's only a county championship.

It's not the World Cross.

I need the loo again.

****

Through those dark, injury-haunted days of 1979 and 1980, even when I was at the point of giving up, running was the light at the end of the turmoil. Running would be my salvation. And if I could run again, everything would be okay. But I would not be satisfied with just okay: I would strive to be the best that I possibly could. For me, that was running well enough in the Scottish Championship to gain selection for the World Cross. It might have seemed out of reach when I was taking my first tentative steps after the operation. A ridiculous, outrageous ambition. But it was *my* ridiculous, outrageous ambition. I felt that I could do it. After all, I was fourteenth (twelfth Scot) before injury halted my progress. If I could get back to that level, push on from there, get into the top six, maybe even get a medal, I'd make it impossible not to be selected to run for Scotland.

How close was I to achieving my objective, to make this dream a reality? This dream that kept me running day after day when feeling great and when not feeling like it at all. This dream that got me out of bed on cold, dark and gloomy mornings. This dream that made me persist with training on calm days and windy days, in sunshine and rain, hail and snow, on the track and over the country.

After that promising comeback season in 1981/82, I had a mini breakthrough similar to my silver in the West Lancashire Championship at Runcorn in 1979. I finished third in the Hampshire League at Havant and someone shouted, 'Which lap did you miss out, then?' Just as the finish marshal at Runcorn had tried to direct me onto another lap, no one expected me to be as highly placed in this strong league down south: I was an unknown.

Back in 1979 I had followed up with a bigger breakthrough at Livingston in the Scottish Championship. In 1983 it was the Berkshire Championship at Caesar's Camp, Bracknell. I already had a bronze from the Berks, Bucks & Oxon Championship a few weeks earlier. Although the Berkshire involved only one county, not three, it was more prestigious and, as the qualifying race for the National Inter-Counties Championship, it was highly contested.

Towards the end of the race, it was down to three of us. I had been 'hanging on', but the closer we got to the finish the more I grew in confidence: I was going to be the one disappearing through the woods into the distance; I was going to run away from them all, up that final hill to the finish; I was going to win this.

That was my first and only county championship win. It didn't lead to national glory: I went off like a scared rabbit in the Inter-Counties—far too fast, far too early—and spent the rest of the race 'going backwards', finishing outside of the first hundred. And then came the Scottish, where in 1982 I had finished a promising thirty-second. Could I finish higher this time or even higher than 1979? Could I break through into the selection places?

No. Because in 1983, despite a much improved season, I slipped to sixty-eighth. Was it a one-off, only one a bad race?

Could I make it in 1984?

****

First of all there's another county championship to run. I feel a pang of terror as I picture myself on the start line, shivering as the wind howls through the woods. I'm beginning to panic. It feels like my heart is in my mouth. My legs are actually shaking and I'm going weak at the knees but it's not the cold: it's anticipation, but not a good kind. I need the loo yet again. I'm scared. Do I really want to do this?

It's only a county championship, so why am I beating myself up about it?

I'm beating myself up because I'm the defending champion. On this morning last year, I knew I had a good chance of winning, but there was no pressure on me: nobody else worried about me as a serious contender. But this year I have a title to defend. And I'm under pressure. It's not from my rivals: it's unlikely that they're giving me more than a passing thought, if that. The pressure is entirely my own doing.

So, what am I going to do about it?

'Did you say tea? Yes, please, Steve.'

****

Months later, Crystal Palace, London. For many years the home of UK athletics.

It's the first round of the Southern Men's Track & Field League, 1984 and it's not going well for Newbury AC. We've been last or second last in every event so far. And it's nearly my turn to run.

Critics say that Southern Men's League matches are boring. Others say that it's a varied programme: there are twenty-five teams in each division, you meet each of the other twenty-four teams once only, over six rounds at six different venues. In that sense, it's not boring. However, there are only five teams at each match. This means that each event has only five competitors or a maximum of ten when the 'A' and 'B' strings are combined. Apart from the athletes, club officials and a few friends and family, nobody is watching. If one man and his dog came along—having watched international athletics on TV, and now inquisitive about what's happening at the track down the road—they would assume that they've got their dates wrong: it looks as though there's nobody there. The athletes are spread out sparsely across the arena, and so are the events. If the man expected to learn anything from public announcements, he would struggle to decipher the tinny sound of the single tannoy, which always seems to emanate from the opposite end of the ground. If he wanted to read a programme to find out what to look forward to, he might be lucky to pick up a discarded A4 sheet but he

154

would be inadequately informed: there would be a timetable and a list of clubs, each annotated by a letter, but without prior knowledge he wouldn't be able to tell which club was which, and he would have no idea who any of the athletes are.

Many athletes stay away because of the long journeys by coach and all the hanging about, especially if you're in only one event. Why give up a whole day of your weekend when you could just turn up at an open track meeting or a road race closer to home? But I love the Southern Men's League. Initially, I was relieved, grateful, revitalised, excited to be back on the track after such a long absence. And then I was elected as club captain. Whilst my shyness remains, being captain obliges me to at least have a conversation with everyone in the team. Far from being bored during the long day, I start by assisting with team selection and chatting with team members on the coach, taking an interest in their training, wishing them well with their events and sometimes persuading them to 'take one for the team'. As the events begin, I follow the tall, lanky Simon and Bill in the high jump; jog down to the discus circle to support the stocky Tom and Fergus; and be back alongside the home straight to cheer on Tim and another Simon in the 100 metres. This is how I spend the day until it's time for me to warm up for my event.

The excitement builds with announcements, throughout the afternoon, of points earned by each team so far. Which will be the winner? Our team manager, Keith, counts the points from each event— five for first down to one for fifth—and then stands next to the squeaky tannoy to hear his calculations confirmed.

It's partly due to my captaincy but mostly thanks to Keith's man-management skills and organisation that we are here today. We have achieved two consecutive promotions. This is Division One. It's a much higher standard than Division Two. And we're heading for last place. We could be doing better: there's quality in the team. Nick Dorey has run 3:45 for 1500 metres, so close to four minute miling pace. Jon Solly is on the fringe of international selection at 10,000 metres. Richard Rippon has been invited to run the 400 metres at the forthcoming trials for the Olympic team. But Nick and Jon aren't here today, and Richard hasn't run yet: his race is after mine.

Since my first season back from injury, my progress on the track has stalled somewhat. I've improved my 800 metres time to 1:58.2, less than a second outside my pb. My 1500 metres has come down slightly to 4:04.5. I joined Newbury AC with a 5,000 metres pb of 15:20 from that Western District Championship in Coatbridge; it's now 15:09, not a huge improvement from someone who five years ago thought that he could run close to fourteen minutes.

Today at Crystal Palace, each member of our outclassed team may have done his best, may even have run, jumped or thrown a pb. He may also be despondent. Perhaps he's looking for inspiration before his next event of the afternoon. It's part of my role to inspire. And I'm running 5,000 metres. Twelve *and a half laps. That's a long way to run if you're being outclassed. I know: it's happened to me before.*

But it doesn't have to be like that today at this iconic stadium. Can this gladiatorial arena inspire me to inspire the team?

****

By the time the cross-country season had finished only two months earlier, any hopes of realising my ambition of selection for Scotland this year had well and truly fizzled out. After all that fuss leading up to the Berkshire Championship, I finished ninth and scraped into the county team, the only runner to do so on three consecutive seasons. At the National Inter-Counties I improved on last year's performance but was only just in the top hundred. Following the disappointment of dropping from a promising thirty-second to sixty-eighth in 1983, I made the long journey to the Scottish National, confident of a return to form. My confidence was misplaced: I endured an even longer journey back to Newbury after an underwhelming eighty-third place. How could I possibly entertain hopes of international selection when I finished eighty-third? Whom was I kidding?

I ended the season in overall second in the Wessex League for the third year in a row. A good team man, dependable but not outstanding.

But then my fortunes changed. There was a race called the Combe Gibbet to Overton, held between the cross-country and track seasons. It was sixteen and a half hilly miles on varied terrain, by far the longest race I had ever run.

I won. It was at least a week later before I could run properly again, but it was only muscle soreness, not injury. I recovered to win the West Wight Three Hills race on a club weekend on the Isle of Wight. Five years after arriving late for my pot washing shift, having nearly run off the island, I *did* run off the island. My third success was on completely different terrain: the Thruxton motor racing circuit where we won an interclub road relay and I ran the fastest leg.

I had been struggling to build on the early promise of my debut season with Newbury AC. There had been interruptions caused by colds and viral infections, niggling injuries and lingering, biomechanical problems dating back to a time before my operation. There had also been encouraging performances. And now I had just achieved three wins in a row. Could I prolong this winning streak, her in Division One? It was a tough ask.

****

We're running together, tightly packed, down the home straight for the penultimate time, about to hear the jangling of the bell for the final lap. Is it going to be a signal for one of us to make a decisive move at last? We're down to a group of four from the original ten. There's been nothing to separate us for the first eleven and a half laps and I've been on the shoulder of the leader the whole time: the perfect place to cover any move. But whose move will it be? For the past three laps I've had to hold myself back to avoid tripping on

158

the heel of the leader: a sure sign that I'm running within myself, desperate to change pace, but waiting, waiting. I'm ready, but wait, wait, not yet.

The timekeeper calls out 'split' times as we approach the bell: 'thirteen fifty-seven, fifty-eight, fifty-nine, fourteen minutes...'

The sudden change of pace takes me by surprise. And it's my change of pace. A gap opens up immediately but 100 metres later I can hear footsteps and laboured breathing close behind. Someone has recovered from his surprise and has rallied. But he can't maintain the pace. I can: at the crown of the final bend, I'm a few metres ahead and I'm not slowing down.

'Keep going!' Geoff shouts as I enter the home straight. 100 metres to go in my first track race of the season, in the lead at Crystal Palace, focused on holding my form, staying in front; keep going? That's the kind of thing shouted by well-meaning non-athletes, not knowledgeable runners. Of course I'm going to keep going: what else does he think I'm going to do?

I risk a glance behind: the gap is still a few metres; I haven't won yet. I need to maintain focus, eyes on the prize, visualise myself crossing that finish line with no one in sight, keep sprinting, increase the pace if I can; keep going.

I can hear the team yelling encouragement from the stands. These stands that have held thousands of fans. Marvelled as David Bedford broke the world record for 10,000 metres. Stood up in astonishment as

Brendan Foster destroyed the opposition with a mid-race surge. Gasped at Steve Ovett's electrifying injection of pace as he breezed past his rivals down the finishing straight, waving to the crowd. These *stands.* This *finishing straight.*

Except today there's no crowd. I can hear every shout echo around the empty stadium. From our sprinters, distance runners, jumpers, throwers. And Keith, the proud manager of our team. A team that is losing heavily. But I'm winning. I'm team captain and I'm going to bring us our first victory in Division One.

And then I do something weird that feels wonderful.

I start waving to my team in the stands, punching the air, whooping, still sprinting. I must look like an idiot. I'm going to be a prize *idiot if I don't win now. Keep going. Only a few metres more.*

I cross the line and push down an imaginary finishing tape with both hands. It's an inadequate gesture after all that punching and waving and whooping all the way down the home straight, and I can hear the team clapping and laughing; with me or at me, I'm not sure.

It's probably my imagination that most of the team are in the stands, watching my race, cheering, applauding, laughing, sharing the significance of the occasion. It's more likely that most of them are resting after their event or preparing for the next one or having a coffee in the café under the stands.

But I am our first winner. And I've run a big personal best of 14:58.0. With a fifty-eight second last lap. *It's a breakthrough. Finally, I've beaten the fifteen minute barrier. It's fourteen-something, not fifteen-something. It makes a difference.*

Does it make a difference to Richard in his blocks at the start of the 400 metres? Probably not: he knows his business; he doesn't need to be inspired or distracted by a skinny distance runner. He wins. It's our second win of the match. We don't win any others, and we end the day in last place.

But nothing can take away my sense of achievement. I'll never forget this day. I've run a good time, and I got my tactics right. I can race. Where can I go from here? Can I bring my time down to the low fourteens? Can I be competitive in the Scottish 5,000 metres, show them all what I can do? Can this track campaign be a springboard to success in next cross-country season? Can I finally make the World Cross?

All of these questions, hopes and desires keep me buzzing all the way home from the first track competition of the new season.

This is only the beginning.

****

Training diary entry:

'Sunday 1 July 1984

'Scottish Championships, Meadowbank, Edinburgh

'5,000 metres; sixteenth; 15:23.0

161

'A nightmare! I seemed to do everything right in the early stages, running 70s and 71s, making up places. After about six laps, the leading group broke away, and I was at the front of everyone else. I was still on schedule for the low 14:40s with five laps to go, but I was slowing down. I really suffered during the last mile and slowed down so much that I was lapped by Nat Muir and Allister Hutton during their last few metres. So the TV and newspaper pictures will show this scrubber with a lap left to run. What went wrong? I was trying hard enough. I suspect that my form has just blown. If that's correct, I'll have to find out why I'm getting worse exactly when I want to be at my best. This has happened before. I think I need some expert advice.'

What had caused the shift from ecstasy to despondency within two short months?

There was no gradual decline. My next race after Crystal Palace was faster: 14:53.9, only fourth in the Berkshire Championship but at the end of a week of stomach upsets. The one after that was even quicker: 14:44.3 for a close second in the next round of the Southern Men's League. I had planned my training meticulously. My big mileage of the winter had been a foundation for progressive track sessions, changing only one variable at a time: increase the number of reps, reduce recovery time or increase recovery time so that you can increase the pace. I was also training at different paces in different sessions: 800 metres, 1500 metres, 3,000 metres, 5,000 metres, longer runs. It was all textbook stuff. All building towards a peak at my most important race.

With the benefit of hindsight it's glaringly obvious that there was too much racing, too soon. The beginning of July was too early for a peak performance unless I had started the build-up much earlier. But I hadn't: following a late cross-country season, I went straight into an early track season. My training may have been sensible and progressive, and I may have gained tactical awareness, but my competition schedule was far from sensible. Those three pbs at 5,000 metres were all in May. They should have been more spread out but I was ignorant and unaware. I even ran a mud splattered Thirteen Mile race along the Ridgeway only two days after my third 5,000 metres of the month. From 1 April until 1 July I ran fourteen races: seven on the track, one road race, one road relay and five 'off road' races. Far too many, far too close together, far too early.

I might have got away with it if I had eased off before the Scottish. I knew about tapering, and had used it successfully before, but not this time. I ran five races in the fortnight leading up to the championship: an 800 metres pb of 1:57.3 (at last, shaving a tenth off my previous pb of eight years before) and a 9:56.8 pb in a brief return to the 3,000 metres steeplechase on the same afternoon; ten uncomfortable miles in an off-road race over the South Downs *the next day*, after being sick in the night; a Five Mile road race six days later (a pb of 24:14, although the organisers knew that it was forty metres short: why didn't they just move the start or finish line by forty metres?); four days after that and four days before the Scottish, a 3,000 metres in 8:38.4 on a late night in London; two days later I was on the bus to Airdrie. I was running well and on a roll of good performances (South Downs excepted). Nevertheless, in those circumstances, how could any sensible person believe that they would be at their best in their most important race of the season? It's so clear now that I had run myself into exhaustion.

I was an idiot. No wonder my training diary told me to get expert advice. But did I?

No. The trouble was, there were no endurance running coaches at Newbury AC. There were good coaches at other clubs but that could cause a clash of interests. And I didn't have a car: I relied on team coaches or lifts from teammates to races, but neither was an option for training at a different club. In ignorance I blundered on.

But with surprising success.

Only three days after my humiliation at Meadowbank I took a second off my 1500 metres pb (from the Roger Bannister experience of 1978), running 3:57.8 in only the 'C' race at West London. I went on to run 3,000 metres in 8:28.5, just missing my pb by a tenth. And I found a new event: 10,000 metres, making my debut with 30:58.0 for second place and my only medal on the track at Berkshire Championships. I was collecting a set of respectable pbs but I was still an idiot: for instance, that midweek 10,000 metres was sandwiched between two weekends of light-hearted half-marathon races.

Then I went on holiday for a fortnight. And that's probably where any sensible athlete would end their season. Not me: I was club captain, there were more races to run, more matches, more points to win for the team. I couldn't let the team down, could I? My season petered out with performances which were at best average and at worst mediocre. I had run a grand total of thirty races in under five months.

I was tired but amazingly, uninjured. Looking forward to the forthcoming cross-country season and another shot at glory. And looking back on a whirlwind of a track season full of contradictions.

I had run far too many races, planned poorly and performed badly in my most important competition of the season.

On the other hand, I had enjoyed myself. It was a huge thrill to win on the track or run faster than I had ever run before. It was also fun to race far away from the track in beautiful locations. I enjoyed the training, too: pushing myself to the limit in track repetitions or relaxing on runs across country, being at one with my surroundings. This was my hobby. Hobbies are supposed to be fun. Did I have to tie myself in knots, planning to succeed, striving to be one of the elite? Was I over-thinking things? Could I not just go for a run?

Well, no.

I was improving.

I had ambition.

I could give this one more try.

It was the Golden Age of Distance Running in Britain. I had just set a group of personal best performances which meant nothing to the elite but everything to me.

I had no idea that I would never run those times again.

Chapter Twelve: Tragedy

One last throw of the dice.

That was my approach to the 1984/85 cross-country season. The mistakes of the track season would not be repeated. For one thing, it's impossible to run thirty races in a cross-country season: there aren't that many weekends. The focus would be to get a simple training and racing programme right. It's not rocket science: build up your mileage gradually, make sure that your reps sessions are progressive, ease down towards the most important race.

And be aggressive in races.

AGGRESSION. I wrote the word in BIG LETTERS in my training diary, just in case I forgot that it was a key component of success.

'I don't like this aggression you're talking about,' Mum said when she and Dad came to visit me in my new flat on the edge of Northcroft Park in Newbury. I was still her nice wee boy. I wasn't aggressive in real life: it was a persona reserved for races. You had to keep aggression leashed during the early stages of a race, then release some of it in that difficult middle section where there's a long way to go but you have to stay in contention. The last lap would take care of itself, which wasn't strictly true but with that final unleashing of the beast it was 'all out' to the finish line. You had to know how to 'spend' yourself. Nothing was left on the field.

Meanwhile, Dad had built up steadily from that fun run in Cumbernauld back in 1980 to run the Glasgow Marathon in 1983. That was Dad's way: methodical in his planning and determined to succeed. Tired of falling asleep in the armchair after work every evening, he started night school and studied for his Highers, finishing the course with better grades than Susan and I achieved. It wasn't one-upmanship: he wanted to share our experience and understand what we were going through. When we were learning to drive, Dad followed driving instructors around the test course so that he could help us practise in the most informed way. And now he was living the running dream.

But Dad wasn't able to run that autumn. He asked me to show him some of my training routes on long walks together, so that he could imagine me running there. At the end of the visit he drove back to Airdrie having shared something of my new lifestyle and seen me settled into my first property. But he couldn't run: something was wrong with his insides. Dad was in pain.

****

The first half of the season had been respectable, even promising. For the first time I was in contention for an end of season medal in the Hampshire League as well as the Wessex. Determined to complete the Hampshire series, my clubmate Andy and I travelled together to Bournemouth for the December round when no one else in the club was interested. Neither of us had a car, so we planned the journey by trains and enjoyed our day at the seaside.

However, I was battling with shin soreness, and had to ease down in training sooner than planned to get rid of the pain. Twice I had to stop running altogether for a few days. Shin pain is caused by one or more of three things: running downhill, running on hard surfaces or a sudden increase in training. I had been much more sensible this autumn and winter than last spring and summer but the damage had been done long before this season. I had noticed shin soreness last winter but I ran through it: it wasn't too bad; if you don't get aches and pains, you're not training hard enough, are you? I thought I had got away with it but now it had come back to haunt me.

And set in motion a sequence of events that would not conclude until more than eight years later.

****

The rutted ground was frozen solid at the Berkshire Championship in January 1985. On a steep downhill section of the course, after the third time of going over my ankle, I dropped out.

After a rest, I returned to running on a much reduced capacity. My heels hurt too, but I chose not to contact Doctor Walker: I wasn't ready to accept that this was a serious injury. Take it easy, wear heel pads, I'd be okay, wouldn't I? I'd be back racing soon. I might not make it to the Scottish this year, but I could end the season with medals in the leagues, couldn't I?

I was modifying my goals. My dream of the World Cross on hold, I was compromising, taking stock and already looking ahead to the following season.

By February I had stopped running altogether. The pain in the shins and heels was not going away. It was time to seek help.

I paid to attend a sports injury clinic and received physiotherapy. An x-ray failed to show anything unusual about my shins. I took up swimming and cycling again but without conviction: I still believed that I'd be back to running soon.

A month later, belief had been reduced to mere hope. Swimming and cycling were keeping me fit and didn't aggravate the shins or heels but the pain was always there, reminding me not to run. No longer able to afford private treatment, I went to my GP, who prescribed anti-inflammatory pills and put me on the waiting list for ultrasound.

It was a frustrating time but, unlike the dark days of 1979 and 1980, I was coping in a more mature way. Far from cutting myself off from athletics, I filled a gap in the club coaching structure by supervising our young athletes. Initially there was a group of between twelve and twenty attending indoor fitness and games sessions supplemented by short, closely supervised road runs under street lights.

Meanwhile, at school, I was leading the school running club towards the Amateur Athletics Association 5 Star cross-country awards. I taught a keep fit club for parents, on a voluntary basis, raising funds for outdoor play equipment. I completed the Amateur Swimming Association Teacher of Swimming course and enrolled on the Assistant Club Coach course for athletics. I coached our school football team to win the Newbury & District and Berkshire 6-a-side tournaments, falling one step short of Wembley at the South West tournament. I enrolled on the FA referees' course and followed our local senior teams—Newbury, Thatcham and Hungerford—and became a regular at Elm Park, home of Reading FC.

And all this time, I never lost touch with my friends. I was not hiding myself away this time.

****

Mum phones to tell me that Dad is in hospital. Remembering my own positive experience, when Doctor Walker changed my life for the better, I say, 'Dad'll be okay. They'll look after him there. He'll be fine now.'

'But son, it's a tumour.'

'Wh- what does that mean?'

'It's cancer, son.' She's crying. 400 miles away, Mum's crying. And here am I, useless, comparing cancer to my trivial operation.

I catch the next train to London and then the coach to Hamilton, where Susan picks me up and drives us straight to the hospital.

****

The three of us are crying outside the ward. Dad's never been ill before. Can the doctors help him?

A few days later Dad comes home. He should be relatively comfortable for quite some time, possibly years. But the long term prognosis is not good.

****

Back down south the young athletes moved out to the track and up to 100 were turning up every week. Having devised a rota to incorporate the skills of running, jumping and throwing, I recruited former training partners, other coaches and friends to help. Each session ended on a high with a shuttle relay between ten teams of ten. I also managed the women's track & field team as well as the young athletes. Almost going back to my Boys Brigade roots, I was the Berkshire Boys Clubs team manager at the National Championships.

Finally admitting that this injury was long term, I arranged a consultation with Doctor Walker. He diagnosed Compartment Syndrome, a thickening of the bone inside the sheath of the shin, which causes pain when the muscles expand with exercise and creates pressure in the limited space within the sheath. (I think that's what he said.) He disagreed with my GP's recommendation of ultrasound, so I took myself off that particular waiting list and joined a new one for a bone scan in Portsmouth. Doctor Walker also recommended a new pair of orthotics to help ease the pain: I would be seeing my old friend Mr Ball again, eventually.

It was a lot to take in but there was much worse to follow. Dad was back in hospital. The consultant said that he should have enjoyed months or years of relative comfort but the cancer was growing. Dad was suffering.

****

I'm at Dad's bedside with Mum and Susan. It's the end of the spring half term and I'm about to return to Newbury. Beckoning me closer, Dad shakes my hand and says, 'Bye, son. I love you.'

'But I'll see you next time, Dad. I'll be back in a fortnight.'

****

It was denial. I couldn't face the fact that Dad was saying goodbye for the last time.

He knew.

Why didn't I tell Dad that I loved him?

The regret would stay with me forever.

Only a few days after I arrived back at my flat, Mum called.

Dad was dead.

I said I was sorry, so sorry. What an inadequate thing to say: I was grieving, too.

Why hadn't I told Dad that I loved him?

He had always been there for us. Supporting us through school, work and hobbies, joining in when he could. Driving us here, there and everywhere. Taking us on holiday. Providing for us, even when he lost his job and spent the last years of his life unemployed. He

173

saw his daughter married a year before he died, but he would not see his son married. He would never meet his grandchildren. He and Mum never had a cross word in all their years together. Now Mum would have to live on her own. Dad was gone.

And I had not told him that I loved him.

Mum did most of the funeral arrangements without our help. She was protecting us. We did not read a family tribute. We did not see Dad before he was cremated.

I did not tell him that I love him.

****

Mum won't come out of the bathroom of my flat. Wails of despair from behind the locked door. The only other time she's been here was last autumn with Dad. To see my new home. A new beginning. There would be no new beginning for Mum and Dad together.

It's been too early to invite Mum down.

Another regret.

****

The triviality of my injury resumed. The bone scan confirmed signs of stress. Bone injuries take longer to heal. Mr Ball took new casts of my feet. I would have to wait until October for the orthotics. Doctor Walker made no mention of surgery.

By August I had built up my cycling mileage to over a hundred per week and was enjoying exploring the countryside again, discovering new places with almost every ride. And I was a regular at the swimming pools, indoor and out, only a five minute walk from my flat.

****

One of my clubmates is on the phone, reporting back from a long distance trail race that afternoon.

'How did you get on?' I ask.

'Andy collapsed and died.'

'What? Say that again.'

Did he say that Andy died? It's impossible to comprehend. Runners don't die. We're fit and healthy.

I remember well our train journey to the sea back in December and how Andy helped with the young athletes' programme in the summer. I knew that he had a big heart, but no one knew that it was a weak heart. A heart that stopped beating, at the same time as he stopped running, for the last time in his life.

And here am I, worried about sore shins.

****

With the arrival of winter came a hot and infuriating itching, spreading across my chest and made worse by exercise. Cycling and swimming were put to one side while I tried to find a way to stop the itch. Antihistamine tablets and cream had no effect. Was I allergic to something? A blood test provided no answers.

The first Christmas without Dad passed.

January 1986: a whole year of injury.

Stretching, elevation, ice, pills, cream, more pills.

Mr Ball advised me to do what I could for three months. I should be able to run again eventually but not as well as before. I would have to be aware of my limitations. He gave me a new garlic-infused lotion to rub into my shins, warning me that there would be a garlic taste in my mouth afterwards. Six years after Mum signposting me to that clinic of alternative therapy, had the homeopath been correct, after all? It was worth a try. Within seconds of applying the lotion to my shins, a strong taste of garlic was right there in my mouth. How did that happen so quickly? I stank of garlic for weeks. I laughed about it but the shin pain remained.

A skin specialist suggested that the itch was a nervous condition caused by stress. Rest assured, the specialist said: it will go away. Stress, that made sense. A whole year after Dad died, why hadn't I realised before? And with that realisation, the itch started to go away.

As the young athletes returned to another season on the track, I was working towards my Club Coach qualification and I enrolled on the Swimfit award scheme. It was simple: you logged each swim and received badges at cumulative distances such as ten, fifty, all the way to 1,000 miles. It would keep me motivated for years.

Doctor Walker offered me a place on the waiting list for a new operation to relieve shin pain. It was a simple procedure called (bilateral) lateral compartment decompression: a small incision along the length of the anterior side of each shin would relieve the pressure. The operation would take place within a few weeks or up to a year's time and could allow me to run again. Mr Ball used me as Exhibit A in front of his students. He described me as an ex-athlete whose legs were wrecked.

Well, we would see about that.

Suddenly, after a year and a half of waiting—longer than the interminable time between my knee injury and the successful operation—there was hope again.

****

The Commonwealth Games returned to Edinburgh, and I had tickets for every athletics session. My old running mate from Chester, Dylan, was coming up to join me. Heavily boycotted because of the UK's sporting links with South Africa during the era of apartheid, the medals were shared amongst only seven nations. Nevertheless, there were many stars on show such as Kathy Cook, Sally Gunnell, Kirsty Wade, Yvonne Murray, Judy Oakes, Tessa Sanderson, Fatima Whitbread, Daley Thompson, Ben Johnson, Linford Christie, the famous 4x400 metres relay team of Akabusi/Black/Bennett/Brown, Steve Ovett, Steve Cram and Peter Elliott. Finishing between Cram and Elliott for silver in the 800 metres, and no longer a wee nyaff, was Clyde Valley's Tom McKean. But the events that thrilled us most were the 10,000 metres races.

During the women's race we were sitting behind a coach, who was chatting with his friends and giving them the benefit of his opinion. Although with the England team, he was Scots, and as the drama unfolded he became more and more impressed by Scotland's Liz Lynch, a relatively unknown athlete who had nevertheless been making a name for herself on the US college circuit.

'Liz Lynch is doing well... I think Liz Lynch can win a medal here... Liz Lynch is definitely going to medal... It looks like Liz Lynch can win this... I think Liz Lynch is going to win...'

It was a bit annoying to listen to him state the obvious. He was right, of course, and Liz Lynch won Scotland's only athletics gold of the Games.

I later discovered that the coach was John Anderson, mentor to many international athletes, including Dave Moorcroft, world record holder for 5,000 metres in 1982 and one of my heroes. John Anderson would go on to coach Liz Lynch (later McColgan) for two years before she won gold in the World Championships at 10,000 metres and half-marathon as well as winning the New York, Tokyo and London marathons.

Just before the start of the Men's 10,000 metres, Dylan and I bumped into Simon and Bill, the Newbury high jumpers. We made Dylan an honorary member of Newbury AC as we settled down in the stands to support our own Jon Solly. We weren't settled for long. We yelled, 'Come on, Jon! Go, Newbury!' every time he passed our seats. The longer the race went on, the louder we yelled as, lap after lap, runners dropped off the pace. When the bell sounded, Jon and his England teammate, Steve Binns, were inseparable. But Jon edged ahead and, to tumultuous applause, maintained the small gap and crossed the line below us as Champion of the Commonwealth.

Newbury AC held a welcome home celebration for Jon, and a strange letter from Doctor Walker dropped on my doormat. He was going to be featured in a TV series about sports injuries. If I agreed to have my operation filmed he could see me sooner: in two weeks' time.

Meanwhile, down at the track, the mother of one of our new young athletes and I were having a chat. Nothing unusual about that: it happened all the time as children settled into the routine of the club. You got to know the regular parents.

The vivacious young athlete was Clara and her mother—open-faced, supportive, interested and *interesting*—was Jane.

****

Given the events of the year, my feelings on arriving at hospital in September for this operation were less ecstatic, in 1986, than in 1980. I was looking forward to a return to running but I was more pragmatic now. If Mr Ball was correct that I had no chance of returning to my previous form, it would be disappointing but it wouldn't be a tragedy. Some say that when an athlete has to give up their sport it's like a bereavement: they mourn the loss of an important part of their life. This was not bereavement. I knew about bereavement. I was mourning, but not for running.

Within a couple of weeks of the operation I was cycling and swimming again and, for the first time in a year and three quarters, jogging. By the end of the month, my exercise routine was more like proper training than rehabilitation.

The young athletes' training programme was well-established at the club, my Club Coach award was on its way, I was teaching new coaches on Assistant Club Coach courses at venues as far away as Crystal Palace, and I applied for a place on a forthcoming Senior Club Coach course. It was an exciting time, but, in contrast, the honeymoon period of teaching at my first school was well and truly over. My career needed a boost: either get a job in a different school, preferably a promotion, or a different job altogether. When a vacancy for an athletics development officer job came up, I applied and was invited to interview at the British Athletics head office in London.

****

Waiting for the interview, sitting on a park bench, head between my knees, feeling ill. It wasn't nerves: I hadn't eaten anything for two days. I thought about cancelling, but this opportunity would not be repeated, so I caught the bus to London and made my way on the tube across the city. All I wanted to do was curl up in bed, but I was a long way from home and I had to pretend that nothing was wrong: I wanted this job. This could be the fresh start that I needed, working in the sport that I loved.

There was a hand on my shoulder. It was a police officer.

'Are you all right, sir?'

He must have been used to homeless people sleeping on park benches, but a guy in a smart suit?

The interview proceeded through a haze. I remember only two questions. When asked about the national coach education scheme, I remarked that I thought new coaches were asked to specialise too early: they had to choose a discipline on only their second day of the assistants' course. It was my opinion that introducing children to athletics should be one of the most important roles of a club and that the best coach should be leading the young athletes' programme, which should be wide ranging and not specific to standard events. It followed that, as well as middle-distance, sprints, jumps and throws, there should be an option for children's athletics in the coach education structure. I also told them that I didn't think that league athletics was the 'be all and end all', and that it was more important to focus on the needs of the athlete rather than the team. There was often conflict between coaches and team managers but, in fulfilling both roles, I once left both 400 metres Hurdles places blank, rather than humiliate an unprepared athlete just to get a point or two for the team.

The panel wasn't impressed with my assessment of the flagships of British Athletics: leagues had been set up to provide regular, meaningful competition and improve standards. However, children's athletics was introduced into the coach education programme in later years.

I didn't get the job but that was the least of my worries: I thought I had cancer. Dad's illness had started with what he believed were stomach pains. It was all I could think about for the rest of the week, while still not eating. The doctor came out to see me, tried to reassure me that it wasn't cancer but that they would run tests to eliminate certain conditions.

It wasn't cancer: it was irritable bowel syndrome. Eventually, with the help of medication, more rest and a change of diet, I recovered and was ready to return to school. Having already missed the first two weeks of term because of the operation, I hardly had time to settle before this illness. After over a month's absence I was anxious about my return.

Meanwhile, Doctor Walker advised that I needed to get well, and then train.

The sun set on 1986.

After two years of injury.

A new dawn awaited.

And there was still no sign of a return to running.

Chapter Thirteen: Modern

A pile of training shoes on my front doorstep.

At the end of our Saturday morning cross-country training sessions in Northcroft Park, the young athletes and their parents would pile into my front room for tea and biscuits. I made them take off their muddy trainers; hence the pile. The neighbours must have wondered what was going on.

One of the parents was Jane.

I never did find out what the neighbours thought.

I had regained my health and was running about twenty-five miles a week supplemented by swimming and cycling. I was getting quite fit again.

March brought a return of shin pain but it felt different this time and reduced my running to ten miles per week.

Another bone scan. The same injury but on the posterior side of the shins. One side of both legs wasn't enough: I had to complete the set.

After six years of teaching at the same school I made a career move and started the spring term in a new school near Reading. No longer cycling a mile and a half to school, I became a commuter, driving Dad's old car forty minutes or so each way. The extra travelling and responsibilities meant changes at the club: I wouldn't have time to oversee the young athletes' programme or manage the teams, so I mentored other coaches to step into my roles. Everything was in place by the start of the new track season.

However, I wasn't turning my back on the club. There was a gap in our coaching structure: middle-distance. Keith, as head coach as well as men's team manager, was strong on squad training, getting people fit for a range of events. An accomplished veteran sprinter, Keith had a great saying: 'You'll never run faster until you run faster.' It sounds like nonsense but it's not. It means that you have to train fast to race fast. His sprinters would run short reps at top speed, complemented by longer reps and more generic training. Keith's mantra also applies to middle-distance running: multiple reps at faster than race pace, with short recoveries.

It even applies to marathon running: it's amazing how many marathon runners think they'll run their target time by magic. For instance, if all their training up to their longest run of twenty miles is at eight minute miling pace, how do they expect to achieve seven minute miling for twenty-six miles on race day? That would be magic. Which doesn't exist. They have to complete some of their training runs at their target pace and faster.

Some of my friends, who were marathon runners and wanted to try the track, became my first coaching group. Another was made up of young athletes, including Clara, who were old enough to graduate from the children's group and wanted to be middle-distance runners. The two groups followed different programmes, of course. The marathon runners were introduced to the delights of repetition running with short recoveries, while the younger group's training was more varied and with a fun element, learning the skills of middle-distance running without multiple reps, and never neglecting other athletics disciplines. Both groups enjoyed success and improved their times. Eventually, other coaches joined the groups and the provision for middle-distance running expanded.

My new orthotics arrived in July and allowed me to run between ten and twenty miles per week alongside coaching. And there was a letter from Doctor Walker, embarrassed that his request for a bone scan had gone astray.

Two months later, the bone scan showed nothing helpful. Baffled, Doctor Walker referred me to a clinic in London for a gait analysis. Oh well, that was something we hadn't tried yet.

That autumn I saw my operation on TV. At the club on the following day, I overheard: 'There was this bloke having an operation. You should have seen it: the surgeon just unzipped his shins and zipped them up again.'

'Excuse me,' I interrupted. 'Those were my shins.'

The day after that I received an unexpected cheque in the post: my appearance fee. £15, I'll have you know. £7.50 each leg. Not only was I a TV celebrity but I was now a professional athlete.

More significantly, Jane and I were now a couple. We moved into our new home in Hungerford and started our life together.

Meanwhile, I was unhappy at my new school. I enjoyed the extra responsibilities in PE and was hosting a well-received course in athletics for primary school teachers. But I had no freedom to express myself in the classroom. Nor had the children. I had been warned about the moods and micromanagement of the headteacher and the school's formal methods, but I hadn't listened. Having felt stagnant at my first school, I was convinced that this career move would revitalise my career.

I was wrong.

****

January 1988. Three years of injury.

Jane and I were married in April at Newbury Registry Office. In attendance were both of our mums, my old housemate, Steve, as best man, Susan and her husband Alastair, Clara and her sister Sarah, and most of Newbury AC. If only Dad could have been there.

Two months later I accepted a job offer from Swindon. It was a progressive school with a good reputation for topic work and teacher development. It was ideal but my then headteacher would not allow me to start until January 1989. She was sticking to the rule of a term's notice, so I wasn't able to start afresh in the new school year in September. I would have to wait for more than six months after giving notice of my departure.

At last the news came that I would be having surgery again: the same operation as before but on the posterior side of both shins. Soon afterwards I was called in, and was home on the same day, surgery techniques having developed somewhat over the years.

Only three months later I was lining up in the first round of the Wessex League, on the Lawns of Swindon: my first cross-country race in almost four years. Standing much further back than usual in the field of three hundred runners, I was soaking up the atmosphere: the earthy smell of turf under my training shoes (not wearing spikes yet); the less earthy scent of hundreds of males in close proximity; the throng of small talk amongst nervous runners, becoming a murmur as we were called to our marks, and then silence before the crash of the starting pistol.

Over half an hour later I crossed the finish line.

In eighty-fourth place.

I improved to fifty-sixth in November, then nineteenth in the Berks, Bucks & Oxon and twenty-first in the Berkshire in December. I was running around thirty miles per week, with no sign of shin pain.

January 1989: now up to forty miles per week, I improved to twentieth in the Wessex League. And finally I started teaching in Swindon. It was a far from ideal start: although the school was renowned for team teaching, my classroom was a single hut at the end of a lonely path, as far away from the main building as you could get. Already playing catch up due to my late start (no change there), I struggled to settle in.

One month later I was injured again. Not shins: knees. Again. But not like before. Sharp pain behind the joints reduced my running to almost zero. How cruel to have a taste of running after such a long absence, make good progress, and then have it all taken away so soon.

I was struggling at school. Recognising a need for support and collaborative teaching, my new headteacher appointed a mentor and with her help I began to find my way. The difference in approach between this school and my previous one was matched by the subsequent improvement in my teaching.

It was March, and Doctor Walker diagnosed Peritendonitis, prescribed anti-inflammatory pills, referred me to short-wave physiotherapy and signposted me to Mr Ball again for yet another pair of orthotics. However, this news was not on my mind as I drove Jane to the maternity ward. Within minutes of our arrival, Sam was born. He nearly lost his Dad and Jane nearly lost her husband, as I was in a car crash on the way home. I braked for a pheasant and the car behind smashed into the back of mine, instantly writing my car off and giving me whiplash.

The pheasant was fine.

There was no indication of when my knee injury would be treated but, with a new baby in the house, was there any time to think about it?

At an appointment in July, Doctor Walker asked me to cross my legs, which made the pain worse, and he changed his diagnosis to Poplitius Tenosynovitis. He offered to inject Cortisone into the back of one of my knees; the other knee would be injected two weeks later. The pain was relieved by the first injection and had disappeared after the second.

I resumed running in August. And, as cycling and swimming had been part of my recovery and training for a long time now, I was thinking about having a go at triathlon.

My first beginners' triathlon was in September. I enjoyed it but lost a lot of ground on the cycling. However, I had heard about biathlon. There were two types: a continuous swim/run (later renamed duathlon) and a shorter, points-scoring event derived from modern pentathlon. One of our advisory PE teachers was reigning National Masters Modern Biathlon Champion. In a masterful display of motivational speaking, he told me that I'd do okay at running but would be 'hammered out of sight' in the swimming.

My debut at modern biathlon was a few weeks later. On low running mileage and with no experience of competitive swimming, I finished eleventh of thirteen. I had indeed been 'hammered out of sight' but I had caught the bug.

Now running thirty miles a week again, I made another return to cross-country: thirty-fourth in the Wessex League and twenty-ninth in the Berks, Bucks & Oxon. But when knee pain returned I was back down to under ten miles per week.

January 1990: five consecutive years of injury.

Following a stuttering return to twenty miles per week of running I made yet another comeback. My first track race for nearly six years was an 800 metres in 2:07. This was my time to beat the following month, which I did with 2:04, and also ran a 1500 metres in 4:19.

Still on only twenty miles per week I won a tactical 5,000 metres in the Southern Men's League Division 3, outsprinting everyone to win in 16:10. My next 5,000 metres was also a win: a noisy, desperate 15:56 in the Club Championship.

My track season ended in September with a 1500 metres win in 4:12 and a season's best of 2:02 for 800 metres.

And I heard that if I learned to shoot, I could take part in a modern triathlon.

At the end of the year I won a cross-country race without surpassing thirty miles per week but also training for multisports. I joined a masters swimming club, immediately improving my stroke technique and therefore my training times. And, on modern triathlon coaching days, I learned to shoot, then incorporated shooting practice into my training, pinning a target to a tree on Hungerford Common.

Many years of recovery and rehabilitation had led me to a sport that I had never heard of before. Would this multisport cross training (not to be confused with cross-country training) prevent further injury? Had I replaced my now defunct World Cross dream with a more outlandish one? Had all those years plagued with injuries reached their end at last? Had I finally found an approach to training that would keep me injury-free?

These thoughts occupied my mind as another New Year approached.

Runners think that when their running is going well, everything is going well. As far as I was concerned, it was absolutely true at the end of the summer of 1991. I had run 5,000 metres in 15:47.4, more than a minute slower than my best, but my 1500 metres was under ten seconds slower at 4:06.9 and my 800 metres was as close as three seconds at 2:00.6, all on thirty miles per week, plus swimming three times per week, regular shooting practice and cycling as often as I could. I was learning quickly at the masters swim club, completing up to 2,800 metres per session. Unlike running repetitions, swim reps, at distances from 50 metres to 400 metres, had a target time that included a short recovery. We varied the programme with drills, kicking and pulling practice and other strokes.

My final 'endurance' triathlon convinced me that I would never be competitive at swim/cycle/run: I was sixteenth in the swim and first in the run, but unfortunately in between those two I came sixty-second in the cycling. I competed well in duathlons and finished second in my first modern biathlon as a master: I had turned thirty-five earlier in the year.

Meanwhile, I was enjoying a purple patch at school. A deserted village in the Marlborough Downs called Snap was a perfect inspiration for the summer term topic for my class of eight and nine year-olds. It started with a site visit, picking up artefacts from

Victorian times scattered amongst the ruins. Then, like my own season in multisports, the topic grew in excitement and intensity. The children wrote illustrated letters to historians, local residents, nearby schools and libraries, writers: anyone with a possible connection with the former village. They interviewed descendants of the last residents of Snap, and were interviewed themselves by the local paper and regional television. The classroom was transformed into a museum, with a huge model of the village as centrepiece, all created by the children. The climax of the term's work was a presentation for parents and local dignitaries, and a memorial stone, erected in Snap's former high street. I also gave presentations to other teachers in Swindon and to the Hungerford Historical Society, and had an article published in a national education magazine.

Amidst all this excitement, Jane and I started the next chapter of our lives, moving house to the outskirts of Calne, close to ancient monuments and giant white horses chalked into the rolling hills of the Wiltshire Downs.

It had been an eventful year.

January 1992: seven years since shin pain stopped me running.

But no longer injured.

Preparing for a year of competition in multisports, I reached a new level of understanding. Having completed all coursework for my senior coach award, I decided not to proceed to the case study and final exams. Living so far from my former coaching base in Newbury, and with renewed interest in my own sporting career, I had stepped back gradually from coaching. However, I never stopped learning. Swimming club, shooting, advanced coaching education and the modern triathlon/biathlon competition schedule all led me to a conclusion: in order to compete to the best of my ability, I would plan for a double-periodised year.

Effectively the calendar year was divided into two seasons: modern triathlon and modern biathlon, culminating with their respective national championships in May and November. Each season began with a general preparation phase, laying the groundwork for the specific preparation phase, finally tapering towards the climax of the national championship. The general phase included multi-tier track-type sessions—preferably on grass—at 800 metres, 1500 metres, 3,000 metres and 5,000 metres pace. Key sessions at the pace of the competition distance of 2,000 metres with long recoveries to maintain a fast pace, were introduced during the specific phase. There were also steady recovery runs and a long run at the weekend, but my mileage never exceeded thirty per week.

I placed my trust in the twice weekly swim squad sessions, and planned my third weekly session to include long reps at the beginning of each phase and sprint sessions towards the peak. I also planned a progressive series of circuit training for each preparation phase, practised shooting every week, and cycled now and again.

No longer would there be a haphazard approach to competition. After years of injury, frustration and disappointment, I believed that I had been given another chance to excel: I wasn't going to mess it up this time. The regional qualifiers were always two months before the national. There were also minor biathlons and triathlons and swimming galas all year round, although I limited my number of appearances: I still wanted to *run* races. The second half of the cross-country season was ideal preparation for the national triathlon in May but the next cross-country season had barely started by the time the national biathlon came along in November, so I extended the biathlon phase to take in the Berks, Bucks & Oxon and the County, before taking my end-of-phase rest. I ran some track races at the end of the triathlon season and then during the biathlon general preparation phase. However, track had taken a back seat: it was difficult to do myself justice and, with so many options available, I was not going to make the mistake of over-racing again.

The year was a success, in that I didn't get injured, I won the regional triathlon and finished fifth in the national; and achieved bronze in the regional biathlon and fourth in the national.

However, none of those was the highlight of the year.

Our daughter, Emma was born in July.

And our family was complete.

****

In 1993 could I build on the success of my first full season in modern triathlon and biathlon, and improve on my fourth and fifth places?

The modern way was to complete each discipline separately with long rest periods in between. The swim came first: 100 metres in the pool. You competed in heats, earning points for your time. Next came shooting: ten targets, maximum score for each bullseye and lower scores for hits nearer the circumference. A formula calculated your final score. Finally, the run was a 2,000 metres cross-country time trial; you set off at intervals and your final time completed your overall points score. The masters' championship incorporated a handicap system: the older you were, the more additional points you were awarded. At thirty-seven, one of the youngest competitors, I was giving away points to most of the opposition.

My performances at the regional were:

100 metres swim, fourth, 1:14.96 (1,108 points)

Shoot, third, 65 (850 points)

2,000 metres run, first, 6:16.25 (1,340 points)

Total: 3,298 points, first place

Having retained my title, I entered the specific preparation phase, quietly confident of further success.

The British Championships were to take place at Milton Keynes, spread over two days: swim and shoot on Saturday, and run and presentation on Sunday.

****

At the final turn, swimming in the pack in the second heat,

Something unexpected happens:

A perfectly executed tumble turn,

Push off more powerfully than ever,

Glide more smoothly than ever,

Kick, pull, sprint,

Faster than ever.

Reach for the wall in first place,

A pb of 1:12.58,

1.5 seconds faster than ever,

I've taken 2.5 seconds out of the opposition,

All on the final length.

It's the perfect start. 1,124 points. But, after the handicapped points, only eighth place. But certainly not 'hammered out of sight'.

Shooting is unique. So different from the other two disciplines where it's an advantage to be nervous, to be pumped up with adrenaline at the start. Before the shoot you have to stay calm, almost detached: if you're too nervous, your hands shake: not ideal for shooting at a small target ten metres away. Shooting brings other challenges: if you're short sighted, do you wear your glasses so that you can see the target clearly or do you keep them off to focus on the sights at the end of the barrel? I keep them off.

We wait, side by side, as targets are set up,

Spend as much time as you like,

With the first shot, nerves settle,

Pistols down while the first targets are removed,

And the next ones set up.

I leave the hall with a pb score of 81.

1,010 points. tenth in the shoot. I've slipped to fourteenth overall.

****

On the morning of the run, I know what I need to do to improve from fourteenth to first.

Yes, first: *I'm aiming high.*

I need to beat my two closest rivals by forty-six and fifty-two seconds. Have they done enough in the swim and shoot to hold me off, or can I beat them by about a minute? It's a big ask in not much longer than six minutes. But I'm the fastest runner.

This is what should happen now: the overnight leader sets off first, everyone else follows at timed intervals according to how much time they need to make up to finish in front of the leader. Whoever crosses the line first wins the championship: simple.

But that's not what happens: we line up in a *random order predetermined before the championships began. We're going to be running blind. It's down to pace judgement. Start too slowly, and you'll leave yourself too much to do in the closing stages and finish frustrated, knowing that you could have run faster. Start too quickly, and you'll struggle to maintain your pace just when you need to finish strongly. Factor in hills, mud and wind; and pace judgement becomes even more of a challenge.*

So we wait, each in his own bubble.

Wait for our turn to step up to the line.

Wait for the signal.

I'm waiting.

I'm ready.

Six and a quarter minutes later, it's all over.

Was that fast enough?

****

Peering over shoulders at the results pinned onto a noticeboard at the presentation hall. Every time someone moves their head, you have to move yours or shuffle your feet to get a decent view through the crowd. My time is confirmed as 6:15.0 to complete a perfect set of three pbs exactly when it matters most. How many points including the handicap? 1,345. Where's the overall result? Another shift of feet, bend down to stare at the rows of digits further down the page. Catch a glimpse. Does that say 3,479 points next to my name?

People are patting me on the back. They've spotted it before I have.

I've won.

Eight years after shin pain brought my running to a standstill,.

Eight years of injury, operation, comeback, injury, operation, comeback, injury, injections, comeback, new focus, swimming, cycling, shooting, planning, avoiding injury.

Finally getting it right.

It's 1993.

I'm thirty-seven years old.

I am British Champion.

Part Four

The Closing Laps: Veteris

Chapter Fourteen: Crisis

The summer of 1993 was disrupted by another operation, although not for a sports injury: it was a vasectomy. Recovery was supposed to be easy but, thanks to an infection, it was more painful than the last two operations put together.

Going into the biathlon season, I was swimming more often than running. The climax of this was silver in the National. Then they changed the rules, imposing an additional handicap of minus 200 points on every competitor under the age of forty, effectively taking us out of the reckoning. I had one more year of modern triathlon and biathlon in 1994, unsurprisingly without medals, and then decided to return to running. I had joined the newly-formed Calne Running Club and thought it was time to say goodbye to the track, return to my cross-country roots and enjoy some low-key road races and relays.

The road relays were fun, always ending in the pub. I was elected club captain and also 'player-manager' of the Wiltshire men's cross-country team. My final race of the 1995/96 season was in the Wessex League at Blandford where I clinched third place overall after improving from eighteenth in the first round to second. It was twelve years after my last medal in the same league. The standard in the league had slipped, like most of UK distance running. It was my final race as a senior because two weeks later I turned forty.

And became a veteran.

I wasn't tempted by the disappearance of the 200 points penalty that a return to modern triathlon would bring. Armed with the knowledge gained from coaching and coach education as well as twenty-three years of running, I was preparing for a season at 800 metres and 1500 metres.

Not the marathon?

Here's how the conversation goes, one that has been repeated *ad nauseum* many times since the marathon boom of the early eighties.

'So, you're a runner, then?'

'That's right.'

'Marathons?'

(Notice it's always 'marathons'—plural—as if one marathon isn't enough.)

'No, not marathons. I run track and cross-country.'

'How far is that, then?'

'Well, there's 1500 metres on the track.'

'1500 metres: that's not even a mile.'

'That's right.'

'Not much of a challenge, is it?'

'Well, it depends how hard you run it.'

'But marathons are a bigger challenge, aren't they? You could move up to marathons, couldn't you?'

'No, thanks.'

'Why not?'

'Because I enjoy running 1500 metres and cross-country. I want to try my best to improve my times and win championships.'

'How far is cross-country, then?'

'It varies, usually about five miles.'

'Oh well, then you could probably manage marathons; really test yourself.'

****

Approaching the bell at the end of the first lap of the 800 metres at the South West Veterans Championships, Exeter.

A balding runner moves up alongside me, vying for pole position.

An old balding bloke? I can't let somebody like that beat me. But, hang on: I'm an old balding bloke. (I've been warned that there's something uncomfortable about being at an event when everyone is over the age of forty.) I pick up the pace and hold the bend.

And win in 2:05.0.

An hour later, I'm watching the back of the early leader of the 1500 metres as he pulls away.

But only so far, then I start to reel him in.

200 metres to go, I'm on his shoulder. Do I take it on now or wait until we're in the final straight? I'm feeling good: let's go now.

I win in 4:15.8.

It's my first veteran-only competition and I'm a (double) South West Champion.

So far, so good.

****

On reaching the age of forty, many runners think it's going to be easy: they're the youngest, all they have to do is match times achieved in their late thirties and they'll win. It's not that easy: it's more about managing your inevitable decline than being a slave to your times from younger days. And it's competitive: standards are high at the top level of the 'vets'.

My training was going well. I was following the five-tier system: progressive sessions at 400 metres, 800 metres, 1500 metres, 3,000 metres and 5,000 metres pace. A progressive competition programme was more of a challenge: there was the Wiltshire Senior Championship and the occasional open meeting but Calne had no track team: I was the only one. However, I did manage to run 2:01.2 for 800 metres leading up to the British Veterans Championships and a return to Exeter.

The 1500 metres on Saturday was a straight final. Showing some of my old aggression I led for the middle section and wound up fifth in my fastest time of the season—4:12.38—a pbv (personal best as a veteran). Looking at the results on the board, I thought about changing my name to Dave: all four in front of me were Daves. I won my heat in the 800 metres on Sunday and finished last in the final. This could have been another crying-in-the-showers incident. However, twenty years older, I reflected that 2:03.70 was a respectable time, it was my third race of a weekend that included a season's best exactly when it should be—in the final of the most important event of the season— and it had been a successful return to the track.

Encouraged, I wrote to the Scottish Veterans team manager, asking to be considered for selection in the Veterans' Home Countries International Championship, coming up in November. I wrote about my performances that season on track, the previous season on the country and my fourteenth place in the Scottish in my younger days. Fingers crossed, I posted the letter and waited for a reply.

Meanwhile, we were hosting the first Calne 10K road race, which was to incorporate a veterans' race and a trophy.

Dad's trophy.

The year after Dad died, Mum had commissioned a trophy in his memory for the first veteran to finish the annual road race in Airdrie. When the race ceased to be held, the trophy lay dormant in Mum's attic, from where I reclaimed it and had a new inscription added: *First veteran to finish the annual road race in Calne*. It was a proud moment when I walked up wearing my Airdrieonians shirt to receive Dad's trophy.

Unlike the long-running exchange of letters leading to my selection for British Colleges, there was a straightforward reply from the Scottish Veterans manager. It confirmed my selection for the Scotland over forties' (M40) team and provided details of where and when to meet. With the minimum of fuss, I was on the edge of achieving a lifetime's ambition: to run for Scotland.

It wasn't the World Cross but it was the only international veterans' event of the year when top quality in-depth was guaranteed. Although only five nations gathered for the British & Irish International Cross-Country Championships, this was usually a higher standard than the European and World Championships. Whilst there were stars amongst athletes from all over Europe or the World at the continental or global championships, nobody got there by selection: they all entered as individuals and paid their own way. On the other hand, only selected athletes made the start line at the British & Irish, and competition for selection was fierce.

The championships were hosted on a five year cycle by England, Ireland, Northern Ireland, Wales and, as in 1996, Scotland. In less than glamorous circumstances, I drove to Airdrie after school on the Friday, Susan drove Mum and me to Irvine for the race on Saturday, and I drove back down to Calne on Sunday.

It was a huge thrill to pull on my Scotland vest and line up to represent my country at last. In my excitement I started too quickly but recovered and ran a sensible race thereafter to finish twenty-fourth (eighteenth M40). Overtaking another Scotland M40 in the run-in, I had squeezed into Scotland's scoring four, helping the team to silver medals. It was my first international medal, although I didn't see it until a week later: we left before the presentation, because of my early start and long drive home the next day. Once again, I was an unknown: turned up, ran the race, didn't have time to get to know the team, went home.

But nothing could diminish my sense of achievement. I left wanting more.

****

Looking for more regular races as my second track season as a vet began, I joined the British Milers' Club (BMC), which had been set up to raise standards in middle-distance running by providing regular, meaningful competition. I ran for the BMC Vets in a successful world record 4x1500 metres attempt at Watford. Unfortunately, I was in the 'B' team, which failed to finish. It was no compensation that we ran a decent 3x1500 metres. However, 4:10.6 was a promising start to the season, nearly two seconds quicker than my best.

But I would run no faster.

It was nothing to do with injury, bad planning or over-racing.

It was the start of a long period of illness.

Brought about by stress.

At school.

It was another crisis.

I came to the village school in January 1996 with a good reputation, forged during six years in Swindon, where amongst my post-Snap projects had been writing and implementing a new Physical Education policy and scheme of work, and grounds development. Raising funds from grants, I coordinated the planting of thousands of trees, hedging, shrubs and flowers. Together with new fencing, bird boxes, extensive pathways and a redevelopment of the pond area, the grounds were transformed from a featureless 'green desert' into a haven akin to a nature reserve. Every child in the school was involved: from planting a bulb to designing plans.

It was in the midst of this transformation that the headteacher of the village school came to observe me in my classroom. She was visiting all candidates who were due to interview for deputy head at her school. She liked my style of teaching and saw in me what she felt her school was missing: a leader with a firm understanding of the curriculum.

I should have heeded the warning signs but, excited by an opportunity, I was in denial.

It was my tenth interview for deputy headship: could I not see that the previous nine were trying to tell me something? There were ninety children on roll in the village school but the headteacher did not teach a class. Did that not ring any alarm bells for me? She wanted a deputy head with a firm understanding of the curriculum. Is that not the headteacher's job? What had she been doing with the curriculum so far? The Swindon school was in a relatively poor area where most parents took little interest, whereas the village school was in a middle-class area, where most parents wanted to be involved, not always in a positive and helpful way. Could I not see that transplanting ideas and methods from one school to the other was going to cause problems?

If only we could benefit in advance from hindsight. In ignorance I blundered into the crisis. As well as teaching my class full-time, I developed policies and schemes of work—none of which was already in place—in every subject area. Inevitably, in the limited time available, this work was rushed, without full consultation or involvement of staff and governors. Everything had to be in place by the end of the year and a half between a worrying pre-inspection review (before my time) and a forthcoming Office for Standards in Education (OFSTED) inspection. I tried to teach my class with the same methods that had brought success before, not giving myself time to think that this school and these children required a different, bespoke approach. Almost idiotically, and shortly after joining the school, I volunteered to coordinate another grounds development project.

The number on the school roll increased to over a hundred during that year and a half.

And still there were only three classes, not the more obvious four.

My own class grew from thirty-three to thirty-nine, made up of all of the Years 2, 3 and 4 children.

And still the headteacher did not teach a class.

It was a recipe for disaster.

By the time the inspection week came along, I was running ragged.

The school did not fail the inspection.

Neither did I.

The school was not put into special measures.

Neither was I.

But strong recommendations were made.

And it appeared that I was to be the scapegoat.

Had I suddenly changed from being a good teacher to a poor one?

****

'It's not our job to advise; would that it were'.

'Improve the teaching in the middle class.'

'This is down to you.'

'If you walk out of that classroom now, you'll never come back.'

'Go and have your nervous breakdown somewhere else.'

****

Driving home on Friday at the end of OFSTED week.

I haven't failed, but I'm a failure.

As a teacher.

As a husband.

As a father.

As a person.

When I get home and walk through the door, what am I going to do?

What do I say?

How am I going to get through the weekend?

And go back to school on Monday?

How do I face that?

How do I face…

Anything?

On the edge of a steep drop.

Why not…

Drive the car…

Over the edge?

Turn the steering wheel.

Crash through the fence.

Let go of the wheel.

213

Let go of everything.

Let myself go…

Over the edge.

End it all.

Is the drop steep enough?

****

The edge of a cold loch.

I didn't do it then.

I found a way forward.

I won't do it now.

I'll find a way.

But how, what?

****

Friday evening.

I'm sitting on our kitchen floor, rocking back and forth.

Jane makes an appointment with our doctor.

For Saturday morning.

****

'*You're ill. You're not going back to work. I'm signing you off. Taking you out of the situation that's causing you this stress.*'

I've never been off with stress before.

I've always kept going.

Have to keep going.

Can't let the children down.

Can't let the family down.

Have to keep the income coming in.

'You're ill. Your priority is to get better. It's the only priority.'

Okay, I'll go off sick.

But after I write the reports, after I take the class on a planned trip, after I finish...

'No. Someone else can do all that. You're ill. Go off sick now.'

****

I'm in my classroom.

On Saturday morning.

We're all there: Jane, Sam, Emma and me.

It's a compromise.

Put things in place to make it easier for a supply teacher to take over.

Then go home.

Phone the head.

Go off sick.

215

Stay off.

Three hours later, that's exactly what I do.

****

Three weeks later.

Sixteen years of teaching plus four in training.

Twenty years.

I had never been off sick for three consecutive weeks before.

It had never before occurred to me to go off sick, despite the obvious signs and symptoms that I was suffering from work-related stress. I had responsibilities to the school. I had to keep working, get through the OFSTED week, do my best to take the school forward.

Nor had it occurred to me to give up teaching altogether. I had responsibilities to the family. I had to provide for them. How would we manage without an income?

I had responsibilities to myself, too. I had trained for four years and had been teaching full-time for sixteen. It was my vocation. It was part of me. I couldn't give it all up after twenty years.

Could I?

Then I discovered that income wasn't an issue: I would be paid 100% of my salary for six months and then 50% for a further six, when sick pay would make up the difference. For a whole year we would be no worse off.

A whole year.

Would I really be off sick for a whole year?

Then what?

'Deal with that when it comes,' my doctor advised. 'I'll keep signing you off. Concentrate on getting well.' He prescribed anti-depressants and referred me to a mental health consultant.

I thought I was the only one.

'You're not the only one,' my doctor assured me. 'There are hundreds, maybe thousands of teachers just like you.'

This was 1997.

People *still* didn't understand mental health, especially men's mental health.

But there were exceptions, including our GP. It could have been so different: he could have been dismissive. And I had experienced enough of that when I was first injured. But he understood, knew exactly what to say and what to do. Set me on the road to recovery.

A long road

Chapter Fifteen: Tribunal

Who were these thousands of teachers like me? I'd never met any of them. Never heard of anyone. Were we all in denial?

Until I bumped into a former colleague from Swindon, outside the Co-op in Calne. She was off sick too. Her feelings were similar to mine: despair, uselessness, anger, wanting to blame someone, blaming herself, feeling alone despite the support of family. So, I wasn't the only one but did that help?

At this point I should be able to recount how running saved me: how it provided a release from stress, a distraction, a different focus, time to think and make decisions about the future, a new way forward, a happy ending.

That's not what happened.

My GP had recommended exercise. That wouldn't be a problem, I had assured him.

But it was.

At first I hung up my spikes and went out for a run over the hills, trying to relax. I went swimming, cycling and walking the dogs, all at times when I would have been in school. It was a relief. It was almost revenge: doing something that I wanted to do instead of being a slave to OFSTED. If only the inspectors knew how they destroyed lives.

After a few weeks I started to train for the track again. Released from the physical exhaustion of teaching, I had much more time to recover from training, which was going well. I resumed my racing programme.

Which didn't go well.

My 5K road relay times were a minute slower than pre-OFSTED. Meanwhile on the track, I would get into good positions but when the time came to dig deep and find another gear, there was nothing there. There was no competitive urge. It felt like adrenaline had run dry. Aggression had disappeared.

I hung up my spikes again and went for a run.

This should be when I describe how I connected with nature, reconnected with myself, rediscovered…

Something.

I didn't.

I described my feelings to the mental health consultant. Were the drugs suppressing my competitive instinct? Did they have an effect on adrenaline? The consultant confirmed that there was some truth in what I was suggesting. Drugs were supposed to be help me feel better and recover from illness. If they were having an adverse effect on running, it was like putting up barriers, a roadblock on my alternative route to recovery. It was counter-productive.

We agreed that I would wean myself off the drugs.

By the end of the summer I was drug-free, and preparing for my second cross-country season as a vet. Having regained some confidence, I had started to volunteer at our local sports centre. Where, after a career of working with young children, I discovered that I had an affinity with older people. Months after withdrawing into myself, I gradually crept out of my shell and chatted with the older people. They were happy that a younger person was taking an interest in what they had to say, and they were interested in me, too. Although I never revealed the full story of what brought me to their group as a volunteer, they seemed to know. Life experience brings perception.

I took them on weekly walks, which usually ended at a café or a pub for lunch, and I started to assist the fitness instructor in the gym. The manager wanted to keep me on and, as he couldn't pay me, the centre funded my attendance at courses: fitness instruction, the National Pool Lifeguard Qualification (NPLQ), exercise referral, older people's exercise, even an IT course. Over the course of a year, I was setting myself up for a career in leisure and fitness.

I sent a new doctor's note to the headteacher every month without fail. So far, there was no pressure to return to school. I was beginning to relax into volunteering and running. One step at a time, I was starting to feel good about myself again: doing something useful, being liked.

And running well: I was called up for Scotland again.

It was odd that the British and Irish always took place in November, much nearer the beginning of the season than the traditional place for major championships at the end. The selectors either had to arrange an early trial race or rely on current or previous form. In my case, it had to be previous form: I had done nothing since the beginning of the track season. Scotland put its faith in me, which made me feel even better about myself.

I wasn't going to let Scotland down.

It was Northern Ireland's turn to stage the races. Curiously, Scotland arranged a coach journey, not flights. My journey was longer than most but I saw it as a continuation of my recovery. It was my first time away from home since going off sick. I would miss the family but I was looking forward to an adventure.

Train to Glasgow, then Airdrie to stay a night with Mum. Then train back to Glasgow, Mum coming with me to see me off. Team coach to Stranraer, ferry to Belfast, coach to Ballymena.

On the back of good early season form I ran confidently, finishing seventeenth (fourteenth M40) and third Scot. It was an improvement on the previous year. More significantly, I belonged. The long journey by coach and ferry, the two-night stay in the team hotel and the presentation and dance all fostered team spirit. Unlike the mad dash of my international debut, there was time to get to know my teammates: Archie Jenkins, our top runner, always up for it; Davie Fairweather, team manager, always there for you; Iain Stewart (not *that* Ian Stewart), always close to my standard; Colin

Youngson, another teacher, always eloquent; Jane Waterhouse, an adopted Scot, always there or thereabouts; Hazel Bradley, always cheerful.

I took my good form and renewed confidence with me on the long journey home and into the remainder of the season. Sixteen years after my first attempt, I finally won the senior title in the Wessex League, with two first places and two thirds. I then returned to Scotland for the Scottish Veterans Championship and drove back home two days later with a bronze medal in my pocket. I remember having last year's winner in my sights in the run-in. It was Fraser Clyne who, as a student, had beaten me in that representative match in Camberley and went on to become one of Britain's top marathon runners. I was in exalted company again, knowing that one final thrust would take me past Fraser and into the medal positions. It was a proud moment when I walked onto the stage to receive my first national cross-country medal.

As a successful season drew to a close, I completed my leisure and fitness training. I had been shy at the beginning of the fitness instructor course, amongst a group made up mostly of ex-forces personnel and PE student-types. Slowly but surely I found my way. Passing the practical assessment, which required a demonstration of perfect technique in free weights, was a landmark achievement for me, such a contrast from the destructive nature of OFSTED. In regaining my self-respect, I also earned the respect of the rest of the class, particularly at the final assessment when I led them in a circuit training session.

The course enhanced my own exercise routine, adding quality weights training to my usual long runs, cross-country and hill repetitions supplemented by a weekly swim and regular cycling. My mileage had crept up from the thirty miles per week of my modern triathlon days to around forty-five: not excessive. I had been able to maintain quality and quantity for a whole season and I wasn't injured. It proved beyond doubt that a sustained period of regular, sensible training leads to good racing.

Running was helping me recover from the trauma of OFSTED, after all. Volunteering and vocational training were providing me with a new purpose in life. However, school was never out of my mind. The end of a year off sick was approaching. By now, I had decided never to return to the classroom. What was I going to do when the salary stopped coming into my bank account? Working in leisure wouldn't pay the bills. Even if it did, I couldn't get a job until my contract at school had ended. Rather than let it happen to me, I decided to influence the way that it ended.

History was repeating itself. My recoveries from injury had taught me resilience, proactivity and determination. I sought advice and guidance from my GP, my mental health consultant and my union rep, Craig.

Together we formed a plan.

The doctors agreed that, when my teaching contract ended, I should be eligible for retirement on the grounds of ill health. And yet, they knew that I was getting better. It was a dilemma. At the one extreme, I was volunteering, training for a new career and running internationally; at the other, I needed to show that I was unfit to return to the classroom. Which was undeniably true: no matter how well I seemed on the outside, each and every thought of facing my demons again filled me with dread, caused palpitations, loosened the bowels, made me feel physically sick.

In order for me to extricate myself from teaching, fully recover from the crisis and start again, both extremes had to be in place at the same time. This was the challenge faced by my union rep and me as we attended a tribunal at school.

****

It's the first time I've been at the school gates since that Saturday morning almost a year ago, when I was here with the family, preparing to leave it all behind.

Conspiratorially, Craig and I turn to each other. He sighs, gives his shoulders the slightest of shrugs, his facial expression saying: here we go, good luck. Taller than me, he pats me gently on the back, almost fatherly, and we walk through the gates and into school.

Two and a half years ago I walked anxiously through these same gates, relishing the opportunity that my first deputy headship would bring, anticipating a turn of fortunes, an advancement of my career.

How could I have known that those fortunes would turn against me? That, far from an opportunity, it would be a nightmare? Far from advancement, it would end my career?

And now, anxious again, anticipating a different turn of fortunes, I hope to walk away again at the end of the evening with another opportunity: to receive an ill health retirement pension. Then I can afford to start afresh. Just like the interview nearly three years ago, everything depends on how I present myself in the next hour.

We're in the library, the same room as the interview. Once again facing a panel of judges. Do any of them understand how I feel? Do they realise that they hold my future in their hands?

I'm here tonight to shape my own destiny. It's a job interview and OFSTED inspection rolled into one. It's 'down to me' again.

The preamble describes events since OFSTED: no interim deputy head, only one of the original trio of teachers left (ironically, a previously failing teacher whom I mentored so well that she performed better than all of us during OFSTED), a switch from three to four classes, the number on roll continuing to rise (but still the headteacher doesn't teach), poor standard attainment tests (SATS) results, a lowly place in the school league tables, parents up in arms. Some of the governors are looking at me as though it's my fault, the OFSTED scapegoat their obvious target.

But hang on, the Year 2 stats, which I coordinated, brought better results than previous years, and the school roll began to rise at a rapid rate when I joined the school, so I can't have been all bad. I decide not to comment. Let them ramble on.

'I wasn't consulted on this,' states the headteacher of the (hypothetical) phased return that Craig and I sent in advance of the meeting. Her letter, inviting me to a pre-meeting, arrived on the same morning as the meeting. And sent me into a state of shock. Luckily I managed to contact Craig, who phoned on my behalf to cancel the meeting.

'I fail to understand how, after all this time, you could be shocked by an invitation to a meeting with your headteacher,' one of the governors, a vicar, tells me in accusation.

You don't understand mental health, I think. For a man of God, you don't understand much about human beings, do you?

But I say: 'May I remind you that I'm off sick?' This isn't the time to be confrontational.

There are two vicars, representing two churches. The other tries a different approach, not unkindly: 'Do you really think that this phased return will be the best thing for you and the school? Do you honestly want to come back?'

He knows. I like him. When I was teaching, I liked him. During the week after OFSTED, I trusted him, arranged to meet him, went to the vicarage, described how I felt, that it wasn't all down to me, that they should also look to the headteacher. I confided in him. I admire the compassion of this other man of God.

I lie.

'Yes.'

****

Craig and I return to the library when summoned. We've been waiting in the staff room while the panel deliberates. It's so like a job interview that it's uncanny. Only this interview is to lose a job.

They have made their decision. They tell me, with regret, that they have decided to dismiss me on the grounds of ill health.

I hold my head high as I walk around the room, shake hands and look each and every one of them in the eye.

Eyes down, the headteacher avoids my gaze.

So does the first vicar.

The second vicar returns my look. Is it sadness? Is it disappointment? He may well be the only governor who truly understands what happened here tonight. We understand each other.

****

'You coped well. Remarkably well,' says Craig afterwards. We're now in the pub, and I'm sinking a pint in relief. It's possibly the best pint I've ever tasted.

I treated the tribunal like a competition. I had my race-mask on the whole time. It was an act. I had trained for it and Craig was my coach. We had prepared well, and it appears that we have achieved the desired result.

Surely I can't be denied an ill health *retirement pension after the school has dismissed me* on the grounds of ill health.

****

I could and I was.

My application for ill health retirement was rejected. The panel (yes, another panel) suggested that as I had been volunteering, I was well enough to work and therefore not unwell enough to receive an ill health pension.

My GP and consultant intervened on my behalf, and there was another anxious wait.

Meanwhile, my year of volunteering over, I took on some paid work at the leisure centre. Not surprisingly, the relationship altered and there was less work for me. It was the odd shift in the gym and lifeguarding now and again. It wasn't enough. I needed to find another job. But even if I found a full-time job in leisure and fitness, it wouldn't pay as well as deputy headship. It wouldn't even pay the bills. We needed that retirement pension. The wait continued.

And then, like a knight in shining armour, the old mantra rode to the rescue: when your running is going well, *everything* is going well. Two letters arrived on the same day: I was selected for Scotland for the third year in succession, and I was going to receive a lump sum and annual teachers' pension.

Shortly after another improved performance at the British & Irish, and a sizeable deposit in my bank account, I was offered a new job in a leisure centre in Swindon. It was temporary and part-time, but my hours would increase with overtime and coaching, and there were many opportunities across the borough for permanent work.

At last, after the nightmares of the last three years, the crisis was over.

It was a new beginning.

Chapter Sixteen: Targets

An ex-deputy headteacher sitting in a lifeguarding chair, I was leaving myself open to ridicule. I was the oldest member of the team, an oddity. However, I was accepted for being different. I soon settled into my new role and routine, and seemed to be well-liked by customers and colleagues. It was the beginning of six mostly happy and contented years.

And safe: I didn't have to go back to school. I would never have to face that stress again.

As promised, the hours of work increased to full-time in the gym, plus coaching and overtime. I taught older people's exercise classes every week, re-establishing a rapport with older people. I learned how to climb and qualified as a climbing instructor. I also helped to start an exercise and social group, to support adults with mental health problems. Some of my colleagues looked upon the group with suspicion. When they saw 'mental health' on the duty sheets, they stood back, frowning and said, 'Mental?'

'They're not mental,' I explained. 'They're people dealing with challenges, just like you and me.'

It was the turn of the century and people *still* didn't understand mental health. But here in Swindon they tried: they changed the name on the sheets to 'Health'. The name stuck and the group is still running to this day.

My own mental health was improving. The pension, coaching and overtime supplementing my fitness instructor salary, we were no worse off financially than when I was deputy head. That brought security to the family and to myself.

I was respected for being good at my work and more importantly for being myself.

But I was having nightmares.

****

There are no children. It's the middle of term and I'm in the staff room, preparing lessons. I've returned to teaching on a trial basis and I'm doing okay. It's a turning point. Do I keep going, rediscover my vocation but run the risk of another breakdown? Or do I give it up at the end of the trial period and return to the comforts of my job at the centre? I don't know, because I wake up, the bedsheets drenched in sweat. The nightmare, with minor variations, returns another night, and still I don't reach a decision. I never do.

The nightmare comes back again and again at times of stress.

And still does.

Twenty-five years later.

****

The hours were long at the leisure centre, but the environment and routine were conducive to training. I had free use of the gym, pool and climbing wall before and after shifts. On days when an evening shift was coming up, I enjoyed running in daylight, free at last from turmoil and stress. Over the hills and *Far*

From the Madding Crowd, I was finally connecting with nature.

I never wore headphones: I wanted to enjoy the full experience. I didn't want to block out one of my senses. As well as admiring patchwork fields from a hilltop, I wanted to listen to the skylark singing high above. I didn't only smell the earth: I heard the squelch of mud underneath every stride. I felt the wind on my face *and* heard it chasing leaves along the trail. I tasted rain on my tongue *and* heard it splashing in the puddles.

One day I ran above the clouds. The sun was shining high but the valleys were shrouded in mist. Coming across some people enjoying a spot of flying with model aeroplanes, I thought: me too; I'm flying. That's what it felt like. A natural high.

Once a week I trained on the track with Swindon Harriers, including Pete Molloy, World Veterans Champion at 1500 metres, a member of that 4x1500 metres world record team, an inspiration if ever there was one, and an ideal training partner. Although a few years older than me, Pete was faster but not so much faster that I couldn't stay fairly close to him. A friendly Yorkshireman, he always had an encouraging word for me.

Minor injuries and illness aside, my performances in competitions were consistent. I won the Wessex League veterans cross-country title every year and was a regular in the Scottish Veterans team. On the track, I was often in the minor medals at the Scottish Vets and once at the British. I wasn't slowing down much, and age-graded tables demonstrated that in age-related terms I was improving.

I ran a faster actual time for 5,000 metres (15:40) in my mid-forties than I did at any time in my thirties. That was the season of my first taste of international track competition, when the World Veterans Championships came to the north east of England. Without overseas travel and accommodation, I could afford the entry fee. The 5,000 metres was run on a heat-declared winner basis: three heats, based on submitted entry times. My best performance at the time of entry was slower than sixteen minutes, placing me in the 'B' race, which I won. It was a huge thrill to win a race at the World Championships but I was outside the top twenty overall. Not exactly setting the world alight.

A strange aspect of veteran athletics is that you look forward to growing older and moving into the next age group, when you'll be the youngest and therefore in theory have more chance of winning. Entering my final year as an M40 I decided that, rather than wait until I was a year older, I would set myself a new challenge: join Swindon Harriers for regular competition on the track. Returning after a long absence to Southern Men's League Division One, I was a consistent points scorer for the team in my first season and improved steadily, from 16:16 for 5,000 metres in the opening round to 15:51, alongside 4:14 and 9:07 for 1500 metres and 3,000 metres. Meanwhile, the team had performed so well in the league that we were invited to the British League qualifying match at Bedford. Selected for the 5,000 metres, I had a problem: I was recovering from minor injury and a wasp sting, and working a morning shift at the gym. To cut a long story short, I drove to Bedford after work, arrived just in time for my race, finished second 'B', we qualified for the British League, and I won the Club Athlete of the Year award.

At the age of forty-five, I was going to make my debut in national league athletics.

But before then, there was a season of cross-country, and it was Ireland's turn to host the British & Irish. True to form as a late starter, it would be the first time I had ever been on an aeroplane. The thought of flying didn't worry me at all: it was fear of being in the wrong place at the wrong time that made me feel anxious. It helped that Clara was going to collect me at Dublin and take me to Scotland's team base near Navan, County Meath. Clara was making a life for herself in Ireland. Long after her early promise as an athlete, she was now a Leinster hockey player.

My spikes caused a minor commotion as I made my way through airport control, but apart from that it was a smooth operation. The bustle of the departure lounge was exciting. Where were they all going? Were they on holiday, business or a stag/hen weekend? It wasn't difficult to spot other runners going to an international running championship: we all had that lean and hungry look about us. I loved the anticipation as we shuffled from the departure lounge into the queue to board the plane. Excitement building like the buzz of the engine under the seats. That unique feeling in your stomach as the plane left the ground, and then you peered through the tiny window at the map-like view of city, then patchwork fields, then shimmering estuary. Into and above the clouds, waiting to relive the experience in reverse as your destination neared.

While the other teams were enjoying the comforts of hotels in Navan, the Scotland squad was accommodated at the race venue, in a building something like a cross between a youth hostel and a monastery. It had character but it was dark and cold. We were asked to turn the lights off whenever we left a room or corridor, which later caused more than one of us to bump into walls as we fumbled in the dark to find the switch. The heating went off automatically but too early: we felt cold. When one of the team went to reception to ask if we could have the heating on, the reply was: 'Well, yeez only paid for bed and breakfast.'

The course was on the side of a hill leading down to the river, not far from the site of the Battle of the Boyne, where in 1690 King James II of England and Ireland and the VII of Scotland lost to King William III, sealing James's failed attempt to regain the throne. There were no such problems for the England cross-country teams: as usual, the most populous nation won most of the individual and team honours. I won my own honours and personal battle to improve, year on year, in this race. I loved that hill as I picked off runners one by one, feeling like I could pass people all day. I entered the finishing straight in eleventh place, only losing out in a sprint finish to Ireland's Colm Rothery, which was no disgrace as Colm would, the following summer, achieve his targets as World M40 Champion at 800 metres and 1500 metres with 1:52 and 3:55.

My own targets were more modest but unique to me and achievable. Working in a leisure centre brought me into contact with coaches from different sports, and it was a swimming coach who introduced me to tiered targets. Setting single targets such as 'win the national' or 'beat four minutes for 1500 metres' will result in disappointment if you fail to achieve them. On the other hand, setting targets that are achieved too easily can reduce your motivation. The tiered method sets targets at three different levels: *should*, *could* and *just might*. There are targets that you *should* achieve if you stick to your training and racing plan and don't do anything silly. Then there are those that *could* be achieved if you stay relatively clear of injury and illness, and build up to and approach the major competitions with confidence. On a perfect day, when everything in place and all is right with the world, there are dream targets that you *just might* reach.

At the beginning of the season I had set myself the following targets:

Wiltshire Championship (senior): *should* – top eight; *could* – top five; *just might* – medal

Wessex League (senior): *should* – third; *could* – second; *just might* – win

Scottish Vets: *should* – top five; *could* – medal; *just might* – win

British & Irish: *should* – top twenty-five (sixth Scot); *could* – top twenty (fourth Scot); *just might* – top fifteen (second Scot)

So I achieved my 'just might' target at the British &
Irish. Twelfth overall was twice as good as my debut
when I was four years younger. I was eleventh M40,
which meant that only one M45 (Nigel Gates) beat me.
Four months before my forty-fifth birthday, I had a lot
to look forward to as an M45, but there were a few more
races to run before then. I went on to finish second
senior in the Wessex League (*could*), third senior in the
Wiltshire Championship (*just might*) and third M40 in
the Scottish Veterans Championship (*could*).

Alongside these triple-tiered targets, and five-
pace training (in the track season), I had been following
a triple-periodised year's plan since first gaining
selection for the annual international match. Much like
the double-periodised year with twin peaks at the
National Triathlon and Biathlon Championships, the
'triple' was designed to help me reach a peak three
times per year: the British & Irish in November, the
climax of the cross-country season in March and a
series of track races in the summer. Unimaginatively I
called the phases: Cross-Country 1, Cross-Country 2
and Track. In theory, the system made sense. In each of
three short seasons, I would lay a training base,
introduce progressive sessions of good quality, and
then taper as the key races approached. In practice it
was fraught with difficulties. For instance, most races
didn't slot themselves conveniently into the schedule,
and the peak races were not exactly four months apart.
There were few opportunities for cross country races in
the build-up towards the most important race of the
year: the British & Irish. Most significantly of all, if you
succumbed to injury or illness during a six-month
season, generally you had time to get over it, but if the

same thing happened in a four-month season, the key competitions could be upon you before you've had a chance to recover.

It may sound complicated. Distance running isn't complicated, is it? You just run distance, don't you? But I was learning from experience, including painful mistakes. I was doing my utmost to get the best out of myself.

Cross training provided variation. There was a weekly swim, consisting mainly of general endurance in the early stages of each phase, followed by more specific endurance in the later stages. Twice weekly gym training was in two parts: endurance, on the rower or treadmill, and strength.

As a fitness instructor I had mixed feelings when I saw customers walking or running on a treadmill. It's better than doing nothing but it's not as good as the real thing: why pay for an hour on a treadmill, going nowhere, when you could do the same outdoors for free? However, many customers don't have the confidence to exercise outside, and appreciate the security of the gym and, I like to think, the support they receive from the instructors. At least they should put the treadmill on a 1% incline or higher, when there is less assistance from the rolling belt and less chance of their legs feeling like lead weights if and when they do venture outdoors.

For me, as an athlete, the treadmill opened up a new realm of training opportunities. I designed my own programmes, such as a continuous run with set changes of incline: a tough, hilly challenge during the early

238

stages of each training phase, and a programme with set changes of speed for the later phase. The treadmill belt is relentless, similar in a way to a faster opponent in a race as you try to keep up with him. I endured some really tough sessions, exceeding my theoretical maximum heart rate and pushing myself to my psychological limit to maintain the set pace, willing the treadmill to hurry up and get onto the easy bits. They were emotional times. Customers saw a different side to their quiet instructor: divulged of bulky tracksuit, stripped down and skinny, giving the appearance of floating (so they told me) through the easier sections but gasping for dear life at crucial points in the programme. Those 'points' seemed to me more like hours of pain, and there was huge relief and a sense of achievement at the end of each session, which I'm sure prepared me well for races.

My strength training, all with free weights, was also progressive: fifteen reps of all exercises in the first month; three sets of ten, for example legs/biceps/triceps/abdominals for session one and back/chest/shoulders/abdominals for session two, during the second month; sets of ten/eight/six reps at increasingly heavier weights in the third month; and finally, two or three sets of six reps for the fourth month. There were also strip-sets, where you reduced the weight as you increased the number of reps, eventually working a muscle group to exhaustion, and many other variations.

Climbing introduced new elements of technique, teamwork and daring: I loved how different it was from everything else in an already wide ranging training programme. Cycling was taking a back seat, because I simply couldn't fit everything in.

Despite this wide variety, I still managed to increase my running mileage into the fifties and, a couple of times, sixty. However, as a mature campaigner in my mid-forties, I listened to my body, curbed my enthusiasm, restricted mileage to a sensible level and managed to recover from minor ailments to complete a final, successful year as an M40.

And move up an age group to the promised land of the M45s.

Chapter Seventeen: Promising

I remember a conversation with the eloquent and motivational Colin Youngson, when I revealed that I was proud but frustrated at often finishing second or third but never first in National Veterans Championships. He reassured me that I had established myself as a regular and reliable competitor of a good standard. There would come a time when everything clicked and I'd 'clean up'.

Would that time be 2001/2002, my debut season as an M45, also my first in the British League? Our team manager at Swindon was Howard Moscrop, another inspirational figure and, like Pete Molloy, a World Veterans Champion (at 400 metres Hurdles). Howard was a down-to-earth man manager, who had a knack of encouraging athletes to turn up: no mean feat, with so many other distractions in the modern world. As a coach, he knew how to get the best out of individuals, leading by example and always showing his appreciation of each and every athlete's contribution to the team. I was determined to make my contribution count and leave nothing on the track.

In a promising start to the season, I finished seventh in the 5,000 metres with 15:45, faster than I had run during my last couple of years as an M40. The higher level of competition inspired a self-confidence which I took to the Scottish Veterans Championships at Pitreavie, scene of my Scottish Schoolboys win twenty-seven years earlier.

'GOLD AT LAST!' I wrote in my training diary. Typically, I didn't cross the line first as I was beaten by the M40 winner in both the 5,000 metres and 1500 metres but I was finally a Scottish Veterans Champion, twice on the same afternoon.

I followed up with 33:13 10,000 metres for fifth place overall in the British League Gold Cup at Eton, increasing my confidence even more, as a return to the same track for the British Veterans Championships beckoned in a fortnight's time. I was due to run the 5,000 metres on Saturday and 10,000 metres on Sunday, not a sensible combination, but I wanted to keep my options open in a genuine attempt to win my first British Championship since the modern triathlon of 1993. Frustratingly, I was only fourth M45 in the 5,000 metres, running just outside sixteen minutes on a day when the winning time was slower than my best of the season.

It must be something about that track: my calves had tightened up immediately after the Gold Cup, not surprisingly after twenty-five laps, and now it happened again after the twelve and a half laps of the 5,000 metres. And I had to come back the next day to run another twenty-five.

****

It's so hot that there's a water station on the back straight. There's not a cloud in the sky as the sun beats down on us relentlessly while we circle the track.

Lap after lap after lap.

I'm in a group of four M45s. We seem to have made a collective decision to ignore the M40s: this is not a day for fast times, let's focus on winning medals. One of the four will drop off the pace and miss out, and one of us will leave the group behind and win this race within a race. But not yet. The heat is oppressive, burning from above and radiating upwards from the track with every strike of the foot. Face reddening and eyes stinging, only slightly relieved by splashes of water along the back straight.

Lap after lap after lap.

I should be suffering more than most: my tight calves were painful last night in my sleep. But the pain eased during my warm-up, not that anyone needs much warming up today. It was more of a loosening up, and the heat, like a massage, counteracts the tightness in my lower legs. The tightness disappears, replaced by growing confidence.

Lap after lap after lap.

10,000 metres can be the most tortuous race on the track. If you judge the pace poorly and start too quickly, you spend the rest of the race regretting it, each lap progressively slower than the one before.

Lap after lap after lap.

This is where my treadmill training should prove its worth, maintain this monotonous pace.

But it doesn't need to.

Because, despite the heat, it feels easy.

Because it's not fast.

Because I've run faster.

Because I'm focused.

On the back straight with about half of the race to go, a long way to run. Jostling at the water station. A group of M40s lapping our group. I'm feeling strong, and latch onto the M40s, allowing them to tow me away from the group.

Two laps later. The M40s have dropped me for a second time. I glance behind. I've dropped the other M45s. All I have to do is keep going.

Lap

After lap

After lap.

Until the last lap.

Until the finish line,

Where I become a British athletics champion.

****

It wasn't a great triumph: it was a slow time, I was well down the field, lapped and outclassed by the top M40s. But I beat everyone in my age group, so I was a British Champion.

Two Scottish titles; one British; good times at 5,000 metres and 10,000 metres; points in the British League: it wasn't a bad first season as an M45. Then came a patchy season on the country, interrupted by colds and chest pains. I was diagnosed with supraventricular tachycardia (SVT)—intermittent, rapid heartbeat—but the results from an electrocardiograph (ECG) test were clear. Probably I was simply trying to fit all my training around working too many hours.

Nevertheless, I was in the midst of a decent period of training when the British & Irish came full circle to Scotland for my sixth consecutive appearance and first as an M45. The venue was Callendar Park in Falkirk, where I had represented Airdrie & Coatbridge Boys' Brigade over twenty-eight years previously. I had a solid but unspectacular race, finishing twenty-fourth overall, some way short of my highest of twelfth a year before. However, as fifth M45, I beat my previous age group best of eleventh and, more significantly, helped Scotland win the team race. We were International Champions. It was brilliant for team morale, an achievement for each and every one of us. But it wasn't an individual gold. I had yet to win gold in the Scottish Vets cross-country, let alone a medal of any colour in the British & Irish.

I missed the chance to win the Scottish because of illness. However, I finished fifth in the British Vets at the end of the season and won the senior title in my only season in the Avalon League.

My 2002 track season opened with a reasonable run in the British League: under sixteen minutes for 5,000 metres again, but something was wrong. There was a tugging in my groin, not enough to stop me running altogether, but restrictive, annoying, and which didn't go away after rest. I eased down in training and called a halt to abdominal exercises because of the pain and reduced functionality, which was also making it difficult for me to demonstrate in the gym and at classes.

By the standards of previous delays this injury was dealt with swiftly. The gym's resident physiotherapist diagnosed an inguinal hernia on 11 June, which was confirmed three days later by my GP, who referred me to a consultant in Swindon. On 17 July, the consultant told me that an operation was required and asked me what I did for a living. When I told him that I was a gym instructor, he asked, 'Lifting heavy weights?' A simple nod from me, and the process suddenly accelerated: on the last day of July I was in and out of surgery within two and a half hours.

An inguinal hernia is caused by a weakness in the abdominal wall, perhaps exacerbated in my case by an introduction to weights training relatively late in life (typical), coinciding with long road runs on a camber. Marathon runners talk about 'the wall' at around twenty miles, when their energy stores rapidly deplete. I never ran further than twenty miles, but my wall was breached, and the abdominal contents leaked into the inguinal canal, resulting in pain and a visible bulge in the groin. The surgery pushed the bulge back through the wall and held it in place with a mesh.

Simple.

But with a long and painful recovery.

Worse than any of my leg operations.

Worse even than the vasectomy.

On the first day after surgery, on eleven pain killers, I walked 100 metres.

With a stick.

On the second day I walked two hundred.

On the third day, down to eight pain killers, I had my first bath.

On the fourth day I took an hour and a half to have my first dump since the operation.

Awkward.

But what a relief.

Gradually, I increased my walking and introduced stretching, then gentle resistance exercises, then cycling and swimming.

My first jog (eight minutes) was on 20 August, the day after a scan gave me the 'all clear'.

The next day I jogged a ten minute mile.

Look out, World (Cross)! Here I come!

But progress was slow. Every stride downhill sent a searing pain into my testicles.

Ouch!

I was due back at work after five weeks but I fell down the stairs, damaged my ribs and had to add another week to my recovery. Eventually I was back at work on 12 September, returning quickly to practical duties and reached full training by the end of October.

It was no surprise that I declined an invitation to represent Scotland for what would have been a seventh consecutive year but I did make it to the Scottish Veterans Championships in March to come away with M45 silver, better than my three bronzes as an M40. I also won the Wessex League veterans title for the seventh year in succession and surprisingly finished 175th in the English National senior cross-country at the famous Parliament Hill course in London. That was higher than before I was a vet. Standards had been sliding down those muddy hills for twenty-five years or so.

The 2003 track season didn't happen. I spent most of the summer nursing sore Achilles and hardly running at all. I was able to cross-train, which maintained my general fitness and helped me start to run again in September. However, ongoing niggles and recurring, minor illnesses held me back so much that I missed the British & Irish again and didn't achieve a full training week until the end of the year. It was a pattern that would be repeated many times until the end of my career.

Not done yet, I had a whole month of full training behind me when I made a rare appearance 'on the boards' at the Kelvin Hall, Glasgow, for the Scottish Masters Indoor Championships at the end of January 2004.

Oh yes, we were no longer veterans: we were masters now. I guess 'veteran' had ex-military connotations but we had been veterans for years, and suddenly we were masters. I had an advantage over most others: I had been a master before in my modern triathlon days. But now, masters of what? We used to be addressed formally as 'master' when we were growing up, but now? We were not grand masters of chess. Nor did we play in masters' golf tournaments. Had we attained mastery of our craft? Were we masters of our own destiny?

These thoughts never entered my head as I won the M45 3,000 metres and became Scottish Champion again. The following week I won the Wessex League February race outright. A fortnight later Jane, Sam, Emma and I were driving along the M4 on the way to Cardiff for the UK Masters Indoor Championships, where I would be amongst the contenders for a medal.

It did not go according to plan.

****

For the spectators, almost on top of the action, indoor athletics is ideal entertainment. Whereas in an outdoor stadium with a 400 metres track, you could be blissfully unaware of the shot put or high jump at the other end of the arena, everything around the vicinity of the 200 metres indoor track is so close that you don't miss a trick. The noise bounces off the ceiling, walls and the track itself as the athletes' feet thunder like drum beats, rhythmically, a crescendo rising each time they pass in front of your eyes. Lap after lap after lap.

For the athletes, waiting for their events, indoor athletics is nerve-wracking. You watch the action unfold and wonder when your event will actually start. Sure, there's a timetable, but on this day, in Cardiff, it's way behind schedule. So, what do you do? Warm up at the allocated time and then try to stay warm? Or estimate the delayed start time and warm up for that? To add to your anxiety, there's no space indoors, so you have to warm up outdoors, where you can't keep an eye on progress, or lack of it, on the track; are they catching up with the schedule or falling further behind?

Normally, I would choose the former: warm up on schedule and stay loose. But today, we're about an hour behind, far too long to stay loose and warm. So I opt for the latter.

Big mistake.

I stay in my seat with the family and watch with them, explaining points of interest to encourage them follow and enjoy the action. They retain their interest and are looking forward to cheering me on.

If I ever set foot on the track: it looks like we're still an hour behind.

After a visit to the gents I'm edging my way back to our seats.

But...

What's going on?

The M40s and M45s are lining up

For the 3,000 metres.

My race.

The timetable is back on schedule.

How did I miss that?

'That's my race!'

Emma and Sam's faces mirror my distress.

'Get down to that start now!' advises Jane.

But I can't.

I'm still in my track suit.

I haven't warmed up.

They're all stripped off and under starter's orders.

I've missed my race.

It's the first time it's ever happened.

We decide there and then to go home and not watch the race.

We're in the car park before the bell sounds.

****

To this day, Emma and Sam tell me how sorry they felt for me. They say that they can't forget the shock and disappointment on my face.

Whether by coincidence or not, I developed an uncontrollable itch, just like after Dad died twenty years before. The nurse asked me if we'd changed our washing powder or altered our diet recently. She was looking for an allergy, but I couldn't think of anything.

Blood test results all came back negative. Then my GP, the same doctor who recognised stress at the end of my teaching career, asked me if I was taking any medication.

'Only Ibuprofen for sports injuries.'

'That's it! Now you're going to tell me that you've been taking Ibuprofen for years, aren't you?'

'That's exactly what I was going to say.'

'It doesn't matter how long you've been taking something: allergies can start at any time of life.'

So that was it: no more Ibuprofen. From that day, whenever completing a medical questionnaire, I would always have to declare my allergy. A small price to pay to get rid of the infernal itching.

In time for the Scottish Masters' Cross-Country Championship.

Which,

At last,

I won.

It wasn't an outright win, of course: I was eighth overall but I was first M45.

Finally, I was a Scottish Cross-Country Champion.

Which of course made me proud.

But the next day, I was brought back down to earth.

****

I'm outside Mum's house, cleaning my spikes when a paperboy saunters up.

'Aye,' he says.

'Aye.'

'Whit ur they? Ur they fitba' boots?'

'They're running spikes.'

'Ur ye a fast runner?'

'Quite fast.'

'Ah bet ye couldnae beat me.'

'I don't know. I might: I'm a Scottish Champion.'

'Aye, right.'

'Aye: over 45s.'

'Whit? Beatin' a load ae auld grainfaithers!'

****

And that was the 2003/2004 cross-country season.

Or half a season.

Two golds in the Scottish wasn't a bad return.

For an old grandfather,

Which I wasn't,

But I got the point.

The paper boy thought there was no cross-country for old men.

I was just an old man beating other old men.

And what's wrong with that?

It's better than being overweight and unfit like most people of my age.

We're not the dying generation: we're athletes.

We run: it's what we do.

And as long as there are other old men to beat,

We'll keep doing it.

Lap,

After lap,

After

Lap.

Chapter Eighteen: Building

The beginning of the 2004 track season gave little indication of what was to come later in the year. Flying the flag for the staff in a Superstars competition at the leisure centre, I didn't place highly, but demonstrated an all-round fitness that enhanced my standing with our customers. However, my form was unimpressive on the track, where I was now in Swindon's 'B' team in Southern Men's League Division 3 (West): quite a fall from grace after running in the British League. During four attempts, I couldn't beat 16:14 for 5,000 metres, although one of them was gold at the Scottish Masters in Dumfries. It was some compensation that I now held three Scottish titles at the same time: indoor, cross-country and track.

At the end of a short summer season I showed glimpses of good form. I ran 26:45 to win the Kintbury Five Miles on a hilly course with off-road sections; 15:52 for 5K road, an outright pb and much quicker than my best track time of the year; and a 4:17.4 1500 metres, which was one of my best ever age-graded performances.

A planned break would recharge me for the forthcoming cross-country campaign. Confident, uninjured and in good health, I was nevertheless cautious in setting my goals. I had enjoyed several months of uninterrupted training but had missed most of 2002 due to the hernia, all of the 2003 track season because of Achilles trouble and half of the 2003/2004 cross-country season. Could I stay healthy, regain selection for Scotland after an absence of two years, pick up where I left off and improve on fifth M45?

Training was going well. During a family holiday in Dorset I was up before everyone else and running along the beach and cliff tops. It was impossible to avoid steep hills, not that I had any intention of avoiding them: I targeted the steepest and ran repetitions, building strength-endurance. After each run, I would take our two Springer Spaniels down to the beach to swim. Someone must have taken a stunning photograph from the clifftops of me and my two canine training partners swimming in perfect formation, the early morning sun glinting off the calm surface of the sea.

We'd all spend the rest of the day doing normal holiday stuff, although I did sustain an unusual injury bodyboarding, when a freak wave flipped me over into hyperextension on the edge of a steep, pebbly beach. It was one of several niggles treated on the physiotherapy table, although nothing was severe enough to put me off training.

After that week away I kept doing the basics: long cross-country runs; tough sessions on the treadmill; sustained road runs up to ten miles, touching six minute miling pace; my favourite cross-country reps sessions. You could do reps anywhere: find a field or patch of woodland, preferably hilly, plan a loop that takes between three and six minutes to run hard around, get your first run done, rest, repeat and go again. The exact distance doesn't matter as long as you run the same loop. As the season progressed I would add a rep or reduce the recovery and try to keep the times consistent, although times varied from session to session and course to course because of changes in the weather and conditions underfoot.

There was also a recovery swim and two or three climbing sessions every week. Focused weights training was bringing a new element to the strength-endurance fostered on the Dorset coast. There was a training method called Body for Life that we were promoting in the gym. The crux was that you could complete a quality session in around twenty minutes (plus warm-up and cool down), rather than wandering aimlessly from machine to machine. Leading by example as always, I was following the programme, making full use of free weights and cables.

My weekly mileage never exceeded fifty. Since becoming a veteran, something would always go wrong when I reached sixty miles and I would have to miss some training, unlike my younger days when I could just keep going. You shouldn't look back and try to replicate your training from those days: you should work with what you have now and look forward. I didn't repeat the sixty mile weeks but I didn't regret having done them before. They were part of the journey that had brought me to the brink of achieving something. Not more than I ever thought possible, because I did think it was possible. But more than I had ever achieved before.

Because I had been selected again for the British & Irish.

And I was feeling more and more confident that this was going to be my year.

What caused this improved form and increased confidence? Well, good form and confidence feed off each other like spreading flames. But what had ignited the flames? There was no single spark. It was a combination of circumstances: the successful second half of the previous cross-country season, glimpses of good form in the summer, resting, a week of training in a different environment by the sea, several months of uninterrupted training, and a pledge to improve my nutrition.

Most athletes know what they should be eating, and nutrition training had increased my knowledge. However, it's one thing to know, and another to do. As a club athlete you may need a selfish streak to achieve your goals, but living with your family, you can't always run whenever it suits you or eat whatever you want. There must be compromises. I would never have dreamt of dictating to the family what they ate, but I could organise my own breakfast, snacks and packed meals for work. And I made a simple pledge not to eat sweets, biscuits or crisps. Some say that if you exercise a lot you can eat what you like, but it's not true: you need good nutrition to fuel good training for good results. I still ate cake, though: you deserve some treats when you're in full training.

There was also a career decision.

Working at the leisure centre had helped me get back on my feet after the stress that caused the end of my teaching career. I felt valued, comfortable and safe.

But I needed a new challenge. I wanted to have some stress in my life again, so I started looking for another job. It would be stimulating and I could handle it. And with that realisation came the confidence to take on anything or anybody, including the best in my age group at international level.

****

The first race of the season.

The Highclere multi-terrain 10K, on my old stomping ground near Newbury.

The phalanx of 300 runners tapers down to two abreast as we exit the wide meadow and file into a narrow lane bordered by lush trees.

Nobody seems to be doing anything, so I take the lead and open up a gap without really trying.

And not one of the 299 comes with me.

I'm clear and away. I'm feeling good, so I keep pushing.

In front of the castle, up and down hills, through woodland, on tarmac and along rough tracks.

It feels easy.

Puzzlingly easy. Why am I so far ahead?

Walking through the finish funnel, a gauntlet of well wishers, parents, children, old friends from Newbury.

My winning margin is over a minute and a half, ahead of rivals who are usually much closer. On rough terrain, 33:19 is my third fastest 10K ever and half a minute quicker than my best on the track or road this year.

****

One week later I ran an outright pb of 1:12:01 at the Bristol half marathon. I could see the time on the finish gantry, second by second, all the way down the straight, and I was trying really hard to make it 1:11:59. It wasn't an outstanding time by the standards of masters who were road running specialists, but it was an achievement for me. It was only when I saw the photos and results afterwards that I realised that Nigel Gates, multiple champion on track and country, was shadowing me for miles, eventually finishing some distance behind. I guess he wasn't taking it seriously, but it was another boost to my growing confidence.

Fast forward another fortnight, and my shoelace was undone and flapping about, with a kilometre to go in the South of England (senior) road relays at Aldershot. Conversely, I was far from undone or flapping. I overtook seventeen runners on leg four, beating my own best time on this course by a large margin. Amongst the masters, only two M40s and Nigel Gates ran faster.

When you're in race shape, non-runners think you're not well. Mum might say, 'Are ye okay, son? Are ye eating enough? Ye're looking awfy thin.'

But runners say, 'You're looking lean and mean. You're on for a good run today.'

It takes one to know one, but here at the relays, a friend and rival said, 'That's a huge improvement all of a sudden. Are you sure you're not on performance-enhancing drugs?'

No.

Never.

It was all honest endeavour.

I was well. Not one hundred percent well—I was being treated for various aches and pains—but who is ever 100% when training hard towards a major race? There's a fine line between being very fit and being injured or ill, a line that I had crossed many times. It's not unusual for an athlete to be teetering on the edge. But if you always train the same, you'll always race the same. If you want to do better, if you want to win, you need to take risks. You might overdo it, get injured and miss some races, important races, maybe even whole seasons. But what's better: a career full of consistently average performances, or one with injuries, illnesses, periods away from the sport you love but, at your very best—when you've planned meticulously and worked hard towards a peak—you achieve something far superior to anything before or since?

Something that you'll never, ever forget.

****

So that was a 10K multi-terrain race, a half marathon and a 6K road relay leg. All good. And I hadn't run on my favourite surface yet. How would the first cross-country race of the season go?

The Wessex League opener.

Glastonbury.

I was rocking.

Like a lead guitarist ramping up the volume riff by riff, all the way to the final curtain.

Next gig, please.

The inaugural Swindon half marathon.

On a very hilly course, against the best road runners from Wiltshire and beyond.

Including Swindon's own Matt O'Dowd, who ran for GB in the Olympic marathon that same summer.

****

The roar of the crowd left behind in the town, we've run four miles and are heading for the first big climb. Four of us in the leading group: Derek from Pewsey, my clubmates Nathan and of course Matt, and me. I was a bit worried about a sore throat but not now: what sore throat? I'm feeling fresh and full of confidence, so I take the lead.

I'm running along the top of the hill,

And everyone else is still climbing.

Seven miles gone, passing one of the radio cars reporting back to the announcer at the start/finish area.

'It's not Matt: it's a much older runner, and he's sprinting!'

It must be an optical illusion because I'm only striding downhill. And not that much older.

I'm nearly half a minute clear.

I've dropped Matt O'Dowd, Olympian!

What's going on?

What's going on is that Matt's obviously taking it easy. He can overtake me whenever he likes.

But I can dream, can't I?

Maybe, just this once,

The Olympian will have an off day,

And let me win.

The nine mile mark, another radio car.

'He's not the youngest of runners, you know. Isn't he doing well for his age?'

The ageist remarks don't offend me: I know I'm doing well. For any age. But I can hear breathing behind me, closer with every few strides.

Matt is waking up.

He's going to pass me.

He draws level, makes an encouraging comment, which I return, and he's away.

The next couple of miles are lonely until the noise of the crowd welcomes me back into town. I recognise some voices but don't risk turning my head to acknowledge them. I'm in no danger of either catching Matt or being caught by anybody behind me but I'm on schedule for a pb: I can't let myself be distracted now.

I'm pushing hard, uphill into Old Town. It's tough, it's painful but I'm loving it. The encouragement from the community thronging on both sides of the road drives me forward to the top of the hill, along level ground to the Croft roundabout, left into the downhill finish towards the Nationwide building. Sprinting, really sprinting down the final straight, under the gantry. A volunteer holds out a medal but she's too close to the line. I'm still sprinting while holding out my hand but missing hers. When I finally come to a stop, I retrace my steps and walk back to her apologetically, nod a thanks for the medal. Someone thrusts a microphone in my face, and I realise that I'm too out of breath to say anything coherent yet. 'In. A. Minute,' I gasp.

Since re-entering town, the last couple of miles, about eleven minutes, have whizzed by. I've missed my pb by fourteen seconds, all on that final climb. But on a hilly course, finishing second behind an Olympian, it's been a much better race than Bristol.

'How did it feel,' asks the man with the mike. 'Leading Matt for so long?'

'Surreal.'

Surreal indeed: the Olympian, the community, the atmosphere,

Most of all,

Yet another boost to my confidence.

What next?

****

What next indeed. It was tempting to find a 10K, 10 miles or even another half marathon to see how fast I could run while in such good form. I settled for the Tewkesbury five miles three weeks later.

Two races before the British & Irish International Cross-Country Championship.

I could hardly wait.

'It's like another runner (a better one) has possessed my body,' my training diary declared. 'I'm going into open races believing that I'm going to win.'

I pinned on my race number—Number One—on that cool, still, November morning in Gloucestershire, where I had run my two best races of the summer; the omens were good.

****

The first mile is fast, too fast. I check my watch as I pass the marker: 5:03 and I'm slightly off the pace, behind the leading three. But I'm not worried: I know I'll be stronger in mid-race. The second mile is slower at 5:10 and now I'm sharing the lead at halfway, approaching a bridge over the M5 motorway. I've

never beaten any of these three before but they all seem
to be struggling up the short, sharp incline, and before
I know it I've opened up a small gap on them as we
cross the bridge, traffic roaring underneath. The third
mile is even slower (5:13) and, crossing back over the
M5 further north, the fourth is the slowest of all (5:16),
but I'm out on my own, full of running, holding back,
waiting to pick up the pace for the final mile.

****

On every journey up or down the M5 I can't help but glance up at those two bridges and remember those two key moments during my best ever win on the roads.

The final mile was the fastest—5:02 best ever— as I stretched the lead to half a minute for a final time of 25:43. It was over a minute quicker than Kintbury and, as I found out a couple of months later, the second-fastest five miles for an M45 in the UK in 2004.

'Did you know that you could run that fast?' the runner-up asked with suspicion.

'I knew something was on the cards: I've been running well.'

Indeed I was.

And there was one more race before the Big One.

The week before the British & Irish, my win in the second round of the Wessex League was harder work than the first but the margin was about 100 metres. I had been some way behind the leaders for the first of four laps but was confident that my pace judgment was correct and that they had started too quickly. Sure enough, I took the lead on the second lap and soon opened up a gap of fifty metres, which stayed the same throughout the third. It was only on the fourth and final lap that I pulled away. It had been solid preparation for a much sterner test to come. My training diary boldly proclaimed: 'Six days to the international: can't wait…'

An easy week followed, as I tapered towards the most important race of my life. At the beginning of the season I had set two generic targets: selection for Scotland and a pb half marathon, both achieved. My specific targets for the British & Irish were:

Should… tenth M45

Could… sixth M45

Just might… medal (never achieved before).

It seemed that everything was finally falling into place, one of those occasions when *just might* is possible. Privately, I even dared to ask myself: medal… which colour?

Decades of training under a glorious sun or through rain, hail or snow; good races and mediocre races; injuries, operations and comebacks; successes and crises.

And now,

In the best form of my life,

I hadn't put a foot wrong.

Building towards a climax,

At Croydon in Surrey,

On Saturday, 20 November 2004.

Chapter Nineteen: Peak

We're all jogging on the spot on the start line, trying in vain to keep warm on a cold, damp and overcast afternoon. There's a delay because there's no first aider on duty. This is the British & Irish Masters Cross-Country International Championship: how can there not be a first aider? Well, they're all volunteers, after all. I'm a first aider but I'm not volunteering. Not today, of all days.

The mass of runners breaks away from the line, putting tracksuit tops back on, striding up and down, spiked shoes mushing the ground into a mire.

It starts to sleet.

Earlier I was reunited with old friends and teammates. We compared notes as we warmed up around the course, keeping an eye on the women's race, where Scotland's Sue Ridley finished third overall and first W35. It's a promising opening for the Scottish squad.

Finally, a first aider steps forward and we're back at the start, closely packed: all the M40s, M45s and M50s, a seething mass of humanity nervously wishing each other well.

But I can't speak. I do wish them well but the words stick in my throat, as if letting out the briefest of comments would release pent-up tension and valuable energy stores too early. I need to keep it bottled until the exact moment. Waiting, waiting.

The BANG of the gun unleashes a tidal wave of runners, mud flying up from heels to splatter legs, shorts, vests and faces. Only 100 metres covered; red, white, green and dark blue vests already streaked with mud. It's important not to be dragged along too quickly by this rush of flailing arms and legs. Let them tire themselves out. We haven't even reached the first kilometre mark. There's plenty of time: save your energy. Nobody wins a race after the first kilometre.

Despite the mud, I can make out the numbers on the back of the runners ahead. I don't know how many are in front of me, but I can identify teams and age groups. There's only one other Scot close by. It's Steven McCloone, an M40. He's forgotten to take off his woolly hat with ear muffs and plaits. As if reading my thoughts, he tosses it aside.

There are races when suddenly something goes wrong. You lose confidence, the pain in your legs puts you off, your chest hurts, you start going backwards, the rot sets in, you convince yourself that you're having a bad run, you don't want to be there.

This is not one of those races.

I overtake Steven, and I think this makes me the leading Scot. I'm moving up and it feels like I haven't really got going yet.

Targeting a few M45 vests just up ahead, I start to increase the pace. Or do I? I don't think I'm running faster: more likely they've started too quickly and are 'coming back to me'. I recognise the running style of England's Andy Wetherill, Alex Rowe and I think it's Steve Smith, all grouped closely together. Usually they're much further in front of me but I'm closing. It's the part of the course furthest away from the start and finish area, and there's no one about other than us skinny, mud-splattered harriers, a rare species of wildlife, evading the crowds. Not that there are crowds: if any local residents are even aware that an international running contest is taking place so close to their doorsteps, they've decided to stay at home out of the cold and sleet. The only spectators are a few hardy friends, family members and runners cooling down after the earlier race or warming up for the next one. But none of them has ventured this far out. You can clearly hear the rhythmic splashing and squelching as spiked shoes slide in and out of the mud.

And I overtake a group including three M45s.

It's nearly halfway and someone shouts that I'm second M45. I still don't know how many runners are in front of me but I can spot the leading M45. Who is it? Does it matter? I'm second in my age group, I've never been higher than fifth, second is good, can I hold this position? That would be better than I've ever done before. It's my 'just might'.

Or can I raise the bar and push on?

On a cold hillside in Surrey, awash with mud, sleet falling relentlessly, it's decision time.

I'm going for the win.

271

Leading a group of M40s up the hill, legs screaming at me to slow down, a thought comes into my head, something Mr McLean, my first coach, said many years ago: 'If it hurts you to run up that hill, think what you're doing to those guys behind you.'

I don't know who they are—I'll find out later—but I turn the screw, hurt myself even more but not as much as I'm hurting them. I leave them behind, top the summit, and England's Jon Cordingley is in my sights. I've seen his results in 'AW': he's the only M45 who has run faster than me for five miles on the road.

We're running five miles today.

But it's not road: it's cross-country.

I'm in my element.

Sleet? Who cares?

Mud? I love mud!

Pain? Bring it on!

I'm on his shoulder. I've been in this position many times already in this race, and always I've breezed past, left the opposition behind.

Jon is not going to be left behind.

I'm past him but a gap doesn't open up. He's still with me, draws level, edges slightly ahead.

On another day, I might think: second is good; better than eve; I've done well; I don't think I can sustain this pace; it hurts too much; Jon's a great runner; I could stop pushing myself to the limit; ease back slightly; hold the others off; keep second place; it would still be the best race of my life.

This is not another day.

This is my *day.*

I'm going to win this,

And nobody *is going to stop me.*

I surge ahead; Jon catches up, draws level; I surge again, see a group of four, too far ahead to catch. This cat and mouse affair, now a microcosm of the race, is repeated again and again until, with about a quarter of a mile remaining, a shout from the sidelines: 'C'mon, Scotland! Ye're furst!'

I know *I'm first, and I'm going to stay first.*

Stay ahead,

Eyes forward,

Visualise:

Turn left at that gap in the hedge just up ahead,

Then 200 metres of straight downhill,

Sprint, sprint and keep sprinting,

Leave nothing on the field except the opposition,

Cross that finish line in first place.

Turn that visualisation into reality.

Everything hurts—legs, arms, chest, lungs—everything. You shouldn't be able to run so hard when it hurts so much. But you have to, you have to find another gear to make that final, lung-bursting effort.

Through the gap in the hedge,

Sprinting,

Arms and legs pumping,

Chest heaving,

Am I far enough ahead?

Don't look back,

Keep sprinting,

Eyes front.

I can hear something to my right, is that breathing?

Is he still with me?

I pick up the pace again,

One last effort,

Don't stumble,

Don't fall over,

Just

Keep

Sprinting

All

The

Way

To

The

Line.

I raise my arms in unrestrained joy, let out a whoop.

I'm the British & Irish International Champion.

There are key moments in life that you remember forever. That become your proudest memories. Graduation didn't mean much to me. Getting married was wonderful. The birth of our children was amazing.

But nothing compares with this.

I've worked for this, overcome adversity time after time,

This

Is

The

Proudest

Moment

Of

My

Life.

I turn to hug Jon. He was a few seconds behind. It couldn't have been him that I heard at my side: it must have been the wind in my ears. We walk through the funnel to join the other finishers. Only four of them? That group of four was the leading group? I had no idea that I had overtaken so many runners, that I was so far up the field. I've finished fifth overall, much higher than my previous best of twelfth, when I was four years younger. One of the four is Nigel Gates, who is in an older age group, but it doesn't matter. Nor does it matter that I didn't cross the line first: I'm the M45 champion.

Today, nothing else matters.

It's 2004.

I'm forty-eight years old.

I am an International Champion.

****

The rest of the day went by in a whirl, like the still-falling sleet. An 'AW' reporter interviewed me; that was a first. Scottish runners gathered around. It's not that often that Scotland wins an individual gold, and today we'd won two. It was celebration for the squad, a time for team bonding.

I gave Davie Fairweather a lift to the hotel. Davie had selected me year after year, trusting my judgement whether I was fit enough to run or not. He's always had faith in my running but, after today, perhaps not my driving: the car was so steamed up because of our sopping wet clothes that it was as challenging to see the road ahead as it had been to visualise crossing the finish line earlier. Everything had to be done in the right order: park the car, get the door key at reception, find my room, peel off the saturated gear, shower, text the result to friends and family, meet the team downstairs, relax, get ready for the presentation. My roommate was in the pub, so I negotiated the stairs alone, found our room, and didn't know how to get in. It was one of those card-key things, and in my naivety I didn't know how to use it. So, I dragged my sopping wet bag back down the stairs to ask the receptionist to enlighten me. She must have thought that, coming from the wilds of Scotland, we didn't know about hotels, whereas I had driven along the M4 from the wilds of Wiltshire, and didn't know about hotels there, either. Finally, divested of mud-splattered running gear (no idea how I was going to get any of it dry in time for next morning's pack run with our squad), I showered, clogging up the drains with acres of mud, leaves, twigs and who knows what else, phoned Mum and Jane, texted everybody else and got ready to socialise.

The race had been won by Guy Amos, from Clive Bromhall, Nigel, and Andy Wilton, all of England. Guy was half a minute in front of me, and there were only four seconds between first and fourth. It had been quite a battle up there at the front; no wonder I didn't close the gap. Behind Jon were masters that I had admired and read about in 'AW': Keith Newton, Mike Hager, Mike Boyle and many more. The presentation was an anticlimax, in a crowded room with poor acoustics, but nothing could spoil the moment.

Perhaps that's where the story should end. After over thirty years of not quite making it to the top, this was retribution *in excelsis*. Should I have called it a day then, retired on a high?

Well, no: I was already looking ahead. Could I take my form to the next level and win a continental championship? I had never competed abroad. The European Masters Indoor Championships were coming up in Eskilstuna, Sweden next March. Oddly, the cross-country championships would be run concurrently with the indoor events. It would be the experience of a lifetime. Could I afford the trip?

The answer was yes: it would be expensive but worth it for a chance of further glory. I might never be running this well again.

It was the end of Cross-Country 1, and I had to force myself to take a rest. Back home, after washing my running gear a few times to get all the mud out, I hid it out of sight for a week. But I wanted to *run* everywhere: I *ran* to put the bins out, *ran* to the post box, *ran* from the car park to the gym. Nevertheless, I didn't train for seven days, and headed into Cross-Country 2, rested, refreshed and preparing for a European Championship.

Chapter Twenty: Beyond

At the end of my recovery week, Cross-Country 2 began with a win in a low-key race notable only for its location on my Wiltshire Downs training ground and, because of a painful encounter with an unseen electric fence strategically placed across the line of the course.

One week later, I knew I wouldn't get close to the first two in the Wiltshire Championship—Chepkwony of the Army and Plummer of Salisbury—and so it proved. I held off the second army runner, who annoyed me after the race with a throwaway comment to his mates: 'I knew I should be beating that guy in front of me.'

That guy was me, and he didn't beat me. 'What makes you think that you should beat me?' I asked but not loud enough for him to hear. I wasn't that confrontational. Except when running.

It wasn't the most sensible idea to race in the Wessex League the next day but I was tempted to run on another of my old training grounds at Greenham Common, Newbury, and I wanted to win the senior title again. Tired after the Wiltshire, I was putting myself in a vulnerable position, and knew I was in for a difficult race when I saw Mark Hargreaves of Bournemouth on the start line. A tough adversary, Mark had won the British Masters Cross-Country Championship the previous year, and didn't have too much trouble beating me into second place at Greenham. Someone told me afterwards that, upset at his non-selection for England's M40 team at Croydon, he had sought me out to prove a point. If that was true, I took it as a compliment.

Meanwhile, life was about to take a critical turn. Fishing out a free leisure magazine from the bin at the gym, I spotted a job advert: Physical Activities Coordinator, South Severnside Council. My first thought was: I *should* be able to do that. My second was: where's South Severnside? I looked it up on the map and thought: that's a long way off, but I *could* drive there. After receiving the job pack and phoning up to find out more, I decided to apply, thinking that I *just might* be invited for interview. When I was indeed invited, I went along with the attitude: I don't actually want this job, I can't see me driving all that way every day but the interview will be good experience. Ten minutes into the interview, my opinion took a decisive shift: I *do* want this job. It was the attitude of my potential new manager that swayed me: an ex-teacher like me, he was so interested in what I had to say that I thought, if he's willing to take a chance and offer me the job, I'll take it. The next day, I received an offer of full-time employment. I didn't say yes straight away: I had the bare-faced cheek to ask to start at the highest entry point of the salary scale and with a relocation package. To my amazement, my conditions were accepted and the offer confirmed. If an employer is willing to invest in me to that extent, I thought, South Severnside is the place for me.

Three days after the Wessex League, I was driving along the M4 between Swindon and South Severnside for my first day of my new job, *terrified*.

What was I letting myself in for? Had I made a mistake? Was it one change too many? Was I really ready for a stressful life again? Had I not suffered enough in the past? Adrenaline had fuelled me through the most recent of years of adversity to run at my very best, become International Champion and get the job. But what if the fuel ran dry? What if I lost form? If I wasn't running well, would anything else go well? Could I cope with the new job, the commuting, the new lifestyle?

Full of doubts, nevertheless focusing on one step at a time, I made friends with my new colleagues in the office and started to feel my way into my new project: coordinating programmes to activate thousands of older people. The Christmas break, so soon after starting the job, gave me time with Mum in Airdrie. A time away from everything, to think about everything.

When 2005 came along, I was ready.

****

The job was going well but the new routine was tiring, and my running began to suffer. There were showers at work, so I was able to go out for a short run most lunchtimes, but it always seemed to be a rush and I was missing the longer runs in daylight that I used to enjoy before changing jobs. Running under street lights in the evening, after a long day of work and commuting, was far less enjoyable. When my Achilles started to hurt, I was forced to curtail my favourite long runs over the country at weekends.

Nevertheless, there seemed to be nothing to worry about when I won the first Wessex League race of 2005 by a minute and a half. After three firsts and a second, I had won the overall league title with two rounds to spare.

I entered the Europeans and contacted a tour operator to explain that I was an inexperienced flyer: would any of their regular customers take me under their wing? Appreciating the pun, he put me in touch with a friendly, older couple who offered to fly with me from Manchester to Stockholm. It was doable: the Scottish Masters cross-country was a week before the Europeans; I could stay with Mum and travel home via Manchester.

And Sweden.

There were a few more competitions before that key date in mid-March. I ran two short races in preparation for the unusual distance (for cross-country) of five kilometres to be run at the European. The first was 4K against much younger runners at the Reebok Cross Challenge in Cardiff. The main purpose was to gain experience of a faster race pace in the middle of winter and that was accomplished, although I had arrived in a panic after a delayed journey caused by my old car breaking down on the way. A fortnight later I finished second in an open 5K under lights of Street in Somerset. It was only 16:10 but—on a dark, shadowy course with square corners—not too far off my pb of 15:52. Next came the Wessex League again, where, although well beaten into second by a guest runner, I completed a set of four league wins for the perfect score of four points. Seven days later I returned to Cardiff for the British Masters Indoors, this time turning up to the start at the correct time and actually running the race, which was a relief after the nightmare of the previous year. Third place in the 3,000 metres, albeit with an indoor pb, was slightly disappointing but it was a means to an end.

An end that was in sight, three weeks in the future, but was I going to reach it? The pain in the Achilles was coming and going, and I was missing some training sessions. Could I hold on until the Europeans? Would it be worth it? It seemed unlikely as the pain moved up into my calf. I struggled through interrupted training during the next two weeks leading to the Scottish.

Which was painful.

In previous years I would have been delighted with fifth overall and only two M40s ahead of me. I was also beaten by two M45s—Eddie Stewart and Colin Donnelly—demonstrating the strength of our age group in Scotland. Neither Eddie nor Colin had competed at Croydon; how different might that race have been? I had never beaten either of them before, and today was closer to them than ever, particularly Colin, on whom I was closing rapidly in the finishing straight. However, it was a poor run in comparison with my British & Irish win, and I was struggling with injury. Up on my toes every time I tackled the steep hills of Bellahouston Park, pain shot from the Achilles up into my calf. It was too painful to cool down after the race.

It was only five days until my rendezvous at Manchester Airport.

Six days until the Europeans.

What was I going to do?

What I did was self-massage the calf and apply contrast bathing (alternating hot and cold) three times per day and walk, swim and complete a set of body weight exercises every day. Two days after the Scottish and four before the Europeans, a local physiotherapist, recommended by Mum, applied ultrasound and friction massage to the calf and Achilles, and I jogged two miles on soft ground. The next day it was three miles, more like running than jogging, then five miles, definitely running now, and another session on the physiotherapist's table. It was two days before the race. In only twenty-four hours' time, I was due to travel to Sweden. I made my decision.

I was going to fly.

Whether I was going to *run* or not was still in doubt. The pain had eased considerably but I was postponing the inevitable: to recover properly from this injury needed more time. Time that I didn't have if I was going to race at the weekend. On balance, I thought it was worth the risk of causing further damage to my lower leg. I had paid the entry fees, booked the flight and accommodation, and was committed to the trip. In more ways than one, I had put the miles in. If the Achilles and ankle held up during my warm-up, I would toe the line again. The trip itself was going to be a new experience for me: the first time I would run outside of

Britain and Ireland. No longer in top form but, after the past four days of treatment and self-treatment, I *should* be able to run as well as I ran at the Scottish. And that *could* be good enough for a medal, and I *just might* become European Champion. It was too good an opportunity to miss. If I didn't take it, I would regret it for the rest of my life.

On Friday morning at 2am, I backed the car out of Mum's driveway and drove downhill towards the M74. Next stop: Manchester Airport.

Where I arrived in good time but in a panic. There would be a hefty parking bill when I returned in a couple of days' time: in my anxiety to get to the meeting place, I parked in short stay instead of long stay. It was a relief when I met my unofficial tour guides, Carol and Roy. They were so friendly and helpful, that all I had to do was follow them as we arrived in Stockholm and transferred to the train for Eskilstuna without mishap. Through the windows of the carriage, Sweden looked exactly as I had imagined: people skating on the frozen river; white trees, fields and hills as far as the eye could see. Walking from Eskilstuna station to the hotel, we were greeted by snow falling thickly, something for which the championship organisers wouldn't stop apologising. But we thought it was perfect: this was Sweden in winter and tomorrow we were going to run in the European Cross-Country Championships. Snow seemed such an essential requirement that we would have been disappointed without it.

Lining up at the start, I was the only one in vest and shorts: everyone else was encased in multiple layers. Running with an injury and stripping down to the bare minimum was a gamble but the cold was numbing the lingering pain in my calf and Achilles. I was quietly confident even though, only two weeks short of my forty-ninth birthday, I was one of the oldest in a race which combined the M45s, M40s and the new M35s. Turning to see Scotland's John Brown standing behind me, I gestured to a place on the front line but he shook his head: 'It's okay, I'll no' be up there the day.'

John had beaten me by half a lap in the Scottish Masters 5,000 metres the previous summer and had won the M40 race at the World Cross-Country Championships earlier the same year. Today he was coming back from injury. So was I, but I pushed that thought to the back of my mind, focused on the path ahead and waited for the starter's gun.

****

Two of the younger runners open up an early gap and stretch their lead inexorably, leaving the chasing group to contest third place. Halfway around the fourth and final lap, although well behind the leading pair, I'm in pole position in our group. To anyone watching, I must look like the hare about to be caught and devoured by the pack. However, on a freezing hill in Scandinavia, battered by snow, all I have to do is maintain this pace, stay ahead of the pack until the final straight and then sprint like nothing else matters.

****

At the presentation there was a video of the final stages of the race. I watched myself straining and leaning into the finish, a few metres ahead of the baying hounds. I had hung onto third and more importantly, first M45.

I was a European Champion.

It was supposed to be a step up from the British & Irish but it wasn't: the standard was lower, it was poorly supported, and there was only a handful of competitors in my age group. But you can only beat who's there on the day, and I beat everyone except two M40s. John Brown thanked me for pulling him along to M40 bronze. The winner was twenty seconds ahead and out of sight in the snow. The runner-up, eight seconds in front of me, had run 8:47 for 3,000 metres on the indoor track earlier in the championships, which would have been fast enough to lap me. Yet, I had overcome adversity and injury once again.

But at what cost?

The gamble in the cold might have saved my Achilles and calf in the short term but, in the long term, there could be months of recovery ahead of me. But once they were out of the way, what next?

Britain & Ireland, then Europe, then?

The world.

March 2006: World Masters Indoor and Cross-Country Championships, Austria. I would be nearly fifty years old, almost certainly the oldest M45. It would be more sensible to wait until I was one of the youngest in the M50 age group but I was in the form of my life, or had been until this latest injury. If I could brush that aside quickly, I'd be back on a roll.

Wouldn't I?

Chapter Twenty-One: Decline

During the months following Eskilstuna, life outside of athletics was good, as I settled into my new job. Injury-free running would make it even better but seemed unlikely, even after months of rest, cross training, physiotherapy and a referral to podiatry for new orthotics. Rehabilitation, initially promising after a few weeks of running, led to nothing but further injury. As so often happens, one injury led to another: the ankle and Achilles improved but knee pain made an unwelcome return. By the end of the summer of 2005, I had stopped running but cross training was causing shoulder and elbow injuries, which were treated by cortisone injections. After missing the entire 2005 track and 2005/2006 cross-country seasons, I attended a pre-op assessment, in the summer of 2006, for my seventh operation: an arthroscopy to 'clean out' the knee joint. I had a good record of coming back strong from surgery, my confidence in corrective surgery was high and I was excited again.

Surgical methods had advanced so much, since my last knee operation twenty-six years previously, that I was pleasantly surprised at the lack of pain on the day after this one. Amazingly, my comeback race in October 2006 was an open win, albeit in a low-key cross-country event. My next race was eighth place in the Wessex League, and I was back in the Scotland team for the British & Irish.

And back to Callendar Park, Falkirk.

For my first masters race as an M50.

Only two years after the race of my life in Croydon, I was brought back to earth with a crash in Falkirk: from fifth overall in 2004, I slid down the field to forty-fourth. However, sixth in my new age group wasn't a bad debut, a mere four months after surgery. Before Christmas, I had improved in the Wessex League to third and then second, and was in contention for a series medal as a senior, never mind M50. To round off the year, I won the Wiltshire senior cross-country, sort of. Sitting at home after the race, I received a call out of the blue from an athletics correspondent. It was rare for an M50 to win a county championship, and I had to explain that I didn't really win it. I was on the top of the senior men's results list but I was only fourth: three juniors beat me. Nevertheless, it was a satisfying end to 2006.

Except that I was injured again: I stumbled on a brick and developed what felt like a bony bruise. Months later, after several physiotherapy sessions and visits to two doctors, I was no better informed and still injured. Needless to say, I missed the second half of the cross-country season, and by the time I was fit enough to compete again, the 2007 track season was over. Since taking my first tentative steps after the 2006 surgery, a year had passed, most of which I had missed because of yet another injury. Surprisingly, my comeback race was another open win, in a competitive trail race at Badbury Castle, which set the scene for my most complete and successful season as an M50.

It was a hollow victory when I won gold at the British Masters Ten Miles Championship at nearby Tadley in Hampshire: Tim Hughes, another M50, had finished ahead of me. National titles were obviously not top of Tim's priority list, because he hadn't entered the British Championship, so I won the title by default. However, I beat everyone else and ran a respectable time of 56:24. And the race confirmed my place in the Scotland team for the British & Irish, to be held in Stormont, Northern Ireland, in a month's time.

Mike Hager, a stalwart of this race and probably the top M55 in the world, was the man to beat in the M50-69 race, and I thought I could do it. Winning gold again and crossing the line first would be the perfect comeback and might feel even better than my M45 win. However, I didn't commit myself: I was in second place for most of the race but never close enough to Mike to be a threat. When he pulled away, I was overtaken by Mike Weedall of Wales and my Scotland teammate, Iain Stewart. It wasn't a collapse in form, but an onlooker's description was that my hips 'dropped' and I 'sunk' into the ground. It was something that I would need to work on, but it was another individual medal at international level.

My good form continued into the Wiltshire Championship, where I was up against Dave Bishop and Dan Wilson. Dave was on the fringe of international selection while Dan, a young senior, had been winning locally. It was clear to me that the rest of us should fight for third place and leave those two to get on with it. Dave would win easily and Dan would be an isolated second. Dan, however, had other ideas: he thought he could win. It was much to his credit that he had a real go at it but, inexorably, Dave left him behind. Dan, suffering from his earlier enthusiasm, came back to me, stride by stride. As I overtook him, I couldn't help feeling a wee bit sorry for him but not enough to stop me laughing to myself all the way down the home straight. At the age of fifty-one, I had beaten the young pretender for the first time and finished second.

It was a return to Irvine, scene of my first ever international race, for the Scottish Masters Championships in February 2008. Finishing sixteenth overall after another close battle with my old friend, Iain Stewart, I won the M50 title. Later in the season I won bronze in the M50 race in the UK Masters although, once again, I was fourth over the line, since Mike Hager, as usual, beat all of his younger opponents.

As the 2007/2008 cross-country season drew to a close, I had won Scottish gold, UK gold and bronze and British & Irish bronze, together with a silver at senior level in the county. I had also completed three series: sixth senior and first master in a local 5K road race league; sixth senior and first master in the Oxford League; and third senior and first master in the Wessex League. Now that my club was no longer affiliated to the Wessex League, it was the end of a love affair which began in 1981 at the age of twenty-five. After twenty-seven years in the league, I had run over 100 races, usually finishing in the top six, and with several outright wins but also an eighty-fourth. I had two series wins, five runners-up and four thirds in the seniors; and eleven series wins as a master, missing out only once when injury wrote off the entire season. It was a good haul in a career regularly interrupted by injury and operations.

But neither the season nor the career was over yet.

Because I finally made it to the World Cross.

Not the World Cross of my dreams in younger days, but the next best thing for someone in his fifties: the World Masters Indoor and Cross-Country Championships in Clermont-Ferrand, France. Given the expense of the trip, I would never have travelled it if I hadn't thought I had a chance of winning, but it was only a slim chance. I had been beaten into third place in both the British & Irish and the UK, and I didn't have a stack of titles like those accumulated by more successful and seasoned campaigners, but I was in good form and was enjoying a rare season uninterrupted by illness or injury, apart from a tender Achilles, which is nothing unusual for a runner in full training. It wasn't impossible that, if everything fell into place, on a perfect day, I *just might* become *Champion du Monde*.

Travelling by car, Eurostar, Paris underground, train to Clermont and finally tram, I arrived at the hotel in good spirits and proud of myself for getting there almost independently. It was just as well that I had practised my schoolboy French because in Clermont, unlike Eskilstuna, very few of the locals spoke English. Alone and slightly lost in a beautiful medieval city surrounded by mountains higher than Ben Nevis, I had to settle for an evening meal in McDonalds, not the best of preparations for a World Championship but it would have to do.

Any thoughts of winning disappeared when the fast start took me by surprise. This was no poorly supported race like the Europeans three years before: it was a strong field, and I was already some way off the pace. However, I didn't panic, picked off runners one by one and finished fifth M50. Or it might have been fourth: the Power of Ten website told me I was fourth, often known as the worst place to be in a championship race. The M50s ran with the M45s, so it was difficult to tell on the day, but fourth or fifth, I had run a well-judged race, probably my best of the season. A season that I'd had no right to expect so soon after injury and surgery.

It was strange watching the opening ceremony at the local hall that evening: my championship was already over and I was going home the next day after only two nights. The entry fees, GB kit, travel, single supplement accommodation and food had taken me £500 into our overdraft: obviously not sustainable. Unless I was going to come into a fortune, not to mention better form, this had been my last shot at glory on the world stage.

The Achilles was still tender during the long journey home. The sensible thing to do was to rest and recover but I was enjoying myself, and there was one more race to run: the Grove half-marathon in Oxfordshire.

There's a photograph of me looking confident and running with a relaxed, upright style, in my black and white Swindon vest, and black shorts, gloves and socks on a black road with verges of white snow. The only splash of colour is my pair of bright yellow racing shoes, which I should never have worn that day. A super-light design, intended to be thrown away after a 100 kilometres of running in races of up to ten miles.

Common sense was to run the thirteen miles in a less flimsy pair.

Despite thirty-five years of experience, common sense deserted me.

Nevertheless, I ran a good race, gradually catching all but one of the runaway leaders, and feeling comfortable and pain-free. Until the ten miles mark, when I rounded a sharp bend and felt more than a twinge in the Achilles. The pain increased during those extra three miles, but I held on to second place in 74:43 and completed the season. A season of one race too many, with or without flimsy shoes. I would rest the Achilles, recover and return to form on the track.

Or so I hoped.

****

I missed the entire 2008 track season as one injury led to another and the pattern for the next three years set in: injury, recovery, illness, recovery, injury, recovery. At least part of each track or cross-country season, usually all of it, was written off. Most of the time, I was able to cycle and swim. Once a month during late spring, summer and early autumn I would cycle the fifty mile round trip to work and back. And once per week I drove halfway and cycled the remainder. I swam regularly in the pool and, on holidays and days out, in the sea. Then I discovered that if I cycled to the Cotswold Water Park early enough, I could sneak through a side gate and swim from the beach area before anyone else arrived. I set myself the challenge of the forty mile round trip with a swim at the turnaround point every weekend throughout the summer, which I achieved. Including the Swan Incident…

****

Swimming inside the roped-off area, I'm aware of a family of swans on the other side of the rope. Pool mentality reassures me that I'm in my lane and they're in theirs: we'll get along fine, minding our own business. But Daddy Swan doesn't know about lane swimming etiquette: he thinks I'm a threat to his babies. Hissing and honking, he traverses the lane rope in an instant, rearing and flapping his powerful wings, threatening. I've never swum so fast in my life as I flee from that angry cob. Seconds later I'm standing on the beach, watching him glide away with his mate, with several tiny cygnets in tow. Human families have started to arrive to stare at the spectacle. It's like that scene in Jaws when everyone is afraid to return to the water.

While the swans swim serenely into the distance, I spot a row of large, bright yellow buoys at the other side of the lake.

'That's Waterland,' explains the lifeguard. 'They do proper open water swimming there.'

****

On my fifty-fifth birthday in March 2011, despite minimal winter preparation, I was determined to mark my entry into the M55 ranks with my first track season and injury-free summer for seven years. Seven years of bad luck? There seemed little prospect of that luck changing but I made the same decision that I had made on my fortieth birthday: I would return to the 800 metres and 1500 metres.

When you're one of the oldest in your age group you can't help but look at the performances of the fastest runners in the next one. Surely you won't slow down that much. But you do. The first time I ran slower than 16:30 for 5,000 metres was a shock. How could I run so slowly when I had been able to run under sixteen minutes only a few years earlier? And then I ran 17:00, then 17:30, and wished I could still run 16:30. And now, at fifty-five, how would my 800 metres and 1500 metres times compare to my 2:01 and 4:10 as a newcomer to the masters scene in my early forties?

My early-season efforts were abrupt reminders to look forward, not back. 2:20 and 4:50? Let's focus on the championships, starting with the Scottish Masters at Meadowbank, where (for a change) I was the youngest in the M55+ 1500 metres. The youngest but not the fastest: Alastair Dunlop lined up alongside me. Alastair had been winning national, continental and world championships for years. He was probably the most travelled master of all: even the shortest journeys from his home in the Hebrides to Scottish Championships were, by most people's standards, major excursions. I told Susan and Mum that I would probably be second, but I had a plan. Warming up, I was hit by a strong gust of wind (and a thought) as I turned into the stadium. Nobody wants to lead on a windy day. Nobody expects anyone to go off quickly. If I did just that, nobody would expect me to stay ahead. This early in the season, maybe Alastair would underestimate me and let me build up a lead until it was too late to chase me down. Maybe the wind would work in my favour, like it did for Alan Pascoe on the same track in 1973, when he hit 'a brick wall' but won his European Cup race, while Dad and I watched from the stands. It was a bold plan, setting myself up to be shot down at leisure by a serial international champion. But the plan worked and I won.

It was the only time that I won a national masters championship and crossed the line first.

Alastair would later peak to perfection, finishing second in the World M55 800 metres during a season in which he ran under 2:10. While Alastair used the Scottish as a springboard to success at world level, I made a raid across the border to win the Welsh M55 800 metres and 1500 metres double. Then at the UK Masters I led the first three laps of the 1500 metres but this time the tactics didn't work: I was overtaken by the eventual winner and then in the home straight by the winning M60. It was a limp performance, not the biggest boost to my confidence as I drove back to the Alexander Stadium with Jane the following day for the 800 metres final.

****

'Oh, no! I'm not on the start list!'

298

I turn in a panic from the notice board to Jane. Yesterday I thought I understood the entry-declaration-reporting procedure. I thought that yesterday was too early to declare for today. I was wrong: I've missed today's deadline. The start list has been finalised and I'm not on it. I've dragged Jane a hundred miles up the road for nothing. What am I going to do?

Well, I talk nicely to an official and explain my mistake. She listens patiently, understands, and adds me to the start list.

So here I am. Another start line. Another national championship. There are only four of us but I know that the other three are all good 800 metres runners. This will be a competitive race.

In the home straight for the first time. There's a runaway leader but he's not getting any further ahead. I'm tucked in behind the next two.

The bell. 'sixty-five, sixty-six, sixty-seven...' Faster than I've run for years. I move up to second and chase the leader.

In the back straight for the final time. I'm closing. Feeling the fast pace, but closing.

Round the final bend. I'm hurting but still closing. Push myself, draw level on his outside, the home straight will take care of itself.

Into the final straight and into the lead. If it's hurting me, what's it doing to the others? After all these years, after yesterday's disappointment, I'm leading again, and it's 800 metres; cross-country runners aren't supposed to win national championships at 800 metres. Visualise: crossing the line in first place. Only sixty metres to go. I'm going to win. British Champion. What a comeback!

Fifty metres to go. Oh, no! What's happening? Someone draws alongside, edges ahead. No! Forty metres. Come on! One final effort. My brain works, my will to win is as strong as ever but my legs don't respond. It's a feeling unique to 800 metres: it's been described as 'treading water' or 'tying up'. I'm in a film, playing at slow speed. And there's nothing I can do about it.

****

At the finish line I was a full second behind the winner, Stewart McGregor, another Wiltshire runner returning to the track after a long absence. Entering the final straight, I thought I had timed my race to perfection. But I hadn't: Stewart had. My time was 2:17.87, by far my fastest of a season in which, with the exception of the UK 1500 metres, I improved race by race.

'If someone had told me on my fifty-fifth birthday that I would win the Scottish and Welsh, get two silvers in the British and make the UK top four in three events in the Power of Ten rankings, I would have taken all that.'

So said my training diary at the end of the 2011 track season. And all on no more than thirty miles per week. More significantly, it was without injury, a trend that continued into the 2011/2012 cross-country season, with an increased weekly mileage of forty, together with weekly cycle rides, swims and weights sessions. Bronze at the British & Irish was the highlight of the season, whereas the same colour of medal in the Scottish was a disappointment. I won the over fifties title in the Oxford League, but was finishing in the forties, rather than the top ten of only a few years earlier.

Although I hated to admit it, I was feeling my age.

****

2012 was the year of the London Olympics and much talk of Olympic legacy. There had been little previous evidence worldwide of a resultant increase in physical activity following any host nation's Olympics. Could we buck the trend? My job had moved on somewhat from those early days as a physical activity coordinator for older people. I was managing a large team and leading on projects such as child and adult weight management, exercise referral, health walks and physical activity strategy. I suggested to my manager that the most effective way to establish an Olympic legacy, increase physical activity and develop running in our area would be to start a parkrun.

During an unremarkable track season for me, I ran faster in 5K parkruns (17:29) than for the same distance on the track. But that wasn't my main motivation for running them: it was product awareness. Parkrun was on its way to becoming the global phenomenon it is today. Its ethos was simple: any age or ability, free entry, a one-off registration online, 5K, in a park, 9am, every Saturday, all year round, just turn up. In 2012 it cost £6,000 to start a parkrun: half funded by parkrun's sponsors and the other half from the local organisers. However, local authorities don't pay VAT, so for a one-off investment of £2,500, South Severnside Council would gain a lifelong physical activity intervention run locally by volunteers. We would also have access to any amount of stats to demonstrate its effectiveness. Each parkrunner has a unique barcode which is scanned at the end of any parkrun that they choose to run, anywhere in the UK and in many other countries. Within an hour or so, results are available online: finishing, age-group and gender position and time, all compared to previous performances. With a little help from parkrun HQ, we would also know which postcodes were represented by participants, an important public health statistic.

You have to be there to see the unique appeal of parkrun. Although there are a few good club runners, the vast majority of participants are not athletes: they are people of all ages, shapes, sizes and cultures, who run to improve their health. It's no wonder that parkrun is seen by many as the most effective investment in public health, ever. I listened to the run directors and volunteers talk about the positive impact on their community. And participants told me about the huge difference parkrun makes to their physical, mental and social health.

Without further ado, our senior management put up the cash in principle. Now all I had to do was find a venue and recruit a team of volunteers. After running round in circles in various parks, I settled on

Vale Park and met with the local parish council, in particular one councillor who saw the benefits to the community and was keen to get it off the ground. We held a taster run one evening, which attracted over 100 participants and, crucially, a group of volunteers, who became the run directors under the guidance of the event director. After training, the first event was all set to go ahead in the autumn.

At the same time, a partnership with England Athletics was established, to form Run England groups and set up 3-2-1 running routes in South Severnside. Run England groups were not affiliated athletics or running clubs: they were semi-formal groups, led by qualified and insured volunteers. Unlike the old days when only club athletes pounded the roads, there were hundreds of ordinary people running, many of whom would appreciate the supervision and companionship that Run England groups offered. The project began in our own workplace. Several of us trained as Leaders in Running Fitness (LiRF) and then, on the Monday after Super Saturday, we started our recruitment drive at work. We could not have chosen a better date. The buzz created by Jessica Ennis, Greg Rutherford and Mo Farah, all winning Olympic gold within the same hour in London, spread across the UK, including our offices. Colleagues signed up in droves, so many that we set up three different groups—before and after work and at lunchtime—for a 'go live' date in early autumn. We also established the area's first 3-2-1 route, the same route as the Vale Park parkrun, marked out with posts and publicised online and via an illustrated information board on site.

Back on the track I was almost involved in a row at an open meeting in Cheltenham. Apparently, as Jane told me after the 1500 metres, a couple of young athletes in the stands were making fun of me as I trailed round in last place.

'Look at that old bloke at the back! What's he doing here? He's either gonna be last or the judges'll disqualify him for lifting.' Or some such wit.

'Do you not think I have a right to run, then? Have you never heard of ageism? How about encouraging me? What are your pbs? Do you want to know what mine were at your age? How many international titles have *you* won? How many national? Regional? County? What are your aspirations?'

I didn't really say all that. I didn't say anything. I still wasn't confrontational. Besides, I finished second last, not last.

My undistinguished track season drew to a close at the British Masters 10,000 metres Championship in Oxford. I had no idea that it would be the final race of my final track season.

A race that I still haven't finished.

It was a struggle for twenty-three or twenty-four laps but then I heard the bell and set off in pursuit of the athlete in third M55 position, overtaking and running away from him in the home straight to claim bronze, a consolation prize for a poor run.

Until the bell rang.

Again.

There was another lap to run.

Amidst the confusion of lapped runners in multiple age groups, an official had miscounted the number of laps. And so had I. Exhausted, confused and not entirely convinced that the lap count was wrong, I watched helplessly as the real bronze medallist ran past me and into this final lap. The logical decision was to get up and run another lap, but I was too tired for logical decisions.

So that was that. Twenty-four laps and still not finished. One day, in a parallel world, I might go back and finish the race.

Meanwhile, in the real world, things were about to go from bad to worse.

Part Five

An End to Running

Chapter Twenty-Two: Decision

On holiday in the New Forest, I took a wrong turn, driving to the start of a local trail race. The map showed a road across a dual carriageway but it was closed to traffic, so we had to take the long way around. Arriving too late to warm up, I collected my number, rushed to the loo and reached the start line with only a couple of minutes to spare. It was far from ideal preparation, but I ran sensibly and finished third, one place higher and about a minute quicker than the year before.

A few days later, in the middle of a reps session on the heathland, I realised that there was something wrong with my right knee. It felt different from the pain in the left knee that led to my 2006 operation. This was sharper, with pain lingering into the night, disturbing my sleep. I couldn't blame one race for the injury: there must have been an underlying problem. I had managed to get through a year and a half without injury, but now, older and wiser, I was pragmatic, as my training diary notes show:

'Sooner or later the right knee will need the same operation as the left. There will come a time when I won't be able to run any more. I hope to delay both occurrences for as long as possible. I'm hoping to run well at least until the international.'

The British & Irish was in a fortnight's time, and my taper began early. There was one more race before the main event: the Oxford League, when I exceeded my expectations by finishing twenty-fifth (twenty places higher than the previous season's race) and first M55.

'Amazingly, the knees don't hurt!' my training diary stated boldly. 'I guess it just takes longer to recover from a long race these days (not helped by having no time to warm up in the New Forest two weeks ago). I seem to be coming into form at the right time.'

Pragmatism had been temporarily replaced by optimism as I boarded the plane four days later. Although the race would be in Belfast, I flew to Dublin because Emma was working as *au pair* to Clara's two sons. It was an ideal opportunity to incorporate a family visit into the adventure. Queen's University campus hosted the races, and also their weekly parkrun. Emma missed the first ever parkrun in the Republic of Ireland (in Malahide, close to Clara's home) to run her first in Northern Ireland and support me in the afternoon.

Shortly after the last parkrunner finished, the build-up towards the start of the international race began: light lunch, team photographs, collect numbers, jog around the course, reunite with old friends. One was Dave James, whom I hadn't seen since that British Colleges race twenty-five years previously. He didn't remember winning easily or asking me if I had known his times when we were students. Now we were M55s and Dave was beginning to reignite his athletics career.

While I was beginning to realise that mine was drawing to a close.

****

It's eyeballs out in the approach to the final section. I've held off all pursuers in a long run for home but I can't shake off Ireland's Brian Lynch. I know I'll be out of the medals but fourth isn't bad, and Mike Hager is just up ahead. If I can throw caution to the wind, hurtle through this final expanse of mud, hold off Brian, catch and overtake Mike, I'll know I've done the best I possibly could.

But I don't hurtle, I'm too cautious, I slide around in the mud as Brian overtakes me and Mike stays ahead.

Fifth is good, probably a better performance than my third place of last year, but I'm disappointed. Normally I'd have to wait another year for my next chance. But I can see the future. This was my final performance on the international stage.

I'm bent over double, breathing laboriously. Great gulps of air, chest heaving. Hands on knees, I can't stand up, can't look up, can't respond to Emma saying, 'Well done. Are you okay?'

I should have finished more strongly and left nothing in the mud, that essential ingredient to cross-country, which ironically was the problem today. That and confidence.

In the changing rooms I'm feeling faint with the effort. I must look pale because Colin Youngson offers me food and an energy drink. Dave James and I shake hands. (I beat him at last.) Brian suggests that we swap vests. He hands over a brand-new one because he wants to keep the one he wore today.

'That vest got me a medal,' he says.

'But, Brian,' I reply, *'I'm sorry, but we were fourth and fifth, not third and fourth.'*

I'm not the only disappointed athlete in that changing room. How fickle are fortunes in the sport that we love.

Fortunes lost in the mud.

****

Back at work, our first parkrun went off without a hitch and we were already looking at a second venue. Our three workplace running groups were well-attended. Years since I had last coached running, I was loving it, supporting colleagues and introducing them to the basics of distance running in a fun way. I buzzed all the way home from work every Tuesday evening.

My own performances in competition continued to improve despite the right knee pain and a new injury to the left heel. But I knew that I was running on borrowed time. Sometimes in a cross-country race with multiple laps, I would use a motivational technique of telling myself that I was passing landmarks for the final time—the sharp turn around a tree, the short section of gravel, through the woods, along the river bank, up the hill—one more time around and then it's all over. Just keep running. Finish the race. My whole season, my whole career, forty years of running, was like that race. One more county championship, one more league race, one more Scottish Masters, one more time around and then it's all over, just keep running. Finish the season. Finish the career.

When I was in my twenties, my first significant injury sent me spiralling into depression. By my thirties, I coped with injuries by finding other interests. I came back in my forties to much improved form and my best ever competitive performance. Coming back from injury in my fifties was almost as good. Each and every time it was corrective surgery that gave me hope, a new challenge and increased motivation to carry on. This time it was different. Mid-season, the pain didn't seem bad enough to merit surgery but I knew it was coming. Could I extend my career again: another operation, another comeback? I didn't think so. Not this time. At the age of fifty-six, finally an auld grainfaither, I was looking ahead to old age. I didn't want to be so crippled that I couldn't play with my grandchildren. However, if this season, after years of unfinished seasons, was to be the final campaign, I was determined to finish it.

Susan drove me from Airdrie to and from Forres in the Highlands for the Scottish Masters. My sister had been my driver and number one supporter for each and every one of my races as a master in Scotland: track, cross-country and indoor, all national or international championships. In this, the last one, I improved to second M55 but the next day, running on my old stomping ground in the Monkland Glen, my knee and heel were so painful that I had to stop and walk back to Mum's house.

That should have been the end but it wasn't. After a few days of rest and a visit to the doctor, I started running again. My GP understood my need to complete the season and get to the end. She introduced

313

me to the new 'choose and book' system, which made it easier and quicker to see a consultant, in this case at the new NHS treatment centre in nearby Devizes. Then came an incident at my workplace running group that encouraged me to make an appointment and a decision about the remainder of the season.

I was at the back of the line, jogging from the office to the local sports fields, when my right knee suddenly locked. At first I couldn't move the joint at all but, after a short walk, I managed to 'shake it out' enough to enable me to hobble along and supervise the session. Painfully.

When I got home that night I cancelled all but one of my remaining races. The exception was the final Oxford League fixture. If I could cross-train alongside minimal running training for the next few weeks, I could make it to the final race of my final season, win the M50 league (there was no M55 category), see the consultant and call it a day. I knew that I was risking further, possibly permanent, damage to the knee (and heel) but the risk was balanced by the satisfaction that I would gain by completing the season and winning at the last. All I had to do was finish the race.

****

Every step hurts. To the left: the heel. To the right: the knee. If it had been a flat course on soft grass it might not have been so painful. But it's the worst type of course for these injuries. Stony ground is aggravating the heel, and tight corners and sharp descents are sending jabs of pain into my knee.

It ends here. Come on, the finish is in sight about 100 metres ahead. You've run thousands of miles, it's only 100 metres. Pick up the pace, sprint for the last time, you can do it.

Ow! A sudden pain shoots into my knee. This must be what it feels like to be shot. Just keep going, limp, jog, walk, crawl, do whatever it takes to end the season.

I stagger to a dead stop. I've made it over the line. I can't run any further, not even to cool down; I'm having enough trouble walking. Hobbling to the changing rooms, it feels like my knee is going to snap, leaving my lower leg dangling grotesquely.

It's not another crying-in-the-shower-scene like the one nearly forty years ago in Glasgow. Here in Oxfordshire there are no tears. There is stoicism. Trying to mask the pain, although putting one foot in front of the other is a major effort, I'm focused on making it to the presentation. Then standing and waiting to receive my end of season medal. Because I've done enough to win the M50 league.

Even standing is a feat of endurance. There are no chairs and nothing to lean against. The stuffy hall is overcrowded, and I'm feeling sick and faint. All I want to do is collect the medal, go home, get this knee and heel seen to, and rest.

'Looking forward to seeing you next season,' says the local dignitary as she hands me my medal.

'Thank you, I hope so.'

315

No chance.

There doesn't seem to be much chance of getting home safely, never mind coming back next season. Is it safe to drive? A clubmate offers me a lift home. I'm touched by his kindness, but how would that work? I'd have to leave the car behind. How and when would I get the car home? If I can make an emergency stop I can drive the hour and a half home. It's a dangerous risk but I take it, and bring my medal home. I've completed the season, but at what cost? Is it worth it? This small piece of metal in my pocket? But it's not only about the medal: it's about getting to the end. The medal is a symbol of that final achievement. I have to take the medal home safely.

Often, when you finish a race, when you're allowed to stop pushing yourself, when you've left everything on the field, when the pressure is off, when adrenaline fades to nothing; suddenly you can't run another metre. Except that after a rest, you usually can; you jog, you cool down, you recover until you're ready to go again.

When I parked the car at home, I could not drive another metre. I couldn't remember much about the journey, and the thought of driving again made me feel nauseous. As I struggled to open the car door, and to lift my right leg manually, in an attempt to swing around and climb out of the car, I couldn't. Jane came to the rescue and helped me out of the car. And back in on the passenger side. And drove me straight to the minor injury unit in Chippenham.

As close to the entrance as possible, Jane helped me out of the car again. As I stood there, wobbling, I thought: what am I going to do now? The slightest movement of the right leg sent searing pains into the joint. The left heel wasn't much good for standing on.

'So, it's not an injury, then?'

That's a rhetorical question from the nurse.

'Oh, it's an injury, all right.'

The nurse and I have differing definitions of 'injury'.

'On a scale of one to ten, how bad is the pain?'

The race I've just put myself through, never mind forty years of training and racing, is testament to my high tolerance of pain. But...

'It's pretty close to ten.'

****

I was sent home with a flea in my ear, and crutches, and told to rest and not drive for at least ten days, take paracetamol and get along to see an expert. Which was lucky, as my prearranged appointment at Devizes was coming up.

Travelling to work was out of the question. Turning in bed was painful enough. I worked from home and left the house only for short walks with the aid of my crutches. And to meet my new consultant in Devizes.

I can't speak highly enough of the NHS treatment centre and my consultant. I was treated like a VIP from the moment that Jane and I walked from the spacious, free car park, into the equally spacious waiting room. The friendly receptionist told me to take a seat; it wouldn't be long. She was right: hardly had I time to look at the widescreen TV or leaf through the decent selection of magazines when I was called to the consultation room. Mr Bartok, a young doctor in decent shape and with a pleasant smile, immediately took me seriously and understood how important it was for me to run, even stating that he wished he was as fit as I was. He took an x-ray of the heel there and then and arranged a scan of the knee for the next day at a different clinic. My follow-up appointment was in a fortnight's time, on the second of April: our silver wedding anniversary, when we would be on holiday in the New Forest again.

Jane was understanding: it wouldn't take me long to drive from the forest to Devizes, even though it was nearly all the way home. The appointment was early enough in the morning for me to be back by lunchtime, plenty of time for us to celebrate our anniversary and enjoy the rest of the holiday.

I returned to the forest with good news: I was going to have an operation in only a week's time, a few days after the end of our holiday. Surgery by arthroscopy would repair two torn menisci in the knee. The bruise on the bone of the heel would be treated by anti-inflammatory gel and by experimenting with different shoes and inserts: surgery would be too invasive. There was every chance that I'd be running again.

Running again.

It was a dilemma. During the past six months I had reached a state of pragmatism: this was my final season. I would not be running again; it was more important to be healthy and fit for everyday tasks; enough damage had been done; don't push it again; it's not worth the risk. Yet, here was an expert telling me that I *could* run again. Mr Bartok believed in me and I believed in him. To run or not to run? Maybe I could just go out for a run but not train to compete. The decision would have to be mine.

After the operation.

Is it possible to be addicted to surgery? This would be my eighth operation, seven of them for sports injuries. You're given some drugs, you fall asleep and when you wake up, a part of you has been fixed. You enjoy a cup of tea and a biscuit, go home, doze off, get looked after. Then comes the welcome challenge of rehabilitation and a gradual return to training and, eventually, competition. I was as excited as ever but this felt different. I thought it unlikely that I would be competing again. But at least I would have a choice, something that seemed impossible when in excruciating pain after that final, tortuous race in Oxfordshire.

Diligently, I performed the recommended exercises four times per day, walked with the aid of crutches and took pain killers. After a couple of weeks I returned to swimming, then cycling, and after two months of restricted range of movement, jogging. By the end of the summer, four months after the operation,

I was running between twenty and thirty miles a week, supplemented by swimming, cycling and core stability exercises. There were good days and bad days. On a good day I could forget about the lingering pain, run freely and even raise the pace to complete a set of reps (but no races). On a bad day, I was back on the pain killers and resting. The right knee was taking a lot longer to recover than the left knee did seven years ago. The left heel wasn't much better.

And the left *knee* was starting to give me trouble.

Meanwhile, at work, our recreational running project was going from strength to strength. Two sites were confirmed for our second and third parkruns, several new 3-2-1 routes were set up, and I successfully applied for a grant to train twelve new run leaders who would start Run England groups in six areas of high health need. Other runners stepped forward and started up groups in their neighbourhoods. Progress wasn't limited to running: I made a small Olympic legacy grant available for twenty community groups to organise local sports and physical activity initiatives. In recognition, our County Sports Partnership made me their Shining Light, which led to a visit to the Olympic Stadium and a presentation by Lord Sebastian Coe. I also won the South West Run England Project of the Year award, presented at a special event in Exeter. I was helping hundreds of people to help thousands more to become more active. It was an exciting time.

However, for me, becoming more active came with a price.

On one of my good days, in September, I was running freely around the course of one of our imminent parkruns. It was a warm, clear and sunny day; the air was clean, and there were far-reaching views over the rooftops to the hills beyond. It was only a run in the park but I could imagine hundreds of local residents enjoying this experience in the months to come. In that sense, it was the perfect run.

How was I to know that it would be the last of its kind?

I should have known: for years, I had spent more months not running than running. What happened the next day should have been no surprise to me.

There was something far wrong with my right knee again, and my running ground to a halt.

Again.

Ironically, I had been back to see Mr Bartok and was looking forward to another operation to my *left* knee in October. But here was a new problem with my *right* knee. It felt different than any of my previous injuries: the knee was 'catching' or 'hanging', especially when descending stairs. I tried cycling but couldn't push down on the pedals without pain. The same thing happened when I swam and tried to push off the wall.

When I phoned Mr Bartok to tell him of this new development, he offered a postponement of the operation until he could examine the right knee. He also proposed an alternative: I could go ahead with the surgery to the left knee, then he could examine both knees at my follow up appointment. I chose the latter option.

Two months after left knee surgery—followed by a scan, thousands of lengths of the pool, some cycling and a painful confirmation that the right knee would not take any more running—Mr Bartok's demeanour told me that it was not good news.

'There is worsening of lateral femoral condyle bone bruising or stress oedema. The stress reaction is most likely to be degenerate but spontaneous osteonecrosis is in the differential.'

In other words, part of the thigh bone was dying due to a lack of blood supply. It was only a small section of bone but if I wasn't careful the bruising could spread. And if that happened, the only option was a total knee replacement. Mr Bartok told me that I was doing remarkably well, considering the serious damage to the joint. He would reassess the knee in three months' time but only if I promised not to run or cycle in the interim. I could swim, as long as I didn't push hard off the wall, and I could walk. With a stick.

All this from the same person who had previously complimented me on my fitness, praised my perseverance and given me hope that I could run again. But now he was telling me that if I didn't look after the joint, it would have to be surgically replaced. Three times he said, 'I'm sorry about the bad news.'

It was a shock. Osteonecrosis: that was a new one on me. One that I had to take seriously. A knee replacement was not an option I was ready to consider.

That's what happens to old, unfit and overweight people. It wasn't going to happen to me. I wasn't having that.

I did everything he advised.

Except walk with a stick.

I wasn't having that, either.

Oh well, at least my heel was much better.

The reassessment was on 2 April 2014, exactly a year after our silver wedding anniversary. A scan showed no change to the osteonecrosis on the lateral side, but there was a new, smaller bruise on the medial side. How had that happened? I had followed instructions to the letter (except the one about walking with a stick). Surely this new bruise hadn't been caused by unaided walking.

Before I had a chance to pose this question, Mr Bartok explained that there was, after all, an alternative to total knee replacement: retrograde drilling, which would give me a good chance of a return to unrestricted swimming and walking, cycling and possibly low level running. The drilling would go in from the side and wouldn't damage or even touch the cartilage, which, despite all the battering I'd given it, was still intact.

Here was an unexpected opportunity to return to an active lifestyle. Probably not to running, despite Mr Bartok's intimation. At last I was lowering my sights. Avoiding a knee replacement, *saving the knee*, was more important than running.

On 6 May, on the anniversary of Roger Bannister's sub-four minute mile and my first metric equivalent, I was back at the treatment centre, waiting for a second operation to the right knee, my third in just over a year, and the tenth in total. Unlike my tenth interview for deputy headship, I was not going to disregard the lessons of the previous nine operations. Enough was enough. No more painful hobbling. No more struggling to get in and out of cars or up and down stairs. Stop all this self-harm before it's too late. Welcome this opportunity with open arms. Take the active lifestyle. Save the knee.

During the operation, my heart rate dropped so low that the anaesthetist gave me a drug to bring it back up. As if I wasn't drugged-up enough already. If I'd been awake I could have told him that my resting heart rate was always low: down in the low forties; below forty was not unknown. It must have been *really* low. I awoke in some pain, so I was given another drug, which made me feel sick, so they gave me yet another drug to stop me feeling sick. No tea and biscuits for me. I had been there for hours and hadn't had breakfast yet.

Considering how many drugs had been pumped into me, I wasn't allowed to leave until the team was sure that I was fit and well enough. Eventually, Jane was allowed to collect me at six o'clock in the evening, over ten hours after she had dropped me off.

The drilling had been a success, and Mr Bartok had also given the meniscus another clean-up. That was a concern because there had been no sign of meniscus damage when the knee was scanned in November. Had six months of walking and swimming caused meniscus damage as well as that new bruise to the femur? I hoped that this surgery would prevent that from happening again.

And I knew that I had made the right decision not to attempt another running comeback. No more beating 'a load ae auld grainfaithers'. There would be no more cross-country for this old man.

There followed six weeks of walking with crutches and wearing a leg brace.

And then an active lifestyle.

Without running.

There was no fanfare whatsoever when I announced my retirement from athletics and gave notice of my resignation from Swindon Harriers.

I was resigned to a life without running.

No more competitions.

But there was a problem.

I was still competitive.

What could I do instead of running?

Remembering that day when an angry swan chased me out of a lake and a lifeguard told me that they did proper open water swimming further along the shore, I made a decision.

I was going to buy my first wetsuit and take up proper open water swimming.

And enter a race.

Chapter Twenty-Three: Lake

Ten days after the leg brace was removed, and just over two months since the operation, I pulled on my new wetsuit, walked into the lake, felt the cool water seep under the suit, stretched out and began my first *proper* open water swim. The lake was so different from the pool. Turning at buoys instead of pushing off a wall every twenty-five metres. Fresh water rather than chlorine. Sunshine and clouds, not artificial lights. Glimpses of trees, hills, fishermen and wildlife instead of lane ropes and the same old wall, length after length. It was a privilege to be given this chance to enjoy a new sport so soon after retiring from the old one, which wasn't only a sport: it was a way of life, it defined me.

And now here I was, immersed in a lake, starting a new way of life.

A world of neoprene, wetsuits, dryrobes, increased buoyancy, chafing, tow floats, sighting, drafting, lakes, lochs, sea, river, nature, companionship and much more.

And I was loving it.

As soon as I got home after that first swim I entered an end-of-summer race.

The summer of the 2014 Commonwealth Games in Glasgow. Twenty-eight years after the same Games in Edinburgh, I enjoyed the athletics at Hampden Park and (in the marathon) on the streets in Glasgow city centre. Sam, formerly a club swimmer and now a hockey player, kept me informed during the hockey on Glasgow Green. At Emma's request, we went to the women's weightlifting at the Armadillo: she had been following the progress of former beauty queen, Sarah Davies. Although it was a sport that I had never followed before, I could relate to the effort, tactics and achievement. It was fascinating to watch the drama unfold and it brought a lump to my throat and a tear to the eye. If any more inspiration was required before my first open water race, it came in the triathlon at Strathclyde Park. My main interest was in the swim, where Jodie Stimpson, Vicky Holland and the Brownlee brothers made it look easy in the loch. It wasn't going to be easy for me in a few weeks' time but I couldn't wait to get into the water.

Turning up for my first open water race, I noticed how similar it was to cross-country or the highland games: parking in a field; registering and collecting race numbers (in this case, a swim hat); changing in a tent; music pumping (dance music, not bagpipes); the smell of tarpaulin, cut grass and burgers. Even the start was similar except that, instead of lining up on the track or shivering in a muddy field, we were treading water, trying to keep warm before the starter's signal.

There had been a space on the entry form for your expected time for 1500 metres. Knowing that my pool swims took around half an hour (30 seconds per 25m length) and thinking that I would be slower in a lake, I had put 35 minutes. Since then I had improved but was still very much a novice.

****

Nothing could have prepared me for this stramash of massed arms and legs, thrashing, kicking, splashing, slaps to the face, kicks everywhere, people almost swimming over the top of you. It's not completely strange to me: I was used to jockeying for space, elbows out, at cross-country races, but in the water I'm less comfortable in my space, more vulnerable. It's scary but exhilarating, and I'm holding my own.

When gaps open up and there's some clear water ahead, I settle into my stroke. Barely two months since discarding crutches and leg brace, I'm grateful to be given this new chance to compete.

Sprint to the finish jetty. Slap the timing board with the wrist band. Clamber out of the water and walk up the slope to collect my finisher's medal. Huge smile splitting my face. It feels like life has begun again.

****

So that was my first open water swimming race, and I was thrilled beyond expectation. I had finished tenth (second master) in 25:23, ten minutes faster than my submitted entry time. That winter I was going to join a swimming club, get some coaching and improve technique and fitness, ready for a full season in 2015. I would enter more events, including championships. Could I improve so much that I would have a chance of winning medals in my new sport, maybe even at national level?

But my new training programme would have to wait: I was ill throughout most of the winter.

****

At the same time as I was being treated for sports injuries, and before, between and after each of my three recent operations, I was also under investigation for possible prostate cancer. I didn't have it—don't have it—but my prostate-specific antigen (PSA) level was too high and climbing higher. A biopsy indicated that there was no cancer, but it's not a foolproof test. And so began years of regular blood tests, other procedures and watchful waiting. During the period between the last two knee surgeries, I was taking medication for the prostate, which made me feel like I had flu and almost postponed my final knee operation. I took myself off the pills and enjoyed several months of relatively good health while recovering and then training for the race in the lake. And then I contracted a urine infection, which spread to the testicles and was followed by a bout of diarrhoea. Swimming was out of the question. A computerised tomography (CT) scan, ultrasound scan and cystoscopy were all clear, but by this time (also remembering the vasectomy and hernia repair of years earlier) I was thoroughly pissed off with people poking around my private parts. I missed five months of swimming in 2014 and ended the year in bed with a chest infection.

The New Year was well underway before I joined a club and also arranged 1:1 coaching. When my first full season of open water swimming began in May,

I wasn't as well-prepared as I had hoped but was looking forward to the new challenge.

There were two main types of event: wetsuit and non-wetsuit.

The wetsuit events tended to be quite relaxed, with a wide range of ability amongst participants: from super-fit triathletes to people just having a go; I was somewhere in between. Some of the distances were strange. I was familiar with 1500 metres, but 750m? Why not 800 metres? It's because 1500 metres is the swim distance in Olympic triathlons, so 750m is half of that and called a sprint, although how anyone could call 750m swim followed by 20K on the bike and a 5K run a sprint, I would never know. 3.8K is the Ironman distance and it's 1.9K for Half Ironman, although I couldn't understand what was half-measure about swimming 1.9K, cycling 90K and finishing off with a half marathon run. At least all I had to do was swim.

Championships were always non-wetsuit in 2015, and that's where the medals were to be won, so I entered the Wiltshire, South West, Amateur Swimming Association (ASA) and Scottish Championships. Did I have any chance of picking up where I left off running, and win a medal for swimming? My quest started promisingly at the County Championship, where I also found that ageism was alive and well in Wiltshire swimming. All age groups swam together and swimmers were numbered according to age. If it wasn't already obvious that at number one I was the oldest, the organisers made us enter the water in number order, starting with me. The hooter would sound when everyone was in position. In other words, I had to wait in the cold until the youngest swimmer was ready. Luckily it wasn't *too* cold and I didn't have long to wait, and I laughed it off. I enjoyed the race, and even beat two women in a sprint finish, although we were well behind the winner. And I won a medal: second over forty. I believe there were only three male masters, but I beat someone. My time for 1500 metres was over two minutes slower than my wetsuit best, which was to be expected. This skins thing—swimming without a wetsuit—wasn't too bad. I was ready for more.

Next were the South West Championships at Weymouth. In the sea, which was colder, although I was more worried about the huge, blobby, dead jellyfish scattered along the waterline. What if their pals were lurking offshore, waiting to sting innocent skins swimmers? The men and boys started together, followed five minutes later by the women and girls. There was nothing I could do about it as nearly all of the male swimmers disappeared into the distance, and then nearly all the female swimmers overtook me. I was outclassed and shivering.

No jellyfish, though. That was one good thing.

I was shivering again at the ASA Masters Championships at Rother Valley Park in Sheffield. And that was *before* the race. Wanting to enjoy the full experience of a national championship, I accepted an invitation to warm up before the event, although warming up was in no way an accurate description: I cooled down rapidly on exit and got colder as we queued up to walk along the jetty to the dive start. Cold shock hit me as I dived in, and I never recovered. Sometime later I was relieved to reach up and tap the finish arch and stagger up the slipway, outclassed again.

On the way to the Scottish Championships, we spent a few days visiting Jane's family in York, which was also the home of Matt, my old pot washing mate from the Isle of Wight. Now an accomplished masters triathlete, Matt invited me to swim at his regular training lake in Allerthorpe. Where it was cold and pouring with rain but where I insisted upon swimming without a wetsuit. It was only a small, shallow lake: I'd be okay.

Wrong.

Later in the pub, while Matt was supping pints of foaming Yorkshire ale, I was huddled in the corner, nursing a hot chocolate and shivering. Again.

How much colder would it be a couple of hundred miles further north, in the vast depths of Loch Venachar in The Trossachs?

A lot colder.

****

'Do you know where ye are?'

'Loch Venachar!'

'What day is it?'

'Saturday!'

I know what the rescue team are doing: they're asking me questions to find out if I'm hypothermic. I'm clambering aboard their speedboat only seconds after waving my arm to the nearest kayaker to signal that I was in trouble. He signalled the speedboat, and now, only a minute later, we're speeding back to the start area.

I'm momentarily confused as the speedboat draws up at the jetty: there are swimmers at the start of the second lap. Were they behind me when I was swimming? No: they've finished already. That's how far ahead of me they are.

I'll be okay now. Get changed, have a hot drink, shiver for a while, I'll be fine. But I'm losing my balance on the jetty as two kind volunteers guide me over to the first aid station: a van with EMERGENCY MEDICAL AID in large letters on its side.

I'm an emergency.

And I'm not the only one: hunched up in foil blankets are several of us who have found the water too cold for comfort. If only the first aiders would let me go to the changing rooms, but they're just doing their job: they have to carry on observing my recovery. Which doesn't seem to be happening: this foil blanket just isn't cutting it. A volunteer passes a hot drink to me but I'm shaking so much that I can't hold it. The event organiser looks on, worried. I'm the oldest person in the van; I suppose I'm a particular concern. Jane and Mum are feeling sorry for me. I'm feeling sorry for myself.

This is what I do for fun?

'It's a shame, son, but ye just wanted to compete.'

****

Mum was right: I just wanted to compete but I had learned that I can't stay warm enough to be competitive in non-wetsuit events. It was all very well swimming in a nice, warm wetsuit, beating most of the other participants in a low-key event but, as soon as I came up against experienced club swimmers, I was completely outclassed. Even if we were all wearing wetsuits, I'd still be outclassed. I was an ex-athlete with forty years of running behind me. It was time to stop pretending that I can match similarly experienced swimmers.

But I gave it a go, didn't I?

And I continued to give it a go, but only in wetsuit events.

However, despite my self-inflicted near-hypothermia in ASA events, most of my training swims were still in skins. Swimming without a wetsuit is invigorating. There's something pure about being engulfed in cool water, nothing between you and the environment but your skin. That tingling sensation. At one with nature. It's well documented that cold water swimming improves your immune system and reduces your susceptibility to colds and flu. It also improves mental health as endorphins are released to create a feelgood factor. It makes you feel alive and in love with life.

It became my choice to train in skins and compete in a wetsuit. The only choice in non-wetsuit competitions is swim or don't swim. But, training in the lake, you develop ownership of your choices. If it's too cold to stay in the water too long, you can either put on your wetsuit and swim for longer, or swim without one and stop when you want to. Dad always used to say that you should get out while you're still enjoying it, although he was talking about swimming pools. It was good advice and even more appropriate for outdoor swimming. The swim doesn't end when you leave the water: your core temperature continues to drop; you have to make sure that you're not too cold to dress yourself and start to warm up.

Back in my wetsuit, I was making good progress in events. I competed twenty-two times that summer, by the end of which I had improved my 1500 metres time from 25:23 to 23:34. My best performance was the 750m swim in a triathlon relay at Bowood, only a few miles from home. We entered as a family team: I swam, Sam cycled and Emma ran, supported by Jane and our children's partners. Surprising everybody including myself, I came out of the water well ahead of all the other swimmers. There's a photo of me running out of the water with style. It looks like I know what I'm doing but there's no image of me bent over and holding onto a rail a moment earlier. Nor does it show how worried I was about the run to the transition area. Sam had offered to run that part for me, but after a long slog uphill in my wetsuit, probably the slowest 400 metres I've ever run, I was proud to hand over to my son in first place. Sam handed over to Emma, who brought our team home to a family celebration. We hadn't won but it was a lovely exercise in family bonding, capped off by a barbecue in our garden on a perfect summer's evening.

The season ended in October with a night swim. There is nothing on earth like night swimming. From the shore it's spectacular. Hundreds of bright, bobbing lights snaking out into the darkness. (We're all wearing glow sticks inside our swim hats.) From the water, it's thrilling. With your sense of sight much diminished, your other senses are heightened: the sounds of splashes are clearer; the water feels, smells and tastes fresher. All you can do is swim to the first buoy until you spot the next one. Jane said I was like a wee boy, grinning like an idiot as I walked over to hug her after the final event of the year.

What a way to finish.

Except it wasn't over.

My last training swim in skins was on the final day of October: 400 metres in 9.9 degrees.

Then it was time to add layer after layer until I was encased in neoprene: wetsuit; hat; gloves; socks; tri-suit and rash vest underneath my wetsuit. I kept swimming throughout the winter as the temperature dropped. I heard about the days when you had to break the ice to swim, although I managed to miss those occasions. I did swim in one degree water once, though. How some of my friends manage to swim all winter in skins I'll never know: it was quite enough of a challenge for me in my neoprene cocoon.

The busy summer of swimming events becoming a distant memory, I never lost my thirst for competition, so when I heard about the Chilly Dippers series at Waterland, I jumped at the chance. Once a month, we raced unofficially for penguin-shaped finishers' medals, hot drinks and most of all, cake. Lots of cake. It's part of the culture of open water swimming.

A culture that I would never have discovered if I hadn't been forced to give up running.

However, running was never far from my thoughts. Running was a culture in which I had been steeped for most of my life. It wouldn't go away. I didn't want it to go away. I had accepted that I would never run again, but I was helping hundreds of others to enjoy running, and I was a strong supporter at big athletics events.

And then something happened that turned running into a nightmare.

And I didn't run a single step.

It was the debacle of Vale Park parkrun.

Chapter Twenty-Four: Debacle

It wasn't only a debacle. It was devastating. It was an international scandal.

The Vale Park councillor who had supported our first parkrun had left the area. The remaining councillors did not share his enthusiasm. Far from basking in the reflected glory of a hugely successful physical activity phenomenon in their park, they decided, without any public consultation, to charge participants. This of course upset the volunteers, who came to me for advice. Some of them were angry. Understandably. But no matter how much I understood, I had to tread carefully. If we were going to reach an agreement, it was important not to annoy the parish councillors. Nothing would be gained by lecturing them about the benefits of parkrun or threatening them with the consequences of not allowing parkrun to continue. Besides, I had a duty to my employers: South Severnside Council would have to work with Vale Park Parish Council long after this debate had ended.

At first, I acted as diplomat, trying to find a middle ground. Would the parish council run a café, like other parkruns, therefore raising income and negating the need to charge participants to run?

Their response was unenthusiastic: 'Other groups pay to use the park, why not parkrun?'

'But the volunteers don't hold any funds.'

'Parkrun HQ has funds. They employ people. They can pay.'

'But parkrun is free. That's what makes it accessible to all. It removes barriers to participation. Nowhere in the world does a landowner charge parkrun. If there's a charge in this park, it will have an adverse effect on the future of parkrun worldwide.'

'Well, they *should* charge. parkrun is an organised group with income. They should pay. There's no such thing as a free lunch.'

Inevitably, the volunteers, led by the parkrun regional ambassador, started to list the huge benefits of parkrun to the local community.

'But most of the runners are not local: they come from all over to use our park.'

'There are stats to prove that a sizeable percentage of participants are local. People go to their nearest parkrun.'

That fell on deaf ears.

'The more venues there are, the more local the parkruns become. We need more parkruns; we can't afford to lose one, which is what could happen here. If you force parkrun to close, we'll have to inform our many thousands of members.'

Oh dear, that was a threat. It didn't go down well.

It was an *impasse*. The meeting ended with nothing achieved, other than a delay while both sides sought a solution.

Fuel was added to the fire when parkrunners across the world heard of the parish council's intention to charge. It could become the first and only incident of a parkrun closing because a landowner wanted to charge entry. Social media went mad. Local residents and parkrunners wrote negatively about the parish council. They protested to councillors. The news hit local and national papers. It was on national TV and became a worldwide scandal.

An outrage.

The parish council was receiving an email every minute; some of them, apparently, were offensive. Emotions were running high. The parish council enlisted the support of their local MP, who spoke on their behalf in parliament. He said that they had no intention of charging parkrunners: they wanted them to apply for a local grant to pay for the upkeep of the park; why couldn't parkrun agree to that? The parish council had already filled in the form for parkrun; all parkrun had to do was sign it.

Parkrun couldn't agree to that because they would have to apply year after year, not only in Vale Park but all over the country, perhaps all over the world. Besides, I knew, and the parish council knew, that there was no such grant: it had been discontinued.

I was asked to write a briefing note to keep colleagues and members informed of developments.

Reluctantly, I agreed. Although the document was proofread, the published version was firmly on the side of parkrun. How could it be otherwise, after all the time and effort I had invested in setting up our first parkrun, all the support for volunteers, all the great work they were doing, all the hundreds of residents enjoying parkrun and reaping the benefits to their health?

Soon afterwards, our director of public health took me aside. He had received a complaint via the Tory rep on South Severnside Council: I was supporting parkrun and making political statements.

'The first part is true,' I said. 'But I wouldn't know a political statement if one fell on my head.'

'I can see where you're coming from,' he told me. 'I don't think you've done anything very wrong, but you have to be careful not to be caught in the crossfire.'

'Who's shooting at whom?'

'The Tories and Labour.'

I was so naïve, that it hadn't occurred to me that this was political. I hadn't even known that Vale Park Parish Council was Tory.

'I just want to say that I've got your back. I told them that you're doing your job, you're passionate about physical activity and you know where the boundaries are.'

I thanked our director for his support, and then booked a day's annual leave at short notice. I was in too deep. I needed a break from the pressure. Once again, stress was threatening to overcome me.

But there was no escape, even at home on annual leave. One of our senior managers called, asking where to find information about our expenditure on parkrun. Later the same day, she called again to tell me that the Tory rep was satisfied with the information, that he was really grateful for my work and passed on my thanks. Wasn't that nice of him?

Really? He hadn't said anything to me. And I was supposed to be having a break from this. Not to be harassed when I'm on annual leave.

The final, fateful Vale Park Parish Council meeting was televised. Each side stood their ground: the parish council would not allow parkrun to continue without payment, and parkrun would not agree to pay.

All the parish council had to do was let parkrun happen.

But they couldn't bring themselves to back down.

'Well, that's the end of parkrun.'

'Shame on you!'

Tears, recrimination, anger, stress, heartbreak.

Which didn't end at Vale Park.

The popularity of parkrun was increasing but, with two or three hundred lost souls from Vale Park looking for somewhere else for their weekly parkrun, volunteers at the remaining local venues were in danger of being overwhelmed. We had to find a new park to cope with the demand.

However, the legacy of Vale Park was making that difficult. Landowners were wary: if they started a parkrun and then had to close it later, they were afraid of a potential repeat of the scandal that had blighted Vale Park. As soon as potential site was identified, word got out, the news made the press, a few residents complained, and landowners took more heed of them than the thousands who supported parkrun. When, finally, it looked like a suitable venue had been found, the volunteers were dismayed to find two of the Vale Park councillors turning up at a meeting to speak against parkrun. They even contacted the landowners of other local parkruns to warn them of the dangers.

In the long run, they didn't win. Years later, with funding from South Severnside Council, another parkrun was set up, then another. With each new parkrun, less and less of my support was required: parkrun is owned by the community, and continues to grow at a phenomenal rate. Every Saturday morning, millions of people in thousands of parks across the globe enjoy the simple act of putting one foot in front of the other for five kilometres. A simple act that has huge benefits to their lives: physically, emotionally, socially.

Which is the way it should be.

Forever.

Chapter Twenty-Five: Crash

We celebrated my sixtieth birthday in Cyprus on our first overseas holiday, joined by Sam, Emma and their partners. At this reunion of the family relay squad, I was the only one swimming in the sea. It was the beginning of the tourist season and the water was still cold but I loved it. In fact, Jane and I both liked the experience of holidaying in the sun out of the UK season so much that we returned to the Mediterranean in the autumn, and fell in love with Menorca. Early morning swims starting under starlight and ending in the sunrise; afternoon swims in secluded bays in warm, turquoise water, multicoloured fish glinting in refracted sunlight. And my first jellyfish sting. Or I think it was a jellyfish; I didn't see anything. There I was, minding my own business, full of the joys of the late Spanish summer, when I felt something brush against my thigh, then my arm, then *ouch*! An electric shock to my chin. The speed of my escape to the shore rivalled my sprint away from that swan years previously. I never did find out what stung me, but my mouth throbbed all the way back to the hotel and was still swollen two days later. We returned to Menorca twice more and each time the swimming was the highlight for me, despite another day when the beach was invaded by tiny jellyfish with electric stings that left scars on my arms for weeks. But it was worth it for the sun, sand, sea and skies of endless blue on the most beautiful of islands.

Back in less infested waters, I took part in iconic events in beautiful locations. There was the Henley Classic: two kilometres upstream at dawn on the longest day of the year; four kilometre swims in Wimbleball Lake on Exmoor and along the River Thames in Oxfordshire; a mile swim in the Serpentine and five kilometres in the Royal Docks; the Great Scottish Swim in Loch Lomond and a swim across the River Forth on the weekend that the new bridge opened; the Holy Isle to Arran swim; an estuary swim in West Wales; the pier to pier swim in Bournemouth; an end of season swim around the lake and along the river at Hever Castle, Kent. They were all hugely enjoyable, all the more so for the opportunity to swim in different places, often where swimmers are not usually allowed.

I won the over sixties category a few times and even won the odd race outright, but only in the swimming equivalent of fun runs. After the rapid improvement of my first full season, I was slowing down, just like I did as a runner. On occasions I could hit my best training times in the pool, and now and again I surprised myself in an event, but the trend was to lose speed year on year. Once again, I was tasked with managing my decline, which wasn't going very well. I was almost obsessed with performance, particularly times, which in open water is silly: not only are no two courses the same but the buoys move—even during the event—therefore accuracy of distance is impossible. I really needed to relax and get back to enjoying swimming for swimming's sake.

And my own.

At one late night club swimming session, it took only a remark from a clubmate, who said that he wasn't feeling up to it and was going to get out of the pool, to convince me that I wasn't enjoying it any more. Not one to give up easily, nevertheless I'd had enough: I left early and never went back.

I didn't give up events completely, but they became fewer and further between. I didn't need to enter races to swim in different places: wherever we travelled, I looked for an opportunity to swim, which wasn't as easy as finding somewhere to run but I found a few: lakes as far apart as the New Forest and Leicestershire, rivers, lochs and different seaside locations. Menorca aside, the jewel in the crown was Brittas Bay in Ireland, where the Irish side of Clara's family own a beach house. A short walk from the back garden, through the sand dunes to a deserted beach, a swim at sunrise. My idea of paradise.

You can hardly be more connected with nature than when you're swimming in open water: you're *immersed* in nature. Back in my 'home' lake I swam all year round. In spring you can swim alongside a paddle of ducklings, through fallen blossoms while a heron, sentinel-like, watches from the shore. With the sun on your back in summer, there are shoals of tiny fish for company, close enough to touch. Autumn brings crayfish, scuttling along the lakebed while you swim above them, safe from their huge pincers. Winter sunrises and reflections are spectacular and sometimes the lake is framed by frost or snow as white as the lake's resident albino magpie.

Idyllic scenes.

Which were about to be shattered.

****

'It's her back: it's covered in bruises!'

Crying in desperation down the phone, my sister is worried about our mum. We're both worried: Mum hasn't been herself for months. When I last visited, in February, she was off-balance because of low blood pressure, and was prescribed medication for that. It's August now, and this is something else. Mum has been lethargic, confused and still off-balance. Always independent but nevertheless accepting help from Susan once per week, Mum has been more stubborn than usual lately, almost aggressive. That's not like our mum. Susan, battling against protests, almost dragged her down for a blood test. And this Saturday morning, the results came through, and Mum was asked to get herself to the hospital as soon as possible. This caused confusion, anxiety and panic but, with the help of a kind neighbour, Mum got there. Susan caught up with them soon afterwards, after leaving early from her work. And now she's calling me. And crying.

When Susan watched the doctor examining Mum, she was shocked and upset to see a mass of bruises. She's been living independently for thirty-five years since Dad died, and hasn't told anyone that she's been bumping into walls and furniture for months. And now she's been admitted into hospital for care and observation. The blood test has revealed low sodium levels. Confusion, lethargy, altered personality: we know now that these are classic signs of hyponatremia, which in the elderly can cause seizures, coma or even death.

If Susan had not insisted that Mum had a blood test, the next time she visited she could have found Mum in a coma.

Or worse.

Understandably, Susan, even with the staunch support from Alastair, can't deal with this.

My sister needs her big brother. Mum needs me. I need to go home.

To Airdrie.

But that's going to take some time.

Jane and I are 450 miles away on the Dorset coast. Earlier in the week, when I phoned Mum, I knew she was unwell, I wanted to come and stay for a few days.

'No! I don't want you to come. I'm fine. I can't cope with you coming.'

Talk about altered personality. If only we knew what we know now. But we didn't, so Jane and I drove down as planned to Dorset for this swimming event.

And now we're waiting at Mudeford Quay for a ferry to take us back to Hengistbury Head.

Then a long walk along the seafront back to the car at Boscombe, because the buses aren't running and we can't find a taxi.

Then a couple of hours' drive home to Calne, an hour or two's sleep and another seven or eight hours of driving overnight to Airdrie.

Straight to the hospital ward.

'Oh, hi, son,' says Mum, smiling innocently, pleased to see me, the angry words of a few days ago forgotten. Innocent, frail, but safe, and finally realising that she needs to accept more help.

****

I stayed with Mum for over a week, looking after her, shopping, cooking, cleaning, giving Susan a break, although she was over most days and we were in constant touch with each other. North Lanarkshire Council were first class: as soon as I explained that I was up for only a week or so, they promptly helped to put things in place: key-safe, alarm pendant, rails and other aids around the house, visit from a social worker. Susan and I bought a new, louder doorbell and a hands-free phone, and arranged home delivery of medication in blister packs. Gradually, Mum regained some independence, although not without episodes of denial.

When I returned home to Jane after another overnight drive, exhaustion suddenly engulfed me. I had been operating on adrenaline for nine days and now the reality hit me: Mum could have died. Susan claimed that her big brother came home to rescue her. Suddenly, that's why I was put on this earth. Being a good brother and a good son was the most important thing in the world. Nothing else mattered. However, it was Susan's prompt and insistent actions that saved Mum's life. My sister was the real rescuer. The truth is: we were a team. We did everything we could to love and care for our mum. Dad would have been proud of us.

'We mustn't think that everything's going to be okay now,' said Susan. 'She's still frail. Other things are going to go wrong.'

So we stayed connected with each other and with Mum. Susan visited Mum every Tuesday to help with shopping and to have lunch. I was always on the phone and I went back up to Airdrie for weekends in September and November. Jane and I spent Christmas with Susan and Alastair and of course saw a lot of Mum. She was frailer and still confused but as cheerful, optimistic and kind as ever, always putting the needs of others before her own.

Mum's illness was one of those life-changing events, after which things are never the same.

And then came another.

Worrying about Mum, stress at work.

A car crash waiting to happen.

Which happened.

****

Driving home on a winter's night, I'm waiting behind a parked lorry on a dark, country road. I'm indicating to pull out as soon as there's a break in the headlights of oncoming traffic.

Bam! Smash! Hurtle towards the stationary lorry, swerve left away from the traffic, narrowly escape crashing into the lorry, smash through a gate, somehow avoid rolling the car, and gradually come to a stop in the middle of a field.

Shaken but in one piece, I heave myself out of the car, turn on the torch on my phone and inspect the damage. The back of the car has caved in. It did its job protecting me. It's just as well our dogs aren't in the boot, otherwise they would be nothing but mangled flesh and bone. I squelch my way through the mud and across the field to see how the other driver is. The front of his car looks even worse than the back of mine. What speed was he doing to cause that much damage and send me careering into a field for 100 metres?

'Are you okay?' I ask.

He stares straight through me. 'I couldn't see anything. The headlights were blinding me!'

'Well, why didn't you stop, or at least slow down?' is the obvious response or: 'How did you not see a huge lorry lit up like a Christmas tree?' But I don't say either of those. I'm still not confrontational, despite this high-speed confrontation between two hunks of metal, writing off both cars, causing other kinds of damage yet to be revealed. And which was entirely his fault.

Instead, I call the police, who breathalyse both of us and take statements. The other driver spends much longer in the police car than I do, while I'm waiting for the breakdown services. Two hours after impact, Jane is driving me home, via the accident and minor injuries unit. Again.

****

Apart from the shock and physical pain of a car accident, you just know that you're in for months of problems: accident insurance claim; argument and counter-argument; a temporary replacement car, then a 'new' car; taking out a loan because the insurance money isn't enough to replace your car like-for-like; injury insurance claim; more argument and counter-argument; and, after all that, you're still out of pocket and it *wasn't your fault.*

For me there was also a loss of confidence, low mood and negative effects on work and home life.

And counselling.

One of the first observations my counsellor made was that the car crash was symbolic of stress at work: immovable lorry ahead, car approaching at high speed from behind, oncoming traffic. Caught in the headlights, with pressure from all directions.

What gave me the most job satisfaction was supporting people: participants in our programmes, volunteers, colleagues, especially the people I was privileged to manage. Passionate about nurturing people and helping them to help themselves and develop their careers, I loved guiding their progress and felt heart-warmed by their often positive feedback. However, despite surviving restructure after restructure over the years, the most recent one took away my line management responsibility. The best thing about my job, the thing I thought I was really good at, the thing I was there for. Gone. Instead, we were in the midst of a new integrated health and wellbeing service, and I was leading, but not managing, a team of mostly reluctant workers. I could understand their resistance to a major change that had been imposed on them (and on me). What I was struggling to understand was their lack of co-operation. So, there was I, pulled every which way by the workers, their managers, my manager, the service lead; caught in the headlights of oncoming traffic, immovable lorry ahead, smashed from behind; something had to break.

And it was me.

I wouldn't even have been on that dark road if I hadn't, for the nineteenth time that month, been covering for colleagues who would always find something else to do that was more important than working on a service that was supposed to be a Division priority.

With that dark thought, it all spilled out at counselling: the car crash, pressure at work, Mum's illness.

I was referred to Occupational Health and, for the first time in over twenty years, since the end of my teaching career, I was grateful for the support of a union rep. At a meeting with Human Resources and my manager, my feelings and concerns were at last taken seriously. Measures were ready to be put in place: more flexible working, no expectancy to cover for reluctant colleagues, a car parking space.

It was the third decade of the third millennium, and at last, people understood men's mental health.

And then the measures became superfluous.

Because of something much more worrying.

A global pandemic.

Chapter Twenty-Six: Pandemic

Covid 19 hit us all hard. But, at work, we were the lucky ones. Unlike NHS workers, we were not risking our lives, in direct contact with the public: we were all at home, learning new ways of working. Like many others, I was redeployed to meet the immediate demands of our residents, particularly the clinically vulnerable, who were shielding from the virus. It was worthwhile work, supporting people with food and other essentials such as finance and wellbeing. We were thrown in at the deep end and developed systems as we went along. Once again, I was leading a team of colleagues who reported to other managers. And, once again, I was in the middle, dealing with conflicting needs and demands from workers, managers and the service lead. Some of the challenges were the same as before: the same reluctance from the same people to something new being imposed upon them. But the challenges seemed more manageable. There was no driving to and from the office and no in person contact with disruptive people. Many couldn't cope with bringing their work into their home, but I felt comfortable and safe, with Jane and our dogs for company. Initially my revised role wasn't entirely clear, but I found a way to make it my own, to make it positive and fulfilling. As some colleagues fell by the wayside because they couldn't cope with the pressure, others who understood that 'we're all in it together' joined the team, that it was 'all hands on deck', not 'mutiny under the decks'.

Mum found her imposed isolation difficult. So soon after she had regained most of her independence, the pandemic took it away again. Susan continued to visit weekly as part of her carer's role, and Mum's neighbours were a great comfort. I ordered weekly food parcels from the local supermarket for Mum, and we all supported each other.

With the advent of lockdown, suddenly there was nowhere to swim. Even the lakes were shut. Which might have been a bigger problem than it was: like thousands of others, I relied on swimming, especially in open water, for my physical and mental health. However, confined to the house nearly all day, I increased my indoor core stability sessions to up to fourteen per week: two sessions of fifteen minutes on most days. And I dusted down my old bike and hit the road again. After years of absence, cycling became my daily permitted exercise outdoors.

At first, I cycled after work for half an hour to an hour. It was one of the things that kept me going during the day: knowing that, as soon as I finished work, I could get changed and straight onto the bike and out on the open road in the fresh air. No lengthy walk to find the car wherever you parked it on the industrial estate, no sitting in queues of traffic in rush hour before you even got out of town and, on the road home, no passing the scene of the crash, no fear of being rammed by another car, no nose to tail traffic through the next town, no feeling too tired to exercise after the long commute Simply close the laptop, pull on your shorts and get out of here. The roads had never been so quiet. There was no rush hour; no stream of cars whizzing by, too close for comfort; no fumes, no noise. Only fresh air, cool breeze, birdsong, clear views, enticing scents of spring, glimpses of wildlife and other cyclists. And then relaxing at home in the evening.

Walking downstairs after my first ride, my knees began to lock. This could have been a disappointment: the return of an old injury, still a problem years after surgery. However, a strange thing happened: my knees *got used to cycling again*. They adapted to their new activity, just as we were all adapting to a new lifestyle brought on by the pandemic.

As the days and the rides became longer, I changed my routine so that I was riding before work. Sometimes into spectacular sunrises; darkness and stars fading as orange and red hues illuminated misty landscapes, a huge ball of fire peeking from behind dark, silhouetted hills into a blue and bluer sky. There was no dust, no noise, only calmness and the chirp of awakening birds. And all that before work. What an energising way to start the day.

Living through tragic times affecting millions of people worldwide, supporting thousands of residents through their troubles, my personal problems almost disappeared. And, as they decreased, my cycling mileage increased. After years of planning my training to the nth degree, this progress was unplanned and natural. By the end of summer I was riding a hundred miles per week, not a huge amount by cyclists' standards, but I had never expected to return to that sort of mileage after so many injuries and operations. I was loving it.

****

Before coronavirus spread to the UK, we had booked a summer holiday on the Isle of Arran. But would we ever get there? A holiday anywhere seemed unlikely until the number of infections and Covid-imposed restrictions decreased. It would be a strange holiday in many ways: face masks, hand gel, social distancing, reduced capacity on the ferry, table service in pubs and some facilities closed but, by August, we were on our way.

We stopped for two nights near Girvan on the Ayrshire coast, enjoying beautiful walks with our dogs along the beach, gazing at the sunset over a huge rock growing out of the Firth of Clyde: Ailsa Craig, against a glorious backdrop of the mountains of Arran. Susan brought Mum down to visit us one afternoon. Six months after last seeing Mum, I couldn't help but notice how much frailer she was: she needed to hold my arm during the short walk to the beach, one leg swinging wide in an awkward gait.

On the day of our arrival on Arran, on the beach at Whiting Bay there was not a cloud in the sky, it was warm but not oppressive; sunshine kissing our faces, sand between our toes, dogs romping in delight along the fringe of a gently lapping sea, clear views past the Holy Isle across to the mainland. It was a beautiful summer's afternoon at the height of the tourist season.

And there was no one else in sight.

We had the whole beach to ourselves.

It was paradise on the west coast of Scotland, and it set the tone for a peaceful and relaxing holiday.

And for me, adventurous early mornings before Jane woke up.

And once, a near-death experience.

I had swum in pools and lidos, ponds and rivers, seas and estuaries, docks and locks, lakes and lochs, but never lochans: miniature lochs high in the hills or mountains. What an adventure that would be: hiking up steep, winding trails amongst forests; between crags, through heather; past shaggy highland cattle, inquisitive sheep and elusive deer to a remote spot with panoramic views of Scotland at its most magnificent. The simple pleasure of stripping off and swimming in the purest of waters. Alone and at one with nature. The most perfect of experiences.

****

WARNING: DON'T TRY THIS AT HOME.

It's misty. Not much to see beyond this uniform collection of gloomy, tightly-packed trees. When you've seen one conifer, you've seen them all. If you can see them at all. The higher I climb along this muddy track, the mistier it gets, the less I can see. At least it's not cold or windy.

Emerging from the trees into an expanse of heather. Well, I assume it's an expanse: I can't see more than twenty metres in front of my nose. I check Google Maps to see that I'm heading in the right direction. Maybe five or ten minutes further, difficult to tell: the mist is disorientating.

Check the map again; it should be right in front of me, but where is it?

A few metres more and there it is: the edge of the lochan. A grey tree stump on a grey shore, overlooking grey water in a grey mist. It's all grey.

Grey, but enticing. Exciting. It's just me and this grey temptress. You should never swim alone in open water. And you should never, ever swim alone on a remote hill when no one knows where you are and wouldn't be able to see you in the mist even if they did. I'm breaking all the rules, but I've looked forward to this, planned it, come all this way. The only reason I haven't told Jane is not to worry her. And because she would talk me out of it. But she needn't worry: I'll be fine and back at the cottage before she wakes up. Okay, I can't see much. The map on my phone shows the shape of the lochan but I can't judge the distance around the perimeter. It doesn't look too far, not a long swim, and it's not too cold, even without my wetsuit. If it wasn't for the mist, I'd be able to see from one end of the lochan to the other, it would be easy to judge the distance and aim for the landmark of the tree stump and my clothes. But in this mist, I might miss them and swim straight past. I wouldn't know where I was, I would start to get cold, I'd panic. Okay, so I won't do that, I won't swim all the way around. I'll set my watch, swim along the shoreline for a few minutes, turn back and retrace my strokes to the stump, and if I feel okay I can swim a few minutes in the opposite direction, turn *around, swim back to the stump, get out, get dressed and get on the path back down the hill to the car. What can possibly go wrong?*

The first part goes to plan: I swim along the shore for three minutes only. Even if I get cold, it's only another three minutes back to my clothes, right? I find the landmark of the stump easily. I'm enjoying myself; it's a unique experience in this grey but clean water; a peaty taste, no sound except my own breathing and a small splash with each stroke. It's been only six minutes, I can swim a bit further: how about three minutes in the opposite direction, three minutes back? That's twelve in total, I'm not cold yet, I'll be fine. Oh, the mist lifts very slightly, just enough to reveal a tiny island off shore. How far away is it? Fifty, sixty metres? Instead of swimming along the shore, why don't I swim around the island and straight back to the stump? That would be a more interesting swim. It'll be fine.

Rounding the island, the fog descends again, all the way to the surface of the water. I can't see the shore, but it's okay: I'll just retrace my strokes and swim straight back to the stump, right? Nae bother.

But it's not nae bother. I'm at the shore and climbing out of the water but where's the stump? More to the point, where's my clothes? I'm starting to feel cold. Where are they? Are they this way or that way? Obviously, I haven't swum in a straight line back to the stump but am I on its left or right? Which way do I walk? I stumble through the heather in what I think is the direction of my clothes but after a few minutes there's no sign of them. I don't recognise any landmarks. It must be the other way. More stumbling but I'm not worried, not really; this'll be the right way, any minute now I'll spot my clothes, get dressed, warm up on the hike back down the hill. What's that Billy Connolly joke about marching through the heather? 'Ye cannae march through heather: ye kinda fall through heather!' Heather looks soft and silky but close up it's rough and spiky, and it's tearing lumps out of my bare feet and legs as I stumble, stagger and fall. And here I am, wearing only a pair of trunks, a swim hat and goggles (whatever good they're doing), alone in the mist on a remote hillside on an island, lying down on my side in the heather, legs scratched to bits and bloody. And bloody cold. Is this how it ends? Nobody knows I'm here. If they send out a search party, they'll never find me in the fog. They say that if you're going to die, die while you're enjoying yourself. Usually sleeping, but for the more adventurous, maybe running, climbing, cycling, swimming. But lying in spiky heather, shivering, scratched and cold? This is not what they had in mind. This is not fun.

Okay, you're disorientated, you've walked in both directions but obviously not far enough: one of them has to be the right one. Think logically: it has to be this way, just keep walking (falling) until you see the stump and find your clothes.

So I keep moving,

Keep looking,

And I'm right:

There they are,

Just where I left them.

Where else would they be?

As soon as I get dressed and start walking, I'm feeling fine and warming up quickly. The hike down the hill is uneventful and, unlike my search for an obscure tree stump and a pile of clothes, I have no trouble locating the car.

Mission accomplished.

Scary, stupid, but accomplished.

As I arrive back at the cottage, Jane is just waking up and none the wiser.

She still doesn't know.

Unless she's reading this.

Then I'm really in trouble.

****

At least there were no jellyfish in the lochan. However, in the sea around Arran were huge, pulsing, bulbous globes with long tendrils hanging beneath the surface, beautiful but terrifying. In your space, in your face. If those tiny creatures in Menorca can sting with an electric shock and leave scars for weeks, what could these monsters do? I was so scared of being stung that, unlike previous holidays, my swims got shorter and shorter as the week went on. Entering the water where the Sannox Burn flows into the sea at the turn of the tide, I swam upstream and experienced sudden change from salt to fresh water. It was like a line had been drawn across the water: on one side was sea, on the other, river. And then a horde of jellyfish floated towards me, dozens of them, all being dragged out by the tide. Probably most of them were dead, having been washed ashore hours earlier and now their carcasses were drifting out to a watery grave. But I wasn't taking any chances. I was out of there; as sharp an exit as my escapes from their Spanish jellyfish cousins and my old enemy, the swan.

It was during my final swim on the island that I was stung. I think it was a Lion's Mane jellyfish, a big mauve thing with a vicious, trailing… mane. I was in my wetsuit, so the only exposed parts of me were my feet, hands and face. Luckily it wasn't my face. The sting to my hand wasn't like an electric shock at all: it felt just like a nettle sting. So, was that it? As a runner, I had run through so many fields of nettles that I became almost immune to their stings. What was I so worried about? A tiny, feeble, nettley sting.

I haven't swum anywhere near a jellyfish since then, though.

I'm still scared of the bastards.

****

Vicious predators of the sea and a near-death experience aside, it was a relaxing break from work in relative freedom, considering what we had all lived through before.

They thought it was all over.

They were wrong.

Infections began to rise again, followed, inexorably, by deaths. Back in my substantial role, I was watching and waiting: surely it was only a matter of time before another lockdown, which would mean that amongst many work-related changes, the council would support the clinically vulnerable again. However, everyone else was back in their old jobs, too. Who would be available to support?

When the head of community support phoned me to ask how I felt about the spread of the virus and the need to provide a proactive service, I volunteered immediately to step up and lead a team again, in preparation for the inevitable.

It was an uncertain existence. Life was mostly back to normal: pubs, shops, leisure centres and other amenities were open but we were all still working at home. I was swimming regularly again, although obliged to book ahead for slots at the pool or lake. It was the calm before the storm. I really wanted to see Mum before it broke.

It was October 2020 when I packed the bike in the back of the car and drove up to Airdrie for a long weekend. Mum seemed to have shrunk, and was less mobile and more confused, but we were happy to see each other again. I enjoyed cycling around my old haunts, but Mum and I left the house together only once, for a drive in the countryside and a stop for coffee. Except we didn't stop. Mum enjoyed the drive but didn't want to get out of the car. She didn't feel steady enough on her feet and didn't want to be an embarrassment.

No sooner had I returned to work than the country was in another lockdown and I was in my support role again.

The new team that I recruited and trained was without a service manager, which meant that, effectively, I was manager as well as team leader. Reporting directly to head of community support, I was a member of the project steering groups, and made joint, strategic decisions. Enthused by the additional responsibility, I was highly motivated. The team gelled immediately and quickly became an efficient and caring unit, providing bespoke support for residents most affected by the pandemic. There was anxiety amongst the team—they were out of their comfort zone—but they really wanted to put the needs of others first and support them to the best of their ability, and they were open to different ways of doing so. I listened actively, taking the pressure off them and delegating responsibility to them in equal measures. Alongside team briefing and feedback sessions, I arranged 'coffee and cake and catch-up' meetings, all virtual of course. There was only one rule at those catch-ups: talk about anything except work. At times revealing, at others hilarious, the catch-ups helped us to get to know each other, even though we never met in person. It was a privilege to lead a team of can-do people. They appreciated the way I was guiding them. For me, it was an entirely positive experience. This was the responsibility I had been missing. This was what I was good at. It's what I was made for: supporting people.

I've often wondered how different life would have been if I had been born in 1955 instead of 1956. I would have reached statutory retirement age on my sixty-sixth birthday at the end of March 2021, the same time as the support team was standing down. I could have retired happy in the knowledge that, in the midst of the pandemic, I was the best person to lead this important work. More than half a century after standing forlornly on the side of a football pitch, feeling useless at everything, I could have ended my career on a high.

Instead, I was only sixty-five at the end of March 2021. It would be another year before I could retire on full pension. I was back in my old role again.

And most of it had disappeared.

While I had been away in redeployment, putting the needs of others before my own, my old job had been decimated. An announcement about the long-awaited and much-postponed restructure of the division was imminent. Everyone knew how well I had supported people during the pandemic but now it seemed that, in only a few months' time, there would be no place for me.

I was struggling to come to terms with this contradiction.

There would be proposals, consultations, interviews, opportunities and, for some, disappointment. No matter how buoyed I was by my recent, wholly positive experience, no matter how optimistic I tried to be, I was preparing myself to be one of the disappointed ones.

And then, once again, something happened that rendered everything else irrelevant.

Mum died.

Chapter Twenty-Seven: Grieving

'Did you get my messages?'

'No, I've been out on my bike. Are you okay? Is something wrong? Is it Mum?'

'Are you sitting down?'

'Yes. What's happened?'

I know, before Susan tells me, that Mum has died.

Alastair went over to see Mum this morning; there was no answer when he rang the bell; he used the key in the safe; walked in.

Mum had died peacefully in her sleep.

I remember Mum phoning when Dad died. Uselessly, I had said sorry to Mum. But not this time, to Susan: it's our shared grief. All I can say is, 'Oh no!' This is our mum. We knew she hadn't been well. We knew this was coming. But not so soon. Not now. Mum was always optimistic. She was making plans. I spoke to her only two days ago. I offered to order a present online for Susan's birthday but Mum phoned me to say it was all in hand: they'd been shopping, Susan had chosen something, Alastair was coming over with wrapping paper and a birthday card, everything was arranged.

Did I tell Mum that I loved her? I didn't tell Dad when I saw him for the last time. Did I tell Mum? That's

what usually happened at the end of our conversations:
'I love you.' Did I tell her?

****

What happened next was instantaneous: I shared the tragic news with Jane, told work that I would be away for a while, packed up and drove to Susan's house.

The date was 6 May.

Arriving in Hamilton late that night, there was no time for Susan and I to do anything other than console each other and try to sleep, before starting to make endless arrangements: meet the undertaker; organise the funeral; contact friends and relatives; speak with Mum's solicitor about her will and estate; sort out insurance policies, utility bills, council tax. Once again, my sister and I were a team, we were doing our best for our mum, we agreed on everything.

We had yet to grieve.

After a hectic few days, I drove back down the road for only two days at work and to collect Jane, and then we were back up the road again.

For the funeral.

And still the grieving had not begun.

When Dad died, Mum shielded us. We had very little part in Dad's funeral arrangements. We were almost onlookers. That's the way Mum wanted it to be. We knew what she would have wanted now. Despite ongoing virus-imposed restrictions, we would do our absolute best for our mum. We invited the maximum permitted number of people, and spoke with every single one of them. Susan met with the minister and arranged for her church choir to record songs and hymns for the service, and she prepared her bible reading. And I prepared the eulogy.

I dearly wanted to write our family tribute, and I was determined to read it aloud at the service. With Susan's help, I practised several times. I even practised with Mum's favourite piece of music in the background. And every time, I broke down in tears. How far would I get on the day? It's not a bad thing if you cry at your own mum's funeral, is it? But would I reach the end before my emotion became uncontrollable? The minister kindly offered to stand by to take over, if at any point I was overwhelmed.

****

I'm trying not to look at the faces in front of me, especially Susan, Alastair, Jane, Sam and Emma in the front row. Of all the challenges I've faced, this is the hardest. I want to share my emotion, but I want to get to the end. If I see others crying, I won't be able to carry on. But this isn't about me. I look over a sea of faces, and begin...

'Our Mum.

'Mum was always optimistic. She would point to a small patch of blue in an otherwise cloudy sky and declare that it was going to be a lovely day. Even in her final years, often in pain, she expected that tomorrow

would be a better day. When she was excited, she'd clap her hands and do her wee dance.'

I'm feeling choked, but beginning to relax as I sense that the congregation recognises what I'm talking about. Keep going. This is for Mum...

'Mum spent her whole life thinking of others. She would visit housebound friends and family and offer them encouragement. She was great friends with her next-door neighbour, Jim, and supported him and his wife throughout his illness. And they did the same for Mum. Real good neighbours. Mum loved her neighbours on both sides of her home, which is called Adaline, after a song that she and Dad came to love on holiday. A song that we've chosen for you today.

'Mum and Dad lived in our family home until Dad died in 1985. Last week, Susan and I found a note in Mum's address book: "our perfect home". After Dad, there was never going to be another man for Mum. Some tried, but Mum soon saw them off.'

Muffled laughter. I'm doing okay so far. Mum deserves this. Do your best. Keep going...

'Mum always put Dad, Susan and me before herself. She devoted her life to us. (Even at the ages of sixty and sixty-five, we were still getting pocket money.)'

More laughs. I'm tempted to make eye contact but, if I see tears, I might not get to the finish. I need to focus...

'Jane and I have two children: Sam (named after Dad) and Emma. Mum doted on her grandchildren. Sam and his wife Catherine have two children: Mali and Lucy, Mum's great-grandchildren. One day late in the summer of 2019, before the whole world changed, Sam and Catherine brought Mali to meet her great-gran. Susan and I were there, when for the first and only time, our four generations were together as one. Mum never met Lucy, whose middle name—Rae—is the same as Mum's maiden name, but she looked at a photo of both girls first thing every morning, and it made her smile.'

Crying from the front row. Keep going. Hold it together...

'Mum loved her walking, out in all weathers, climbing hills, crossing streams, getting lost and going twice as far. Once on holiday abroad with her walking friends, they got stuck on an island and had to hitch a lift back. On a fishing boat.'

Laughs again, but there won't be many more of them.

'On a trip to St. Andrews with a group from church, Mum ended up leading them all on a walk, just like a tourist guide. Everyone loved it, especially Mum, because she and Dad had a special place in their hearts for St. Andrews.

Spirited, independent, fiercely independent (stubborn) are all good words to describe Mum. She insisted on paying for herself (and us) everywhere and managed to do almost everything independently. Almost everything: the TV remote baffled her.'

That's it: the final laugh. The toughest, saddest part now. Stay strong. Almost there...

'Sometime after today, we'll go back to St. Andrews to scatter Mum's ashes. It's there, and here in our hearts, that Mum's indomitable spirit will live on. Let's all remember that spirit and optimism, that selflessness, her undying love. Most of all...'

I've never managed to read this far without crying before. Let's finish this. This is for our mum. I begin to choke up, my voice is wobbling...

'Most of all, let's picture Mum under that patch of blue sky, clapping her hands, doing her wee dance and telling us all that tomorrow will be a better day.'

I'm crying but I've made it to the end. I walk slowly back to the front row and put my arm around Susan. We're saying goodbye to our mum, and to our dad, in a way that no one else can.

Now the grieving can begin.

****

Susan and I are sitting on a rock, arms around each other. The sea laps gently against the shore. Someone has made a small tower of pebbles, each one individual in its shape, size and colour. Next to this small beach is a pool, carved out of rocks, framing still and clear water. It's about the shape and size of a typical indoor pool, and I was swimming in it early this morning. Today of all days, there's nowhere else I would rather swim. The ruins of the castle and white, fluffy clouds in an azure sky are reflected perfectly in the pool. The sandy colour of the castle walls complements the various shades of grey, brown, yellow and white of the rocks and pebbles, and contrasts with the blues of sky and sea, all of these watched over by drifting clouds, like tourists strolling along the promenade above the shore.

This was Mum and Dad's special place. And we're here to lay our mum to rest. We scatter her ashes wide, and, with millions of tiny splashes, they gently pierce the calm surface. Concentric circles widening, glinting in the sunlight, until they fade away, absorbed into the sea.

'Mum's with Dad now,' says Susan.

We look up, and there they are, walking arm in arm towards the cathedral and harbour.

Chapter Twenty-Eight: Reflection

The story could end there.

It might never have started if I'd given up at eleven years old, feeling sorry for myself on the sidelines. It could have ended in my teens with retribution at the Scottish Schools, or in my twenties with my first serious injury, or in my thirties with success in a different sport. Maybe it should have ended in my forties at Croydon or a few months later in Eskilstuna. Or in my fifties with my tenth operation or in my sixties after being fished out of Loch Venachar.

Or should the story have ended with more important milestones—career change, marriage, making a home, birth of children, parents passing away—each of which puts running into perspective? Was running only a dalliance? Did it really matter?

Yes. Running did matter. Not necessarily above everything else but it does matter. Running is not a paltry thing. It's a way of life that's made me who I am, for better or worse.

Given limited talent, I tried to be the best I could possibly be. My first ever race was a championship and, from then on, my goals were always centred on championships. Not for me the easy win or being a big fish in a small sea. Never afraid to lose or take a risk, I took on the big fish in the big seas. And usually lost. When I did win championships, I was only the best of those who ran that day. Even then, I was rarely first across the line. But I was there. I tried. I don't think that

I fulfilled my potential, but I'll never forget the time when I planned, persevered and pushed myself to the limit in a muddy field to become an international champion.

We could all do things differently. Be thoughtful, or stop overthinking. Plan meticulously, or go with the flow. Take life seriously, or have more fun. Be independent, or listen to others. Dedicate yourself to the pursuit of excellence, or put the needs of others first. Keep going one more time, or quit when you're ahead. Never give up, or heed your body's warnings. It's not easy to find a balance.

And when you can no longer do what you love the most, do something else. There's always something you can do, if you really want to. It's never too late to start again.

These days, I walk, swim, cycle and exercise at home, but don't run. Often, I look wistfully upon a footpath winding between sand dunes, up a hill or into a wooded valley, and long to be running again. On occasion (sshh…) I have tried, just to see if I can still do it. (Everybody else does.) And at first it's like I've never been away. Wind in my ears; striding; both feet off the ground; flowing; I feel like I'm about to fly… But, after only a few short runs, something always goes wrong. I can cope with discomfort in the knees, but my ankle will hurt or my calves will cramp up and the run will grind to a painful halt. It's not really running, anyway: it's shuffling, a parody of my former running style.

So it's back to swimming. Year on year, I'm slower in the water. I try not to look at the pool clock because I'm always disappointed, so I devise sessions that are varied and fun and where times don't matter. I still love the freedom of open water but I don't compete any more, partly because I'd be embarrassed at how slow I am; not that anyone would bother: it's an inclusive sport. And partly because I don't need to race. I thought this would never happen but, after years of competition, it's no longer part of my reason for being.

And it's back on the bike. Following my return to cycling during the first lockdown, I'm in a prolonged honeymoon period, still improving, but I know I'll slow down before long. And I won't lose any sleep over it. It's a privilege to be able to exercise outdoors at all. Years ago, up against three operations in quick succession, a diagnosis of osteonecrosis and a severe warning from the surgeon, it could all have been much worse. I'm grateful for what I can do now, but I don't regret doing what I used to do.

I've learned to appreciate walking more. I didn't use to see it as exercise, because I was always between runs, but now I understand the value of walking in its own right. You don't have to run to enjoy the outdoors: you notice, *savour* more while walking, the most simple and accessible form of physical activity of them all. Some say it's the perfect exercise.

Running, for me, was all about competing and training for competition. Initially, I wanted only to be good at something, then to be better, then—if I could— to be the best. I didn't run for my health. In fact, often

379

it wasn't good for me at all. But now I do exercise for health: physical and emotional. Finally, after years of promoting physical activity at work, I am practising what I preach.

Unlike those dark days of my first serious injury, when I shut myself away from sport, I'm a better supporter now than ever. Most Saturdays I'm in the stands, watching our local football team, and I still make the occasional sojourn to Airdrieonians to watch the real stuff. Decades after stumbling across rugby league by accident at school rugby union practices, I'm a big fan, attending the Challenge Cup Final every year, and supporting local grassroots teams. Once, Emma and I demonstrated a dedication that probably surpasses anything from my running days: we spent a night in the car, stranded in a snowdrift on the way home from the World Indoor Athletics Championships in Birmingham.

One day, Jane and I drove up to Nottingham and back in a day, to surprise Sam at the Outlaw Half Ironman triathlon on his home course. Some parents ran down the home straight with their son or daughter at the end of their seventy-point-three miles. I didn't, but I looked on with fatherly pride and a lump in my throat as my son crossed the finish line. Clara is an established Ireland Masters hockey player, and Sarah's experience is even more international, travelling the world and emigrating to Australia, before settling down in Essex. Emma is one of those rare beings who has shown the courage to graduate from parkrun to club track and cross-country. She even won her club athlete of the year award, just like her dad. The other day, Jane and I were cheering her on at a cross-country league. Amongst the familiar sounds of footfall and heavy breathing, the feel of cold wind on my face, the smell from the burger stall, it was the sight of wide passages of churned-up mud that really brought it all home. I remembered old races like they were yesterday and imagined that I was there, racing it out at the front. But I wouldn't be: I'd be shuffling along at the back. My time has passed. The baton has been handed on to the next generation.

And the generation after that. Our grandchildren are now swimming, cycling, running, playing football, even Gaelic football. One of my reasons for accepting that it was finally time to stop running, was to be able to play with grandchildren. I don't need to follow the golden rule—let them win—because they beat me anyway.

This story was never meant to be: *look at me, I've lived on the edge, I've turned my life around, you can do it too*. Or even worse: *you can be like me*. How presumptuous.

This is only one person's story,

'Of what is past, or passing, or to come.'*

And it's not the end.

Because the story never ends.

It keeps on going,

Year,

After year,

After

Year

Sailing to Byzantium by W.B. Yeats

Epilogue

It's late summer, and I'm dipping my toes in the lake. I've cycled twenty-nine kilometres from home, into the sunrise. 'Red sky in the morning, shepherd's warning,' so they say, but it's been an idyllic ride. Watching the light growing out of the almost dark into glowing red. Climbing the hills on the bike, mimicking the sun climbing up the brightening skyscape. Anticipation as I pass the sign for the water park. Excitement as I turn the final corner to catch first sight of the lake, shimmering, inviting.

I've parked the bike, peeled off my cycling gear and now here I am, almost naked, vulnerable, at the edge of the lake, looking forward to immersing myself in cool waters. It helps that there's no wind and the temperature is mild, but you can't go plunging in: you have to respect the lake; even in summer you can be surprised by cold water shock. So, I dip my toes in, coolness meeting warmth of shins, knees, thighs; a sharp intake of breath. Head hanging but only because I'm watching my feet, avoiding any sharp stones. Fresh, slightly fishy aroma. Sunlight glinting on gently lapping water. Pale blue sky and a deeper blue water, framed by different shades of green and brown; trees all around the oasis of calm that is this lake, the only place I wish to be on this beautiful morning. Fish darting between and around legs. Ducks, green, blue and brown, passing close by bright, bobbing swim hats and tow floats, orange, red, purple, pink. A soothing chorus of birdsong complementing swimmers' friendly chatter, gasps, laughs and occasional squeal.

I scoop up handfuls of water and splash it over my torso and head. And I'm into the swim. Taking my first few strokes, sighting the nearest buoy, not easy to spot into the glare. No matter how many times I do it, during those initial strokes I can't imagine that I'm ever going to feel warm, even in summer but, after only a few minutes, as I reach the buoy, I'm warm and cool at the same time, skin tingling, savouring the experience. Turn at the buoy, away from the glare and head alongside the treeline for the next one in the far corner. Although easier to see, this one seems a long way off, but I'm in no hurry. Settling into a relaxing rhythm as I breathe to alternate sides every third stroke, looking up at every sixth, metronome-like, it feels like I'm gliding. It's not always like this: sometimes I struggle. But not today. Today is for enjoyment. I'm here to do something I love to do. Now is the time to live in the moment.

As I round the second buoy, the sun dips behind a cloud. Seconds later it reappears, winking through a canopy of leaves at the precise moment I swim under overhanging branches. I'm outside but inside; sunlight, trees, water. I'm alive with nature, one and the same, fit and well. This is what an active lifestyle is all about.

And there's more to come. I swim to the other end of the lake, towards the children's beach and the pleasure boats shaped like giant swans. It's too early for families to be paddling: only fishermen and other swimmers for company. Acres of space for everyone: it's about a mile around the lake perimeter; no overcrowding here. And, of course, the wildlife. There's only one family of swans (real ones) on the lake. A bevy or gaggle of swans, but those are boisterous and noisy words: these swans are graceful and silent, minding their own business as we swimmers mind ours. Harmony on the lake. Moorhens dipping right in front of my face, disappearing under the surface, big fish hiding below. I don't know the names of all the birds and fish, nor do I recognise all the trees and flowers but it doesn't matter: I'm here, it's my swim and I'm loving it.

Turn at the final buoy, the slipway in sight, nearly time to exit the water. The sun is higher in the sky now, and a new batch of swimmers is anticipating their swim, just as I was half an hour or so ago. They ask, 'How's the water today?'

'Lovely.' No more detail than that. Just as you don't want to give away the ending of a story, you don't want to spoil the experience unique to each individual.

I always enjoy walking through the shallows on my way out of the lake. The resistance of the water diminishing with its decreasing depth as you approach the grassy shore. It prolongs the fun but, even with the sun warming your skin, you have to get out, dried and dressed promptly. After-drop is real: your temperature will drop and continue to drop; you will feel cold soon. So, I quickly rub myself dry and pull on my cycling gear again. Within minutes, I'm sitting on a bench, pouring tea from a flask and unwrapping toast with peanut butter and raisins; banana to follow. I'm shivering slightly but that's part of the post-swim experience: it's the body's way of warming up. A hot drink and food help, too, and taste better after swimming. There's a slight breeze now, gently turning the leaves, alternately revealing dark green and the lighter green of their undersides. Rustling peacefully, a relaxing sound punctuated by the happy banter of bathers. I exchange a few words with other swimmers; not many words; I don't have to: I'm happy to be part of a community and also happy in my own company. A gaggle of geese trundle along the shore to join us, honking, begging for scraps. Now, this really is a gaggle: unlike the swans, the geese are noisy, and funny. They seem to dare each other: which of them can stick its neck out the longest, closest, to steal food? I've seen one eating out of a swimmer's hand before. It's been fun watching this family grow up alongside us humans throughout the summer.

Aye, it's been fun, right enough, but it's time to get back on the bike and ride home. It's chilly to start but it takes only a few kilometres to feel warm again. By the map, it's clear that you're cycling along narrow strips of land between lakes, but you can't really see them through the trees: only the odd glimpse of sunlight reflecting on the surface. Leaving the water park, travelling through a village; people going about their business, driving off to work, dropping children at school. I don't have to do any of that today: I'm free to enjoy what I want to do, and that's cycling away from the village and its busy population, into the countryside and along country lanes so quiet that you're more likely to meet a rabbit, squirrel or even a deer, than a car.

Twenty kilometres to go and my knee is starting to hurt. It means that there's less power from that leg, especially uphill, but it's part of the challenge and I can handle it. I'm not quick and I don't mind: cycling nearly sixty kilometres with a 1600 metres swim in the middle, all under my own steam, is an achievement and nothing is going to prevent me from enjoying it. A bird of prey hovers majestically above the roadside. My gaze returns to the road ahead and all of sudden a deer darts out of the hedge and prances across the road, inches from my front wheel. I don't know who's more surprised but the deer clears the next hedge effortlessly and is halfway across the field before I've even stopped to have a good look. After only a few leaps and bounds, he halts at the far hedge line and returns my gaze. For two or three minutes we stand still, observing each other, and then, from a standing start, he jumps the hedge and disappears. Also from a standing start, bike in the wrong gear, I struggle to build up speed again and, slowly at first, continue on my way, honoured to have witnessed such a princely, balletic display from one of nature's born athletes.

Eventually, our home town is just up ahead, and despite the sore knee, I breeze along the final few kilometres and pull up at our house, tired but exhilarated. Cycle, swim, nature watch. I've experienced all that and it's not even midmorning yet.

And there's more than a patch of blue in the sky...

THE END

Printed in Great Britain
by Amazon